Date Her, Dupe Her, Dump Her

The Complete Bastards Guide
to
Online Dating and Beyond

By Marcus Bliss

www.completebastards.com

© Copyright 2009 Marcus Bliss

Published by Informer Books
Farnborough House
Alveston
Stratford-upon-Avon
Warwickshire
Stratford-upon-Avon
Warwickshire
CV37 7QZ
United Kingdom

British Library Cataloguing in Publication Data
A catalogue record for this book is available from the British Library

ISBN-10: 0-9561448-0-5
ISBN-13: 978-0-9561448-0-5

Cover Design by Pearl Bates and Nim Kibbler
Printed by Lightning Source

www.completebastards.com

Table of Contents

Foreword by Papa Bastard

The Easy Route to Overachievement

I wasn't always a Complete Bastard, you know. Then again, life wasn't always as good to me as it is now. But whatever gripes I've got about life, it has given me the necessary experience and knowledge to become a Complete Bastard. I've been down the Path to Bastardom as I like to say.

A man of my years takes to looking back upon the path he's travelled down. That's when I realized, I probably knew a thing or two that could help some young bucks get on a little easier in life.

There's always an easier way to do everything. I learned that lesson late. And you can bet your bottom dollar that some Bastard is taking that easy route already – doing what you want to do, but going at it a whole lot better and a whole lot quicker.

Ask yourself this question: why should you be the one to miss out on the Easy Route to Overachievement?

The thing is – you needn't. With some pointers in the right direction, you too can get exactly what you want out of life. All that's required is a little guidance and some natural animal cunning. This wisdom and more, I've decided to give away through the Complete Bastards Guides. I like to think of it as leaving my Bastard Legacy to the World.

My books cover a variety of topics – all based on the common theme of helping you to get the most out of life. They show you the shortcuts that are available to everyone in the most important aspects of their lives, such as love, career, and money.

To help me offer you the most Bastardly knowledge out there, I've assembled a band of like-minded Bastard writers and researchers. Like me, they've collected advice and techniques from all over to help you get ahead in a range of life situations. We're a growing kinship who firmly believes in that old adage: 'Do it to them before they do it to you!'

So what's stopping you? Go forth, read whichever of my Guide books takes your fancy and take those first inspired steps on the Path to Bastardom.

Who is the Complete Bastard?

The Complete Bastard is a complex and controversial character – admirable and loathsome in equal measure. His major achievement in life is that he gets what he doesn't quite legitimately deserve, but no one can quite work out how he gets there. A born maverick; a man who knows how to swindle any system; a much desired lothario in love; and a success at whatever he turns his devious hand to. He is all these things and more.

Who could fail to deny that anyone who reaches the top in life should be seen as anything other than a Complete Bastard? No one likes a winner. Sour grapes have, of course, always been the preferred food of the born loser.

Until I worked out many of the ways to get ahead more easily in life and became a Complete Bastard, I too was one of those losers. And I've never once regretted leaving behind my old self and a multitude of other losers who don't have the desire and hunger to make the change.

I firmly believe that anyone – with the right guidance and application – can become a success. Anyone can be a Complete Bastard. All the Guides offer practical advice and learnable techniques that really work and show you how they're done.

Below is the Complete Bastards Manifesto: the rules of the game; the dogma; the self-help golden commandments to fulfilling your goals and your true potential. Learn them, obey them and you'll never stray far from the Path of Bastardom.

Complete Bastards Manifesto

The Complete Bastard **always wins,** for there is no merit in not being Best Bastard.

The Complete Bastard is **focused, dedicated** and **ruthless** in pursuit of his goals in order to become an over-achiever.

The Complete Bastard always seeks **audacious** and **maverick solutions** to some of life's greatest challenges.

The Complete Bastard knows how to **turn any situation to his advantage,** leading to more cash, more success, and an enhanced lifestyle.

The Complete Bastard never commits acts that are **illegal, criminal, or cause direct harm** to others. He's way too smart for a life of crime.

The Complete Bastard is an **expert social animal.** He has the charm, the wits and the cunning to understand that he needs others to help him achieve his ambitions.

The Complete Bastards Community

More than just the published word, the Complete Bastards have a real life, fully functioning community where those on the Path to Bastardom can come together in order to exchange ideas and experiences. You can access this resource online via the CompleteBastards.com website.

Here you will find:

- Additional tips and techniques for the Complete Bastards Guide that you're interested in.

- Free-to-register interactive forums where Like-minded Bastards meet and share their devious know-how and experiences.

- Author blogs where you can follow the life and times of every one of our writers and get plenty more behind-the-Bastards-scene insight.

- Latest news about all aspects of the Complete Bastards' book range

So, to put the finishing touches on your Bastardly education, visit the Complete Bastards website today at:

http://www.completebastards.com

So, that just leaves it for me, Papa Bastard, to say: If you think you have what it takes to become a Complete Bastard, then come join us without delay – and take the Easy Route to Overachievement.

- 1 -
Online Dating and the Complete Bastard Way

Self-helping Yourself

Most self-help books are not very helpful – especially the ones that tell you how to be the 'best ever' in whatever it is that you have always wanted to be the best ever at. There are plenty such books that deal with the subject of dating.

Such books try to persuade you that, unless you become a 'Winner with women and quick', you'll never find a partner who loves you or you'll never be valued by anyone in life. Instead, you'll rot brain-dumb and bloated, in front of a television set, living through some 'Groundhog Day' of never-ending cheap food and masturbation.

To escape this slump into a worthless, loveless, lifeless life, you reach out for help. And help comes in the form of some not-very-helpful books that promise to rescue you from the yawning abyss into which you've fallen.

These not-very-helpful books don't at first seem so unhelpful. They use clever phrases like 'emotional intelligence' or 'self-actualisation'. You have no clue what they mean, but the clever people who wrote them must be right, you tell yourself.

Strangely though, you feel no better for reading their words. Only more inadequate and empty. Don't worry about it – there are even more not-very-helpful books you can buy and read that will explain to you why this is.

Soon, you get to thinking: 'There must be other ways to find happiness than success in love?' And there are. You discover more not-very-helpful books with even more not-very-helpful titles like: 'Be the Best and Beat All the Rest at Business'; 'Quit Smoking While Still in the Womb'; or 'Find Your Inner Child and Bludgeon Him to Death'. You read them and not one of these books actually helps you improve your life. Like always, they're all just vapid, soft-centred, gut-wrenching bores.

But there is hope, avid reader. There exists a book that you haven't yet read. One solitary text in among all the millions of bound sheaves of paper, with their preachy proclamations, summary diagrams, smug jargon, and witty, fist-punching-in-the-air cover blurbs.

Date Her, Dupe Her, Dump Her: The Complete Bastards Guide to Online Dating and Beyond' is different. It is a very-helpful book and it tells you all about life and relationships in the most startling, upfront, and direct way. It is brutal, brash and bona-fide in its advice.

The book offers you an insight into the world of men, women, and dating. It shows you how to succeed at seduction and achieve results beyond your wildest ambitions. But, before you start reading and discover all the devious knowledge contained within, let me first introduce you to the very phenomenon that has re-defined how we now meet people, how we attract new partners and what is, this book hopes to show you, the new best place to meet and seduce women. The phenomenon is online dating and perhaps you know a bit about it already.

A brief history of online dating

Online dating has grown from little more than a Web-based forum for informal chats between horny geeks and nerds on early bulletin board systems (BBSs) to where it is today: a multi-million dollar industry that is continually growing every day and is now one of the most popular ways to meet members of the opposite sex.

Online dating is now one of the most widespread activities on the Web. According to leading internet researchers, Jupiter Research, online dating sites earned a massive $900 million in revenues in 2007, with earnings forecasted to increase by 16% over the following five years, reaching $1.6 million by 2012. This makes online dating the third biggest area of paid content on the Web after music downloads and games.

So, just why is online dating so popular? Well, there are a variety of reasons that include the fact that online dating represents:

- Convenience

- Control

- Versatility

Online dating is convenient: Where else can you flirt with someone from the comfort of your own home or workplace? All you need is an internet connection and registration to a paid (or unpaid) dating site and you're away.

Online dating can be thought of like shopping. When you go shopping in the real world, you choose where you'd like to shop based on what you need. You pass the doorway into a mall, where you select the shop that you know sells what you need. You enter it and it's stocked high with everything you need and more. There is always plenty of choice here and new products arrive every day. So you look around, because browsing is fun, and fill your shopping cart with everything you want and more. Then, it's off to the checkout to pay for your goods and you head off home, happy that you got exactly want you needed and more. What could be more convenient?

Online dating is similar in many ways. You go online (the mall) and find the dating site that best suits your needs (the shop). You login and start to browse all the thousands of profiles (piled high goods) before you. Some profiles you like; some you don't. So you choose the faces you do like, save them to your virtual 'wish list' (shopping cart), and start sending them all your first tentative messages stating your interest in them (checkout). Soon, it's time to log out from the site and you happily await their responses. They usually come quickly.

This is the thriving pastime of romance 'browsing' and 'buying' – fast, fun, easy to do, and all from the comfort of your computer. But there's one key difference between shopping and online dating: when did you last go to the store and fall in love?

Online dating gives you control: Never before with dating has it been so easy and efficient to meet and make the first move on girls that you like the look of. You can make the move by messaging them or show you like their profile by 'cyber-tagging' them.

Cyber-tagging is a feature on many dating sites where you can bookmark or electronically 'nudge' profiles that you like. It usually involves an automatically generated message being sent to their inbox telling them of your interest. It can be the first step in getting their attention and winning their affections.

But what happens if the object of your interest doesn't respond? No big deal – you're never going to feel as rejected as you would have done had you made a move on someone in a bar or a club.

With online dating, you can manoeuvre yourself as you see fit within any interaction. Perhaps you want to take it slowly and scope the members out first with careful analysis of their profiles. Maybe, you'll fall head-over-heels and arrange to meet in the real world within days or even hours. It's all possible, fair game, and within your control.

Control extends further. If you don't like what you see or you change your mind about a person, you can simply stop replying to them. Sure, they may start bombarding you with love poems or forlorn pleas for you to contact them, but usually there are additional functions on dating sites where you can 'block' users so they cannot contact you anymore. Furthermore, practically all reputable sites have a team of moderators who will monitor, reprimand and blacklist any threatening or negative misbehaviour from users. Or else there's always the 'Delete' key on your keyboard.

Online dating is versatile: It is highly varied in its user range. The average age of a UK user is 27-years' old but everyone, from teenagers to pensioners, are utilizing the medium. And it's not just to find love. Using the sites, people can expand their social circles; find people who share common interests, and; find new sexual partners or their next husband or wife. There is also a burgeoning niche of married men, mischievously seeking out mistresses for flings online. In short – different strokes for different folks.

Despite its rather unfair historical reputation as a forum for nerds, online dating is an easy and exciting way to meet new people. It's fast, effective, and usually a lot less random than meeting a stranger in a bar, simply because you can search across thousands of people in one sitting in order to come up with a shortlist of those people with similar interests and a lifestyle to match your own.

Online dating is also democratic and open to all. Providing you can get online, it allows you to connect with thousands, even millions, of people from different backgrounds, locations, professions and religions.

This book will show you that online dating sites are places to find more than just your next partner. There is a whole world of new adventures and exciting experiences just waiting for you – if you know how to exploit them.

The pitfalls of online dating

Online dating may be open to all and have lots of potential, but the irony is that, for many people – perhaps for the majority of people – it simply fails to deliver. The reason for this may be that people's expectations are too high to begin with. However, it seems that the main gripes of most women tend to be boredom, disenchantment and borderline disgust at the male profiles that they view and the attention that they receive.

Here are just a few real life comments from women about their experiences using online dating:

'I joined last week and find the whole thing hilarious but also very fake.'

'I'm new to this online stuff and actually thinking of coming off it soon, due to the tedium of the pseudo-intellectuals on this site.'

'Don't actually know why I've persevered actually. I've been on a couple of pleasant enough dates ... What am I talking about? ... I walked straight into some humdingers just on the basis of a pretty face.'

So if women aren't having a good time online, why is it that the men aren't delivering? Well, the experience can be just as frustrating for men too. There are several popular reasons for this:

- Nobody replies to your messages

- You've had bad experiences of dating in the past

- The people on dating sites are weird

- It costs money to join dating sites

Nobody replies to your messages

You write to them in genuine faith and spend some of your time composing that 'killer' message and you get no response back from them. There could be number of reasons for this: perhaps they have left the site but kept their profile live. Maybe they are currently dating someone else but haven't gotten around to replying to anyone else, or could it be, most painfully of all, that they just aren't interested in you based solely upon what little they know about you from your picture, your profile and your initial approach to them. This is a common curse of online dating and a problem this book promises to solve. There's no guarantee that 100% of your messages are going to get replies if you follow the rules in this book, but we can guarantee that you will see a dramatic improvement in your online dating fortunes.

Bad experiences in the past

For many, the idea of dating or being alone with someone who they are attracted to and want to seduce is simply terrifying. There's a good reason for this – dates and relationships **are** terrifying. They challenge you, expose your weaknesses and tend to be highly emotional affairs. Getting hurt while in love is a major fear for most people and happens often enough to put people off getting involved with another. These people haven't grasped the fact that we all suffer. It's part of life. This book will show you that the past can be easily forgotten and a new 'suffering free' future awaits you. By the time you finish this book, your new motto is going to be: 'Nothing ventured, nothing gained'.

People online are weird

Sure, there are some oddballs out there. They exist in every walk of life. But like beauty, who's repulsive, weird or incompatible is in the eye of the beholder. Just because you don't worship Satan doesn't mean that there's no one out there who's the perfect match for that wacky Goth chick whose profile you've just been shaking your head at. These are the exceptions though. In the main, online dating has millions of ordinary, successful, good-looking, witty, intelligent and sane folk online. This is part of the reason why it makes online dating such a great way to meet new people and to take full advantage of them. This book will show you how to maximize your chances of meeting these people while avoiding the weirdoes.

Someone charges money for this service?!

Of course most dating sites charge monthly membership fees. They are businesses after all and a small minority of people are getting seriously rich from doing something positive about the fact that many of us are bored, lonely and longing to meet our perfect match. We are all social animals and friendship, sex and companionship are all vital to our healthy functioning. Online dating sites vary in what they charge and some can be relatively quite expensive – although, compared to a night out cruising the bars, buying drinks for girls who give you nothing in return, it still doesn't seem like too bad value. And, compared to what you stand to gain in return if you master the principles of this book, joining an online dating site should be the best investment you'll ever make.

What is the Complete Bastards way?

Online dating doesn't **have** to be a source of misery for men. There is another route that uses an approach so effective, that, with its full and successful adoption, you'll not only be dating, but 'cherry-picking' the best of the bunch to date.

The Complete Bastards Guide to Online Dating and Beyond promises that, if you follow the Path to Bastardom and do not stray from its core principles, then:

Never again will you look at online profiles of people you want to date but think you can't attract.

Never again will you be staring into an empty inbox because no one has replied to your messages.

Never again will past relationship failures hold you back from achieving your goals and dreams.

Never again will you waste your time talking with and dating people you are not attracted to or think are weird.

Never again will you regret paying the dating site subscription fee just to have it reinforced that you're a loveless loser.

Instead, let this Complete Bastards Guide lead you into a world where you are the one who is in control; where women are highly attracted to you, and; where the women regularly make the first move. And it gets better: you will learn how you can profit in more ways than by just having more sex with more women. There is a whole other world of perks to be gained by knowing how to dupe women for your selfish gain – and how to get away with it. This is truly the Complete Bastard way.

As an approach, it offers you a range of tried-and-tested techniques that have been used to successfully attract women through online dating sites and beyond. The Complete Bastards way is more of a flexible 'bag of tricks' than a prescriptive formula. For that reason, you can adapt it to your own goals, your own personality and your own lifestyle.

Benefits of the Complete Bastards way

There are a number of reasons why the Complete Bastards way is **the** best way for online dating, which are:

- Winning back the power from woman.

- Easy to use techniques.

- No money required.

Winning back the power from women

There is an argument that the Complete Bastard male figure is only winning back the control over dating that has, over recent times, been in the elegant but highly manipulative hands of women. For the Complete Bastard, there is a justice in wrestling the power and control back for himself.

Easy to use techniques

So you don't have the looks of a Hollywood movie star? Very few men do. But you're no Quasimodo either. The Complete Bastards way is not going to tell you to spend seven nights a week at the gym to get that perfect body, to get a hair transplant or to find a new and more exciting lifestyle. Instead, the changes you will make will come mainly from within and are just subtle tweaks to natural behaviour that you are carrying out every day of your life.

No money required

Forget spending a fortune on designer clothes, fast cars and lavish dates in expensive locations. The Complete Bastard way requires little in the form of financial investment. Your investment comes instead from the time and commitment you will spend honing your dating skills. Master the Complete Bastard method in its entirety and **the women** will be the ones spending the money on **you**. In fact the Complete Bastard method is perfect for the more economically unstable times we live in. In the past, a lot of guys' main seduction technique was to simply throw a lot of money at women. Now, with money tighter for a lot of people, many men are going to have to start using their brains instead of their wallets if they want success with members of the opposite sex.

Bastard beware

This book lays out a foolproof method for improving your success at finding women through online dating sites. There are, of course, always those who deviate from the norm and, for every Complete Bastard who can date, dupe, dump and still come out of it smelling of roses, there is a minority who will use the teachings of this book for the wrong reasons.

There is very little to stop these people doing what they want to do, but we recommend that you resist the temptation to participate in any of the following un-gentlemanly behaviours:

- Using crude, offensive or threatening language in any form of communication to other people.

- Using perversely sexual language or imagery in any form of communication where it is not wanted or encouraged.

- Fawning, begging or trying to emotionally blackmail anyone to win their attention, a date and/or sex.

In short, if you want to come out of online dating as someone well-liked, popular and maybe even with the woman or three of your dreams, then it's simple: don't behave like a first-class ass. Instead, act like a Complete Bastard.

What to expect

So now you know the rules. They're not really 'rules' as such. If they were, a Complete Bastard would be the first to break them. Instead, see them as guidelines to ensuring your Path to Bastardom is focused on your goals and not distracted by pointless, no-gain, dead-end journeys. Here are just some of the good things that you may miss out on if you deviate from this book's recommended path:

- You'll find yourself more attractive to women through knowing how to write a great dating site profile and how to flirt online.

- You'll get the attention from women that you desire and learn how to get them to make the first move.

- You'll learn how to make sure online contacts develop into real-world dates.

- You'll meet lots of new people and enjoy flirting with as many of them as you desire.

- You'll get additional perks from women that will improve your social life, bank balance, lifestyle and even working life.

All of these amazing goals and more can be achieved by you. The first step towards getting them is simply believing that you can.

– 2 –
Meet A Complete Bastard

My Bastard story

Men seek different things from online dating. For some, it's just a fling. For many it's a serious attempt at finding the love of their lives. For the special few – those who really know how to play it right – they can have it all. That means genuine fun with as many genuine women as they desire. And never get caught.

These men are an elite group, so primed in their understanding of how women think and behave and so tuned-in as to how to play the dating game that they can masterfully take advantage of all that dating and women have to offer.

This book is about these 'special few', known affectionately as the Complete Bastards.

We begin with one Complete Bastard's story of how he attained such a high level of success with women that it went way beyond his wildest dreams. His good fortune went further than simply getting a few nights of lustful pleasure. His journey was a complete transformation of who he was, of the life he had led up to that point, and his ability to make his dreams become reality.

His story is my story. After reading it, you'll either think me an irresistible cad or a conniving gutter rat. I think I was probably a little of both. The simple truth though is that I'm just like you – an ordinary, average-looking guy who would have traded a kidney to have lifted himself from being mediocre at best with women, to becoming in any way a success with them.

My bad luck with women went far beyond not getting laid. Women were either just not interested in me at all or, when they were, ripped me off for free dinners, dumped me, or just seemed so damn elusive.

My life eventually got to the point where I had a string of failed relationships to look back on and nothing to show for them except bad memories of all the heartache and pain. I was extremely cautious of women, insecure about my looks and my ability at seducing women when I did find one.

But then, as they say, when you hit rock bottom, the only way is up.

Rock bottom

It was a dark, cold, autumn night. The wind blew among the masts of the luxury yachts in the marina. A single light was on in a boat as it rocked on its mooring. Inside it, I sat – listless and alone; the flickering images on the television screen all that moved around me.

It had been three weeks since my ex-girlfriend and I had split – far from amicably. The memory of her was beginning to fade with each passing, gnawing hour and the pain and hardship of splitting up was also beginning to set deep inside me.

I gazed over at a large battered suitcase in the corner of the cabin. Everything I owned was now inside of that case. The rest of my world had probably been dumped on the steps of a local charity shop or shredded by her in a fit of rage. In the end, she took and destroyed everything I owned: my home, my possessions, my friends, and my life.

It had all happened one day as soon as I had arrived home from work...

'It's men like you who make me sick,' she screamed. 'Sick, pathetic little men like you. So selfish. And I'm not putting up with it anymore. We're over.'

The truth was that I'd been cheating on her for months – since we started dating, during our time living together, and even during my lunch hour at work that very day we split. I'd never stopped cheating on her.

Finally, she'd caught me. In some ways I was glad. What would follow, however, would be some of the darkest days of my life.

I stood in silence before her. She grabbed a bag she'd packed with some of my clothes shoved inside it, opened the door, and tossed it onto the street outside.

We began to argue. After an hour of my shouting for mercy and her vowing to avenge me, I called a taxi to take me out of her life forever. The artful shrew still managed to launch a bucket of cold water out of the second floor bedroom window on top of me before I'd finally gone, however. It did little to refresh my jaded spirits.

I can't deny that I did deserve it all. I had cheated on her. Yet, it wasn't with another woman as such. That would have been simple. My sickness lay in the fact that it was with several **women**. Plural. Tens of women. Dozens of women. Maybe even hundreds of women.

Every one of them I'd met and wooed via online dating websites. First it was flirtatious emails and text messages. Then chats and sex shows on webcam, followed by dates in restaurants, bars and clubs. I even entertained one date in a betting shop. There were sexual encounters and one night stands in cheap hotels. Long, romantic weekends in expensive hotels. Everything – from furtive phone sex to amorous adventures overseas to meet women for whom I'd fleetingly fallen – I had seen it all and done them all.

I didn't even have a type. Blonde, brunette, flame-haired, even a couple of shaven-headed chicks. Tall, short, thin, stout. Fair, sun-tanned or dark-skinned. Waif, athletic or curvaceous. It really didn't matter. All that did matter was that they had a pretty face. Every woman had to hold an expression of romantic potential – a smirk of daring in the curl of a pair of full lips; eyes that flickered with mischief; playful dimples in the cheeks – it all strived to arouse and provoke.

From their pictures online, a pose in front of the camera lens was like a gaze deep into my soul. And if that gaze inflamed my desire, so began a thrilling chase to try to win her affections.

I adored and fell in lust with countless women. Yet there was a snag: I was an addict to finding and pursuing them. I craved their attentions and, in my desire to impress and find the right women, I became a victim of their game-playing, their cunning, and their desire to avoid ultimate commitment in a relationship.

Women had cost me money – lots of money. Dating for the Complete Gentleman is an expensive business. And now women had cost me my relationship.

It's hard to understand what has changed in the world over the past few decades, but now it seems that women are the ones on top. They are smart, self-sufficient, have flourishing careers, buy the drinks and don't demand old fashioned gentlemanly manners from us – they hardly seem to need us men at all these days.

Indeed, today it seems to be the men who are suffering as a result of being 'the weaker sex'.

After my latest split from my ex, I slunk from one cheap hotel room to the next. My social life – which had mostly revolved around her circle of friends – had gone the same night she decided to throw me out. What few friends I had left were soon forced to evaluate their friendship with me after she sent poisoned emails to each and every one of them, spelling out in detail what a cheating, lying rat I was.

With each passing hour, my luck seemed to get worse. I lost my job less than a week after the split; I took to drinking and smoking heavily; I was depressed and lonely - unable to cope or even to make the smallest everyday decision. My rudderless life seemed to be on a course to nowhere.

In an effort to avert my demise and escape the unbearable loneliness of hotel living, I rented a friend's boat. It seemed like a good idea at the time – clean air, a pleasant place to live and space to think. But when you're down, the last thing you need is isolation and space. Soon I began to spend every day alone on the boat, drinking and smoking more and more while falling further out of life. It seemed as if there was no escape.

Turnaround

It was as things seemed to be heading fast towards oblivion that Papa Bastard found me. Well, I found him first, to be more precise.

He was my old boss from my time a few years previously when I worked as a copywriter in Eastern Europe. I hadn't seen him for many years. I'd exchanged a few emails in that time, but none of any great life-changing significance. That was about to change.

Always unpredictable, he'd moved on and was living and working somewhere in Africa now. He would be little help to me there, I thought, a continent away.

But sometimes the most useful advice comes from the most unusual places and so, for no reason other than as a desperate howl into the abyss, I wrote Papa Bastard an email so sorrowful and woeful that it would surely shake even his stout, merciless heart.

His reply was one of the cruellest and most savage pieces of advice I'd ever been forced to read.

Papa Bastard wrote:

'Son, it's time to wise up and understand your potential. Finding a worthy woman isn't about having the good looks or good fortune to do so. It's a state of mind and the first person you need to 'pick up' is yourself.'

He went on to tell me that the reason why I was having such negative encounters with women was because of my not putting into play some basic 'life rules' as opposed to my simply picking the wrong chicks. Most of these life rules are to be found within this book.

He also proved to me that, with a deeper sense of self-belief and a few Complete Bastardly goals, I could get far more from women than just their attention or sex. There were riches far beyond my wildest imagination that could be mine for the taking.

I had squandered so many dates and potential relationships because of my attitude and through my not being able to play the dating game. As Papa Bastard explained: I didn't properly understand women. That needed to change.

He helped me to combat other hang-ups too. I blamed my short stature and poor physical appearance for my low self-confidence with women and for the reason why the hottest ones weren't attracted to me. Papa Bastard assured me that wit and cunning win over a lofty stature and good looks every time.

Finally, as it all started to make sense to me, Papa Bastard told me to enjoy what would be the greatest challenge and adventure of my life:

'It's time to play women at their own game, Son.'
'Oh yes, and if you're any good at it, you should write it up as a book,' he added.

Knowing Papa Bastard's cunning ways, I took this as it was intended – not as a friendly word of encouragement, but rather as an order. I realized that I had just entered a Faustian pact with the Devil of Dating. I never dreamt that one day I would usurp him to his title.

Rebirth

And so I went back to online dating again. I'd always had the enthusiasm for it and found it a safe, accessible and easy way to meet loads of women. Perhaps there was always something of the Complete Bastard in me to have worked that much out.

It was now time to put into practice what Papa Bastard had taught me. Within hours of rejoining one site and changing my profile, I became the number one 'Most Popular Male' on their site. I remained there for an amazing three months as other (more handsome) faces came and went around me. And this was just the beginning.

On my journey, I made lots of new acquaintances. Some of these took the form of some of the more notorious women to be found online. They were the super-confident dating game-players, the highly attractive elusive types, the gold diggers – all the ruin of good and honest men.

Then there were the loose women, drunks, debauchees, the flirtatious, the false – those that were just looking for someone to use and abuse or to be used and abused by.

I befriended good women too – strong, bold, confident, warm and witty women – friendly and fun to be around and full of kindness.

It was in the company of every one of these women that I began to truly understand the world of online dating. And it was from all these women that I began to reap the spoils of what it truly means to be a Complete Bastard.

My bargain with the Bastard

I set about not only dating women with a newfound frenzy using the teachings of Papa Bastard, but I also began to document my experiences as the grizzled guru had instructed me to do.

After every online dating profile I craftily composed or message I sent, I saved my work. I was careful to note down the information on every girl I flirted with – who she was, plus details about what was, and what wasn't, winning her attentions.

As communications began to move towards an actual date offline, I recorded every conversation, remembered and noted down the content of every telephone call made and text message I sent.

After every date, I meticulously analysed and wrote up my experiences - how I dressed to meet them, where I arranged to meet them, what body language I displayed, to what I said in their company. Most importantly, I took care to be aware of how my style and behaviour affected these women I dated.

The number of women I began to ask out on dates began to grow – and grow at an extraordinary rate. I was back to my insatiable self, pursuing women with a voracious hunger and loving every second of the experience. But there were none of the old errors and conflicts from the past.

However, it was when I came to documenting the outcomes of my new, Bastardly approach to dating that the greatest revelations came to the fore.

Whereas previously I had been happy to just regard sex as the greatest pleasure these women could give me, I was now on the threshold of a whole new world where I was getting perks far beyond my original, rather base, intentions. Sure, I was getting as much sexual pleasure as ever – and much more into the bargain. The difference was that I now knew there was far, far more to be gained beyond lustful satisfaction.

Now I had become enough of a Complete Bastard to make even Papa Bastard proud. My life was now such a triumph with women in ways I could never have even imagined before that there was no way of ever going back to the weak and naïve man I was in the past.

Some months later, I would meet with Papa Bastard face-to-face once again. Neither of us could have truly imagined at the start of my journey on the Path to Bastardom that he would be so integral to my transformation as a Complete Bastard and my eventual salvation as an Erroneous Bastard. For my Icarian fall, you must read to the end of this book and you will see that there are highs and lows to be had when you make the bargain to become the Complete Bastard.

I also kept the other half of my bargain with Papa Bastard. I dated as many women as possible and wrote up all the details of my life as a master seducer, the content of which forms much of the book that you are now reading. So go forward, read and enjoy my words. They are as much for your entertainment as well as your instruction. If my words inspire you, then why not make your own bargain with the Bastards? The Path to Bastardom, after all, was my Easy Route to Overachievement. Why not let it be yours?

– 3 –
Unleashing Your Inner Bastard

Bastard state of mind
ASo let us begin with Papa Bastard's first piece of advice: picking up yourself before you can pick up any women.

All the negative perceptions of online dating that were covered in chapter one share a common disorder: they are linked to a negative state of mind in the man.

This chapter looks at how, by understanding the make-up of a Complete Bastard and learning how to think like one, you can get into the right state of mind to become incredibly successful as both an online and offline dater.

The rest of this chapter will show you a number of attitudes vital for a Complete Bastard to learn and possess. The principles given here are not only akin to becoming a Complete Bastard in the field of online dating, but can and also should be applied to all other areas of your life – your offline dating experiences and even your career can benefit as a result of following this advice.

The Complete Bastards Basics
We begin with the most important first few basic lessons in becoming a Complete Bastard.

The key lessons that can be learned about dating behaviour are as old as mankind itself – even older, in fact. The way that men act – or rather the way that they are **supposed** to act – goes back to before the time of Homo sapiens. Perhaps they are best explained by means of some anthropological-style monkey metaphors. After all, some may argue that most men haven't really advanced much further in the mating game than a bunch of gorillas on heat.

The Complete Bastards' Basics are five key areas that all relate to your most primal urges. They are as follows: 'Ape the ape', 'Don't go gorilla', 'Avoid Wimp Chimp', 'Pitch the primate' and 'Monkey around' – and you must learn to adopt them all.

Ape the ape

From asking many of the women I dated about their experiences of online dating, I quickly began to realise that it is **men** who are the ones writing long-winded, soppy emails, sending romantic poetry to the objects of their affection, and who are so desperately seeking a relationship that it's almost possible to smell their despair through the computer screen. Meanwhile, women are playing the field, collecting multiple admirers like trophies, and not rushing blindly into relationships.

What's going on? Man – once the gender of the cad, the love rat and now the Complete Bastard – is having an identity crisis.

There is probably a book or three that could be devoted to explaining in-depth the reasons why women are now firmly in control of the dating experience, but let's look at some crude explanations. After all, this book aims to re-address the balance, not dwell on the morbid conclusion that men have lost their place, power and poise in society.

There are two main reasons for men's fall from grace in the dating game:

- Women have more equal status with men in the workplace than ever before. This also means women have more money than ever before.

- Women are more sexually empowered than ever before.

For today's woman, a man is a 'nice-to-have', not a 'need-to-have' as it was for generations before.

However, no Complete Bastard need feel threatened or downbeat about the previous statement. On the contrary, it's sweet music to the ears of every cloven-hoofed little devil trotting down the Path to Bastardom.

With more money, more confidence and more ambition, today's woman is still searching for the man of her dreams as much as she has always been. Or if she is not quite looking for a husband or a long term relationship, she is looking for some playful distraction.

Sadly, most men have not adapted to this adverse swing in gender control away from them. The result is that, today, women are the main players in the online dating game. They attract the male gaze, they get away with all sorts of dating game-play as they have men wrapped around their little fingers, and they profit handsomely in the process.

It's with no shame that the Complete Bastard way to improved online dating success and beyond does draws on mimicking the sophisticated cunning and shameless guile of women. Yet there is a male figure that the Complete Bastard should more heavily look to aspire to and that's the Alpha Male.

The Alpha Male is the leader of the pack. Without going into too much academic mumbo-jumbo, most sociologists and anthropologists agree that women's primary motivation when looking for a life partner is, consciously or unconsciously, to find a specimen that can provide her with high quality sperm in order to produce a healthy child and then to provide for her while she is raising the children. The Alpha Male is the ape to ape. He's the King Kong of the chimp world, with a line of She-Chimps queuing up for some of his hot monkey lovin'. Conversely, the Beta Male (or Wimp Chimp), has to content himself with hugging trees and spanking his own monkey.

So for all you may think that women desire a kind, caring, New Age type man who will help them with the cooking and housework, raising a family and being on hand to give them advice when they spend an entire afternoon looking around town for a new pair of shoes, the reality of the situation, however, is that such a compliant little Wimp Chimp of a man would bore the pants off her in a matter of hours.

It appears, however, that the majority of men have failed to understand this female doublespeak and, as women have really grown, matured and blossomed through the past few decades, the male figure has begun to wither as he tries to become the type of person he **thinks** women really want these days.

So, gone are the days when real men wrestled crocodiles, scaled mountain tops, and poured whisky over their breakfast cereal. Today's man prefers nights in with DVD box-sets, moisturising over-worked, stressed puffy eyes and looking through the soft furnishings section of furniture catalogues at weekends.

This masking of masculinity is a tragic scenario – less power in the workplace, emotionally unconnected compared to women and their gay best friend, encouraged to prance and preen as a metro-sexual by a media obsessed with the body beautiful, and so on. It's all a rather alarming picture for a species which was previously best known for its boorish 'club head then drag to cave for shagging' pick-up routine.

An increasingly smug female populace, who once found solace in cracking anti-men jokes and gleefully telling stories of men's incompetence, now find themselves missing the challenge of interacting with the masterful cad or charming rogue. In short, women miss a Complete Bastard. They miss the Alpha Male and the strong leader of the pack. Aping the ape is the first step in changing your attitude and emboldening yourself in order to impress women.

Don't go gorilla

Before you take to beating your chest like Tarzan, yodelling a warning call out to all the jungle animals that 'Man is back', you should heed the next piece of advice.

One of the joys of seeing women in control of their dating experience is the knowledge that the Alpha Male has lost his man-mantle. I'm not talking here about the strong male figure who thinks with his wits, can dress in style, swig a bottle of champagne and still behave like a heartless scoundrel. Oh no. This other Alpha Male is the cheap-aftershave splashing, muscle-flexing, crotch-grabbing, beer-guzzling monkey-brains who makes the experience of every girl who's ever stood alone in a wine bar a living hell. These tedious, slavering, blunted manbags of dumb-speak are the reason why men deserved and got such a bad reputation in the first place.

Women **do** like confidence. But they loathe arrogance, being talked 'at' and not 'with', and standing in the shadow of some man-hulk being told how many zillion kilograms he can bench-press. It may seem interesting to him as it spills out of his slack, dragging man-jaw but, although that woman may be smiling politely to his face, she is probably imagining his slow, painful, agonising death using a set of power tools and all set to a soundtrack by Wagner.

Why would a woman even consider such a man, you may be asking? Well, it's simple – these types tend to fit the stereotype of what some men still think a man should be: stupid, insular and never backward at coming forward with a ridiculous point of view or statement. For some women, such Neanderthals are a safe bet. Women at least know what they're getting.

This book will show you that all communications, from your first message online to the kiss at the end of the first date, are cues that need to be made **for** the woman and not **at** the woman. It's an easy trick to miss but, learn to not go gorilla now, and let it percolate throughout your woman-wooing repertoire. You won't go far wrong. In short, simmer down your testosterone-driven bravado – you'll rise nicely in the estimations of women.

Avoid Wimp Chimp

You're intelligent and quite the reader too. Erudite. So much so, that you even know what the word means. You're 'green' and care deeply about the environment. You like to strum the guitar. No more rock songs though – perish the thought that the next door neighbours might complain. Booze? Late nights? No. Not for this smart cookie! You'd far rather have a fruit smoothie and get a solid eight hours' sleep. Working nine-to-five plus overtime (because you're scared of your female boss) is where it's at now. After all, it's the only way to get that three-bedroom house in the suburbs, isn't it?

Does the above sound like a great guy?

Pass the vomit bucket. He's no more than a beige spook of a man who has clearly lost his nerve with life.

If there is one date-type who is guaranteed to have the personality of a dead fish, it's the New Man Beta Male or Wimp Chimp. This coming across all sensitive, caring, emotional and reliable isn't going to fool anyone, let alone a woman whose ESP skills could dance rings round Gandalf the Gray.

The Wimp Chimp is one of the most popular character types to be found using online dating sites. He is also the type who is causing women the most confusion. These are the men who are being consistently dubbed by women as 'bores'.

No one likes a dullard. This is one of the cold facts of dating. Charm, pluck and wit go way further than pseudo-intellectual conversation, contrived high-brow ramblings or cosy, sensible chatter. There is nothing wrong with genuinely showing that you care about the environment or that you're intelligent. Just don't try and portray yourself as a Nobel Prize winner. You aren't. That's why you're reading this.

So if there is one stereotypical attitude that needs readjusting, it is the beta-brains of a Wimp Chimp. Women want and deserve better.

Pitch the primate

In all your interaction with women on the Path to Bastardom, you will begin to see that making an impression often means avoiding extreme statements, whether in lifestyle, behaviour or opinion.

This does not mean that, if you have something extreme in your life, then you should hide this. For example, riding a motorbike fast is a cool and extreme thing. There should be no problem if you casually drop the subject into a conversation providing that you don't go on and on about it.

However, saying that you hang out every weekend with a bunch of grease-stained Hells Angels who go out beating up people all the time is something that is likely to go down less well. Unless you met her on bikerkiss.com (That's a real site, by the way.)

It's the same with opinions. Being forceful, intelligent and sticking to your argument is actually an attractive aspect of a man's personality. It shows he has passion and an enquiring, independent spirit. However, banging your fist on the table during a first date proclaiming that, if only the Nazis had worn thicker jackets when fighting the Russians in 1943, then the world would have been a better place, will only show you up as the ranting loon you are. Best hide your ridiculous views until after she's fallen for you.

All in all, the first few steps when two people meet and interact, especially for the women, are highly cautious steps. She is as much looking for signs that you are a latent serial killer as she is wondering if you are potential husband material.

Be warned: the secret is to temper your behaviour and opinions towards a middle ground. From this safe and stable platform, you can ensure that no women get put off by any extreme traits that you may exhibit. One of the secrets of the Complete Bastard method is to lull your potential conquest into an initial sense of security so that she's not on her guard throughout the dating and, later, the duping process.

From this 'middle ground', you can begin to develop the Complete Bastard personality using all the devilish tips and tricks that you will learn later in this book. This also includes how you should write your online profile.

For now though, Pitch your Primate slap bang down the middle right from the start and you'll be 'swinging high' in the dating 'jungle' in no time.

Monkey around

So, you've learnt that the most important characteristic that a Complete Bastard needs within his personality is confidence. Yet you've also seen that too much confidence is a bad thing and can be seen as arrogance. There's one great way to act with über-confidence and get away with it – and that's to develop a **great sense of humour**.

Look through any women's online profile and check what they are looking for in a man. The one much desired trait that you're sure to come across over and over again is good sense of humour (GSOH). Whenever women are surveyed about what characteristic is most important to them, GSOH is at the top of the charts every single time, beating even good looks.

This is music to the ears of any Funny Bastard who doesn't have movie star looks or a fat wallet, because it gives everyone with a brain and an ounce of wit the chance of becoming a real success with women.

Put the two elements together – confidence and humour – and you have the killer combination for your future success with women. Having a sense of humour, especially if you use it in a self-depreciating way from time to time, also has the advantage of again avoiding your being perceived by women as too brash. So bring yourself down a peg or two if you feel that you're overdoing things on the confidence front.

Confidence mixed with humour is the basic foundation upon which most pick up artists methods are built. It's known as a 'push-pull' technique where you have the nerve to approach her with flattery and then, just when she thinks she has you, you put her down or 'neg' her as it's often referred to by other dating experts.

In your own personality, you temper your almost super-human confidence with a healthy dose of self-depreciating humour. You appear confident – not arrogant.

In both cases, using humour – or monkeying around – is a great way to relax the anxiety of dating or picking up in the real world and, with online dating, it will increase your likelihood of being liked and trusted by women.

But maybe you think that you're not naturally humorous and don't know where to start? Don't worry at this stage of the book if you fear that this might be the case – you're going to be seeing plenty of examples of Bastardly Humour in action during the remaining chapters which you should be able to adapt to your own unique style and voice.

So don't forget, next time you want to get serious about dating, make sure you don't forget that monkeying around is your best route into the hearts and minds of women.

Remember your Bastards' Basics and you'll find the confidence to get the women and the perks that you want:

'Ape the ape' – become the man women want and need you to be

'Don't go gorilla' – temper excessive male bravado

'Avoid wimp chimp' – don't behave like a weak man

'Pitch the primate' – get your personality balance right

'Monkey around' – how a sense of humour is critical

The Bastard Basics are not everything you need to instil confidence – but it's the first vital step in beginning to woo the women you desire and getting the perks you want. Next follows my first Dating Diary extract which shows you just how easy it can be to find the confidence you need to succeed.

A Bastard is born

The Complete Bastard is eager to find confidence within himself and around women. The time has come to forge his Inner Bastard.

Papa Bastard had left me in no doubt whatsoever as to what was the root cause of my current problems – I was badly lacking confidence. Unfortunately for me, confidence wasn't a magical elixir available over the counter at my local pharmacy.

Papa had given me wise counsel as to what exactly needed doing with my messed-up mind. The truth was that I'd lost my poise with women. In their company, whenever I tried to pick one up, I felt like a little yellow pee stain. A woman's only cure to rid herself of my amorous attentions was through the medium of convulsive, rejecting laughter in my face.

The time had come for me to Man Up and face my problem head on.

Confidence is a battle with yourself, right? Yet my non-confident side was armed with a greased wrecking ball, clad in death-proof armour, and sitting aloft his gallant steed, while my confidence lay cowering, naked in the corner of the arena, eyes-averted, holding Heavenward a moth-eaten bible, and shrieking the Lord's Prayer in frenzied panic.

This battle looked like it would have only one victor. Something had to change. I had to ditch my old self and rally my confidence. I then remembered something Papa Bastard had said to me:

'Go forth, Son and be the Best Bastard with women you can be. Remember: the first step to seducing women is seducing yourself. If you only think of yourself as a useless, worthless piece of garbage, then every girl you'll ever meet is going to instantly agree with you.'

Papa Bastard was spot on. I had to seduce myself. From that moment on, I took a vow to start respecting myself, to stop behaving like some Half Man, always feeling sorry for me, me, me and whining about all 'my bad luck'. Instead, I would seize full control of my fortunes.

I realized that I was having real confidence issues with both women and men. So I started forcing myself into new social situations; hanging around bars and even going to nightclubs on my own. Sometimes I got the odd, 'Who's the loser on his own?' looks, but I quickly began to start making the effort to talk to people and, over time, it became easier to draw on confidence.

Confidence began to follow me to more and more places – and not just in bars and clubs. I'd practice confidence while out shopping for groceries, with people I worked with, dealing with the landlord and I even found myself getting the upper-hand after I started haggling with a used car salesman. I saved myself a few hundred quid in that encounter. Confidence it seems pays – sometimes literally as well as figuratively speaking.

The secret to being confident is thinking confident. Gaining confidence felt like I was becoming a new person. My inner voice seemed louder, deeper, more resonant. Instead of having a head filled with nagging doubts and fears, my decisions became snappier: 'I can do thus...' or, 'I must try with this chick no matter what happens.'

Going out more and trying to hit on more and more girls, I was receiving more rejections and cold shoulders than ever before. Somehow it didn't feel too bad though. The curious thing was that all the rejection actually served to **strengthen** my confidence. Making the effort – no matter what the outcome – boosts confidence. Why? Because you are in control, master of your destiny and Manned Up.

Another little sideline bonus was that, apart from becoming better at talking to women, I also began winning the respect and friendship of men. This showed me that my newfound bravado was rubbing off on everyone. Knowing that I was being accepted by **men** and allowed back into the sacred circle of maledom was another way for me to Man Up. After all, where better to learn some Alpha Male chat than from Alpha Males?

But, over time, I began to grow tired of conversations with most men. The majority were all 'Booty-Boasters', (i.e., any conquest with a woman and they had to tell the guys about it). I found all this 'kiss and tell' stuff lame and un-gentlemanly.

I also used to hang out with men in groups thinking that it would be easier to hit on chicks that way. But usually women hated nothing more than being approached by a bunch of leering jocks.

Preying as a pack had become limiting. Sure, they'd shout you a beer at the bar from time to time, but I missed the more perceptive, intelligent talk of women. I liked women. I figured that, if the guys genuinely liked me they'd still drink a beer around me whether I went looking for ladies with them or not.

It was time for me to go solo. My confidence had grown and I felt ready. I reckoned that I had more chances and more adventures with women ahead of me if I ditched the dudes. And so I did. As you'll read over the course of my tales, never a better decision was made.

This was pretty much how I conquered confidence. When I drew upon it, it gave me a powerful surge of emboldened bravado. It made me talk better, walk better and people seemed to genuinely like me better. But most importantly of all, women noticed me and liked my confident way better.

It was when I started getting the female stamp of approval that I knew my Inner Bastard had truly been born.

– 4 –
Create Your Bastard Image

Transform yourself in a month

Cosmetics expert Helena Rubinstein once said: 'There are no ugly women; only lazy ones'. And the same goes for men. Fortunately though, looks are a lot less important to men in the dating process than they are to women, so we can get away with being a lot lazier than they can.

Anyone can do well at dating, irrelevant of their physical failings. No person is physically perfect and, while some lucky people are blessed with what is culturally defined as 'beauty', we less physically perfect ones do still date, get laid and find partners. Beauty is only skin deep after all.

Many surveys have shown that the primary reason for a man to be attracted to a woman is how physically attractive she is to him. For women, a man's character including personality, confidence and sense of humour comes at the top of their list. More good news for those studying the Complete Bastard method is that these are the character attributes that we concentrate on teaching you how to improve dramatically.

Still, some effort on your appearance can make an immense difference as to the quality of women that you will be able to attract and seduce.

The time to start your transformation is **right now** – before you take the rest of the steps in this book that will complete your Complete Bastard education. The reason is that you can make rapid changes to yourself in a period of just a few weeks. So, if you start the process now, by the time you are starting to get out on dates, you will already be in a lot better shape than you are in today.

Below are the simple and easy ways of making some quick yet dramatic changes to your appearance:

Getting into better shape

These days many of us are carrying a few extra pounds. But, unless you are so morbidly obese that you have documentary makers queuing at your door wanting to make a programme about you, it's probably not going to be quite as hard as you think to improve your body shape.

The idea of going to the gym fills most people with the same amount of dread as the idea of applying a chisel to their scrotums. If you've never been though, why not give it a try? Not once, but twice. The first time is never an easy experience, but you will probably find that the second time is not quite so bad. And from then on it can often end up as just part of your regular routine. It will probably never be fun, but it should eventually reach the 'necessary chore' level, similar to washing the dishes or cleaning your apartment.

The main problem with going to the gym for many men is that it is just so damn boring – your body might have been getting all of the exercise that it needs, but your brain finds the whole process to be dull. Many good gyms have TVs now that can keep you entertained while on many of the machines, but a solution to gym tedium is to download a variety of podcasts onto your MP3 player so you can listen to them and learn while putting my body through its paces. Of course, checking out the hot, fit chicks in their skin-tight leotards during the process also helps ease the pain and tedium a lot too.

If you can afford a personal trainer, tell him or her that all you want to do is lose your gut and become 'human shaped'. In this way you won't waste time turning your arms and legs into trees trunks which, while nice to have, is very much an optional extra as far as most women are concerned.

Don't expect to have a six-pack in a matter of weeks. You just need to get rid of the beer barrel and, with just a few weeks of effort, it is possible to make quite a dramatic impact on your waistline.

In summary, although the idea of going to a gym might fill you with absolute dread, why not just give it a try and see how it goes? You have little to lose and a whole to gain in the process. And once you see the initial results, it makes it a whole lot easier to keep going back week after week until you really have made a major improvement to your looks.

The other way of quickly dropping a few pounds is through diet. Again, it's not easy and it's not an exciting prospect thinking of trying to live on celery for the next few weeks. In keeping with the Complete Bastard Manifesto, however, there are some ways to cheat.

The way to do so is using a programme like the 'Atkins Method' or 'South Beach Diet', which is how many celebrities have been able to drop weight rapidly. The diet is a relatively easy one for men to use because it allows them to gorge themselves on proteins like meat and dairy, providing that they stay away from carbohydrates and sugar. Nutritionists do warn that this is not the healthiest way of eating, but they can't deny that it is one of the easiest and fastest ways of fighting the flab.

This is just a brief introduction to getting yourself in slightly better shape. If you would like more information on this part of the process, there is a vast industry out there to help you. Either buy a book on one of the diets, or do a little internet searching and you should quickly learn how the systems work at their basic levels.

Through going to the gym a few nights each week and/or going on one of these diets, it's possible to drop two or three pounds a week, so you can see some reasonable results in just a month.

Masking your flaws

Probably even more important than taking steps to change an imperfect body is to change an imperfect head. You need to take care of this faster than your body because potential dates are going to see your head from the profile picture you will be posting as soon as you go online and will make a snap decision as to whether they find you attractive or not from this alone. With your body, however, as long as you don't use full-body pictures, it will only be upon your first face-to-face meeting with them when you will be forced to reveal your full-self to them and, by that time, you should already have begun to have wooed them with your wonderful new Complete Bastard personality.

Fortunately, fixing many facial inadequacies can be arranged in a matter of minutes in many cases, as opposed to the many weeks or months it can take to get your body into shape.

Below is a list of the main turn-offs for women and quick-fixes for each of them:

Scruffy hair: Fortunately this is one of the easiest problems to fix. Learn to spend some of your hard-earned cash on paying for good quality haircuts from top-end stylists. Go for a high-quality cut in a modern style that will last longer and will be easier to manage. Secondly, the act of paying that little extra will be a boost for your confidence too – looking good means feeling good mentally.

A good hairdresser usually also takes care of other minor problems like ear hair or overgrown sideburns, but for most men attention to things like nose hair, sprouting chest hair that peeks out of your shirt, bushy eyebrows or the ones that join in the middle (mono-brows) are physical details often missed and thought of by a careless male dater as 'not important'. Wrong – the Sasquatch look is very rarely popular with women.

Take the time to trim your body hair regularly. Women notice such things and it's a few bucks well-spent to invest in hair clippers or get a professional beautician's help to sort these things out.

Greying hair: For the more Mature Bastard, greying hair is nothing to be worried about, particularly if he is going after some 'cougars'. To the right age group of women,

Sean Connery and George Clooney are as sexy as it gets. If you started to go grey at a young age though, you might want to do something about it. There are various products on the market that help banish those grey hairs quickly and painlessly.

Balding hair: A bigger problem is if your hair is receding. Here there is no quick fix available. The worst thing that you can do though is to try and mask the problem. Comb-overs, toupees and plugs will all get found out sooner or later and will just make you look sad. The best way around the problem is to go as short as you dare. The ideal solution for most baldies is to simply get a razor and shave it all off. In such a way, it's possible to make yourself look up to a decade younger in under ten minutes. Very few women have a problem with shaved heads, whereas many find long, balding hair to be the ultimate turnoff.

Glasses: If the eyes are truly the door to the soul, then many people's souls are those of a half-blind, squinting, myopic mole that hasn't been able to function properly they were a teenager. The prospect of wearing glasses during a date is never appealing. It shows you as weak in the eyes (no pun intended) of the female who is innately programmed to sniff out good, strong, healthy male genes.

One solution is contact lens. Though luckily for the weak-eyed male, glasses now come in a range of fashionable styles that means wearing them is far less of a taboo than some years ago.

Facial hair: The preferred option is always clean-shaven as it shows you have made an effort to scrub up, plus a lot of women don't like kissing men with grizzly faces. There are also lots of extra products on the market that will give your shave an even cleaner look including post-shave moisturisers and balms, treatments to help shaving rash and nicks, face cleansing soaps and gels. Look out for these as they all help to give you that polished, well-maintained appearance that woman will be impressed by.

However, a lot of women like a man to look a little rough around the edges and some 'designer stubble' can do wonders for making your previously clean shaven face appear a little more rugged. The best advice is to scope out whether your date prefers 'the rough' or 'the smooth' look. Then shave to suit.

A lot of facial 'furniture' just looks odd. Intricate sideburns, ornate moustaches, sculptured goatee beards, and so on. What is there to admire of any man who spends a large part of his day grooming his facial hair? Sometimes though, it can be advantageous. Some goatees can make a fat face look thinner in the same way that vertical stripes in clothing make people look slimmer, so it can be a useful accessory if you have a bit of a moon-face. So if it makes you more confident or hides a double chin, then fine, but apart from that, let's leave the funny facial topiary for magicians, IT nerds and circus ring masters.

Bad teeth: One of your most important features is your smile. This means you have to ensure that your lips and teeth are in good condition. Cracked or swollen lips and a set of rotten or crooked teeth revolt everyone. Think about what the gorgeous woman across from you on your date is thinking when contemplating whether she wants to kiss you or not.

It is worth spending the necessary money on getting your teeth straightened, whitened and kept in top shape by regular visits to a good dentist. Things like gum disease can lead to bad breath and a healthy, well looked-after mouth can only be good for your smile and your attractiveness to women. Learn to brush more, eat healthier and floss daily. If this sounds like your dentist preaching at you, it's because we're both right!

Body odour: One of the main attractors between two people is how they smell to each other. Invest as much as you can afford to in deodorant and an expensive aftershave to make sure you smell good. It is one of the easiest compliments for your date to give you and it's certainly something that triggers a positive response in her eyes.

With aftershave, the best advice is to try out a few. There are hundreds of brands on the market with a scent to suit. Just go out and smell some and select the one or two that seem to be popular with buyers. Better still, take a female friend to help you or ask the advice of one of those girls at the perfume counter. Its free advice they are paid to provide.

Blemishes: As with bad teeth, there are many ways to combat the problem of spots. The most effective way is to go and see a dermatologist if you have a serious problem. If that's too extreme, hit the 'Clearasil' or any other products that are designed for minimizing the effects. At the risk of appearing too metro-sexual, think about using a concealer when you are getting a profile picture made (but go easy on it or else you run the risk of looking like a transvestite).

As can be seen from the above, there are usually some quick and dirty solutions for hiding most of your inadequacies. In this respect, a little bit of effort can go a very long way. But don't be overwhelmed by this long list of changes that you could make in order to improve your physical appearance – they are all going to help for sure, but the improvements that you make to your confidence and personality are going to count for a whole lot more in the great scheme of things.

Dress the part

'Clothes make the man' as Mark Twain once said. Whereas, to many guys, clothes are just a way of hiding our nakedness, to women they are a vital part of someone's personal packaging. This means that, if your wardrobe consists of nothing but faded heavy metal T-shirts and ripped jeans, you need to do a bit of shopping.

For the average men with little sense or care for fashion, where to begin can be overwhelming. Should you buy one outfit or mix and match? What cut of clothes does your body and size best suit? Which colours enhance how you look? And so on.

A solid basic strategy has always been to buy a few good quality items of clothing that you like and feel good in, that are classic in cut, and not overly fashionable for the moment.

Don't think that you need to rush out and buy a designer suit because, if you're a college student dressing for campus, wearing a suit is just going to make you look like a pretentious fool.

The secret with successful dressing is **context**. How you dress is your unique expression. It's your 'moving billboard' to the world about who you are and what you are about. So leaf through the pages of the many male fashion magazines – and look around you.

In chapter seven, we will look at creating your Cyber Persona. Whatever you decide upon, you will need to dress the part. To do so, have a look at what the successful guys with similar personae are wearing – the ones that always seem to be the centre of attention, the ones with the hottest girls swarming around them. Note their style and dress in a similar fashion, whether that's leather jackets and tattoos if you want to be part of the biker community, or tailored suits if you plan on hanging around wine bars with the city bankers.

And that really is all there is to it.

Body language

Your body language gives out clear signals as to how you are feeling inside and no amount of soap or silk will hide a man who is feeling low esteem inside. Instead, think tall and walk tall. Recognise how your posture affects the way in which people perceive you. Keep your head held high, your chin up, your back straight, shoulders back, make lots of eye contact with people (it builds trust as well as focus), try not to blink too often and walk like you are in pursuit of the women and not angling to escape her.

Tilting your head upon first meeting someone together with good eye-contact increases your perceived warmth and the impact of your presence.

Then there is the initial handshake. Too weak and you immediately appear to have a weak personality. Too strong and you can appear to be overly dominating – so keep it firm, but not overly so. And make sure that your palms are dry as otherwise she will know that you are incredibly nervous – not a good sign at all.

While talking to her, keep your hands away from your face and avoid scratching your head or any other type of verbal ticks. They will be perceived as signs of nervousness and lack of confidence or, worse still, that you are lying (or ridden with lice).

One gesture that exudes confidence is where you place the fingertips of one hand against those of the other – sometimes calls 'steepling'. This gesture exudes authority and shows people that you are sure of what you are saying.

Above all else, smile. A smile indicates to another person that you are happy, confident, satisfied and in control of the situation. It is also a very simple and obvious sign to a woman that you are interested in her and will make it very easy for her to reciprocate these feelings.

These simple body language tips might take a while to master if they don't come naturally to you but, like everything else in life, practice makes perfect.

Perhaps these details might seem unimportant to you. But you would be dead wrong. With 55% of communication effectiveness coming from non-verbal communication compared with just 7% coming from the actual words you use, all of the Bastardly advice contained elsewhere in this book can come to nothing at all if your body language doesn't match the wit and charm coming from your mouth.

In summary, how you appear to others feeds into how confident you feel inside. It is for that reason that, for every date you go on now, groom yourself like a man who is confident around women; dress like a man who is confident around women; move like a man who is confident around women, and pursue like a man who is confident around women.

Try all the tips given here and, within a month, you'll see a positive difference. The next Dating Diary proves that, if they can work for me, then they can surely work for you.

Dressing up to bring 'em down

A bit of 'self-reflection' shows the Complete Bastard he still has some important changes to make.

Even with my newfound confidence, I was still not making the kind of impact I was hoping for with women. Going up to a great looking girl was a great confidence booster, but it could also lead to instant rejection even before I had the chance to talk her round to my devilish designs.

There was one bar, 'The Merry Jester', that I used to go to a lot. I like bars. They are one of the few bastions left in life where a Complete Bastard can swagger in through the door, get himself a 10-year old whisky on the rocks, and shoot the breeze with any lowlife around him. Not to mention the wealth of possibilities for hitting on chicks.

This evening in the bar, I was feeling a little down. I had been becoming quietly frustrated at not being able to instantly win girls' attention. It was taking me a long time to get their attention during conversation. Just having the confidence to chat was getting me liked, but it still wasn't enough to get me laid. The result of these constant knockbacks was that confidence – that two-bit whore who sleeps with you when the going is good – was beginning to pack up her purse and think about heading for the door.

After chatting to a few girls unsuccessfully and sinking a few whiskies, I went to take a leak. As I went to return to the bar, I caught my reflection in the mirror. A life of trawling bars and clubs was beginning to etch itself on my face. I looked rough, haggard and unkempt.

'Shit!' I thought. 'Is it any wonder women aren't falling over themselves to kiss me? I hardly look like the kind of guy who has success with women.'

And that's when I realised I needed to make my next change. It was time to start **looking** as confident as I was feeling.

The next day I decided to begin my overhaul. I had no idea where to begin. All I knew was that I looked nothing like those hunks who just schmooze on into a room and seem to suck in the fawning attentions of the women-folk like turbo-boosted vacuum cleaners.

I figured that, with limited money to buy myself a wardrobe of designer clothes and no desire for reconstructive facial surgery, I'd have to re-invent myself with what little money and know how I could muster.

I began to think of every successful guy I knew. And men who weren't - just good with women – as well. I thought about the guys who were successful in business, famous movie stars, guys at the bar who won trophies at the golf club, and even Papa Bastard in his grizzled, dishevelled, beat-up old way.

No two of these men were similar in how they looked or dressed, but there was a common theme to them all: you looked at them twice whenever they were around.

Part of this was their aura – their raw charisma. It was confidence again – whenever she was nestled inside your brains, your back snapped upright and your walk went from a Wimp Chimp to King Kong. Confidence made you smile more, gesticulate more, and reach out and touch the world more. She was deep inside me – but I had to start dressing for her.

A better posture soon made me realise that the clothes I wore were a way of showing off my personality. I'd read about other male seducers who used a tactic called 'peacocking'. (This is where men dress to impress by wearing clothes and accessories that would catch women's attention).

The fact that there were men out there scoring using this technique really stunned me. Do women really pluck for some over-dressed, over-preened poseur in wacky pants and a ten-gallon cowboy hat? I can see that it would take a lot of confidence to go wandering around town looking like a complete boob and that seems to be the basis of that theory. I just couldn't see that dressing up like a circus clown was going to work for me.

Papa Bastard had something to say on the subject as always:

'You know, Son,' he growled, 'When a man spends more time in front of a mirror than on top of a woman, then **all** us men are done for.'

I agreed and reckoned I could get together a few outfits – classic in cut, fashionable but affordable – that would stop me from standing out like a fashion faux-pas. They would also help me blend in as a regular guy who understood the need to look smart, but wasn't image-obsessed. How many women wanted a guy who outshone them anyway?

I began to read as many men's fashion and lifestyle magazine as I could. From these, I noted trends, what was 'in', and began to understand what sort of clothes suited my body shape and skin colouring.

I also paid more attention to detail than just simply clothing colour and style. I invested in quality over quantity. I bought one good pair of smart shoes, found a good tailor who made sure any clothes I bought clothes fitted me well, and began to understand which fabrics looked and felt like 'quality' to the touch.

As my wardrobe began to take shape, I began to face up to my face. I wasn't an ugly man, but I was no male model either. Could I really make myself look better without getting some Beverley Hills surgeon to take his hammer and chisel to me?

I began at the top. I've never had the time or the inclination to style my own hair. I'd wake up; shower and pretty much just walk out of the house for work. Now though, I opted to invest in a top hair stylist to give me a cut that was both fashionable and did not need a lot of styling after I walked out of the salon.

The rest was a personal battle between my mirror and me, trying to find ways to look smarter and better. Looking after the rest of my hair became important – keeping clean shaven, looking out for wayward nasal or ear hair and trimming accordingly.

Then, I got into cleansing. There are a mass of male grooming products on the market today – potions, scents, ointments, balms and creams. Check them out and try a few. Some work, some don't – but find a couple of good ones that focus on keeping your skin clean, your body smelling good and any blemishes hidden.

One of the things that women always pick up on is a guy's scent. I learned early on that spending big on a quality scent that tickles her little nostrils can be an instant attraction to her. Why do you think the scent industry is a multi-million dollar market built on sex and seduction? So, avoid those nasty, cheap scents that your grandmother gives you at Christmas. After all, what does Granny know? She smells of her own pee.

Finally, there is the need to focus on the Biggies – the imperfections that can't be cured (or Beta Banes as I call them). It's stuff like baldness, poor vision, short stature, and bad skin. No guy has ever genuinely lost a chick because of being cursed with any of these Beta Banes. Sure they can lower your confidence, but there are plenty of modern-day ways to help stave off the inevitable or hide the flaws. And anyway, there's some balding, myopic short-ass doing perfectly fine with the girls every day of his life without any miracle cure (that's me!).

As time has gone on, I have probably become more vain and pay way more attention than is good for me as to how I look and dress. My know-how of how to look the part has now reached epic proportions. But, if ever that day comes when I strut out into a bar wearing a cowboy hat for the ladies, just shoot me!

– 5 –
Understanding Women As A Complete Bastard

The female enigma

Women are complex and irrational creatures that a man can spend a lifetime trying to work out. Yet a man is still likely to pass away without knowing even half of the answers that belong to the questions posed by these unfathomable creatures.

So if you're expecting to learn all of the secrets to womanhood in just this one chapter, then you're going to be disappointed. It would take a whole book just to scratch the surface of what's going on in their strange, alien minds the whole time.

But before you throw this book away in disgust and demand your money back, read on to learn some quick and dirty tricks for being able to pigeonhole the most commonly encountered types of women online.

Women online

In chapter one, we looked at how the internet has changed the way we interact with one another. In particular, how it affects online dating. It is clear that people do behave differently online. The online environment affects how women behave as daters too.

As a man of dubious intent, I still firmly believe that online dating has been a hugely liberating force for many women. Instead of it being a threatening haven for scammers and perverts, the Net has actually become a safe place for women to both be courted and play seducer.

There are countless chick-lit books on the market where women tell the story of their experience as serial internet daters, dupers, or how they used men for sex. Their accounts are often frank and funny:

> 'Without a doubt, I definitely think online dating is a venue where people who want to meet people gather. Just beware. Be smart. And don't take it so seriously.'
>
> - Jane Coloccia, 'Confessions of an Online dating Addict'

'When you spin up the dating energy, the goal is not necessarily to meet 'the one'. Rather it's to create a new kind of environment in your life where the unexpected can happen.'

> - Linda J Maynard, 'The Savvy Women's Guide to Online Dating'

Some are a little more perceptive as to the threat of the Complete Bastard who lurks in the shadows of life:

'With Internet Dating, the inexperienced cannot only get burned, but also scorched and charred, if not careful.'

> - Trisha Ventkner, 'Internet Dates from Hell'

Even when writers were faced with a negative occurrence, they were savvy enough to know when one was a **real** threat and when they'd just come upon some derivative form of a Complete Bastard. It all goes to show that online dating the Complete Bastard way holds little risk for women other than the occasional heartache and a few lost perks.

Every woman who goes online dating has a unique experience involving a specific set of men – as unique as the person they are and the people that they choose to meet. Yet, in my own experience of meeting, dating, and speaking with hundreds of women who were active daters both on and offline, there were a few dater stereotypes that kept re-emerging over and over again during my many encounters.

The four types of women

I was able to loosely categorise 'female online daters' into four broad character types. These types are detailed in the remainder of this chapter and are stated as:

1. Doomed Damsels

2. Thrill Seekers

3. Virtual Vixens

4. Power Mongers

These types form a framework that offers a portable and surprisingly accurate means to quickly pigeonhole the kind of women you are interacting with. Plus there's additional advice in this section on how best to use the 'Four Women Type' to get the maximum results from dating with any individual one of these types. You'll also find the 'Four Women Type' approach works in both the cyber and 'real' world.

So, let's go meet our first female character type. She is arguably the one who we all recognise as the most clichéd user of online dating sites: the Doomed Damsel.

1. Doomed Damsel

Strapline
More Jones than Bardot

Demographic
25 to 35-years-old

Personality traits
Earthy
Comfortable
Nice
Generous
Easily duped

More about her
Online dating veteran: She's been trying to find 'Mr Right' for years and it's no surprise to learn that she's tried and failed using every means possible in his pursuit.

Utter romantic: The fact she still believes there is that 'Special One' should be enough to convince you that this women is to romance what a well-pinged arrow is to Cupid's bow.

Chosen path: Usually works for a charity or something equally as worthy. Doomed Damsels rarely get to the top in their career, as being 'nearly, but not quite' is what defines them in all aspects of their life.

What she's looking for
In her words: 'Someone to complete me.'
In reality: 'Someone to completely date me, dupe me and dump me.'

Ideal date scenario for her
You and her alone in her attic after Sunday lunch which you cooked together while exchanging stories of past 'bad' dates. You're both giggling and snorting over her childhood vinyl collection and she is overwhelmed when you reveal that you had exactly the same records as her as a kid. (Or at least that's what you tell her!).

Ideal dupe scenario for you
Its 2a.m. You roll into her place drunk and wake her up by collapsing onto her bed. She's furious but, after an hour's arguing, she agrees to buy you that Rolex watch you've been angling for so you know what time it is in future, then gives you her best blow-job performance yet. All in a night's work!

Maintenance levels
Low: Doomed Damsels tolerate loads. This includes partners who are flabby, grubby,

cranky, moody, farty, smokey, drinky, problem-drinky, druggy and Bastardly. It all just adds to a man's charm.

Watch out for

The guilt trip: Novice Bastards should be prepared to resist the guilt trip that this type will constantly hang on them. It's a trick to keep you with them. Look out for lines like: 'You're just like all the other men in my life!' or 'I just want someone that cares... really cares.'

Possible psychoses

No real deep-rooted psychoses to watch out for in her. However, the major problem is that, if you're not careful, she may drive **you** into an asylum. She's just too damn nice. So nice in fact, that any faux Complete Bastard will eventually have to fork out for expensive dental work to repair the molars he's been gnashing with rage as he's dragged around early morning car boot sales or quaint tea-rooms in the countryside, all in the name of 'romance'. No true Bastard, however, stays around that long.

Best advice

Get as much as you can, then get out quick!

2. Thrill Seeker

Strapline

Older but not any wiser

Demographic

39 to 50-years-old

Personality traits

Wild
Wacky
Wanton
Wicked
Warped

More about her

Bring it on!: Whether it's online dating, speed-dating, meeting in a bar or frequenting torture dens in deepest, darkest Soho, this veritable social whirlwind is up for it all. This older, though still highly flirtatious, type is a man eater and boasts openly of devouring men for dinner.

Boring? Me!?: Scared stiff of being seen as dull. Expect her to use all available means to persuade you that she's as mad as a hatter. Examples include phone calls at 4a.m., naughty pictures of her bits by email or MMS, and persistent promises of 'mind-blowing sex'.

Creative-type: She'll probably have some vapid job in the Arts and be constantly names-dropping. A Complete Bastard will make her prove herself and she'll be only too keen (and easily duped) into doing so. Prepare for invitations to gallery openings and guest list parties aplenty.

What she's looking for
In her words: Madness! Mayhem! Mischief!

In reality: Someone to cure her awful fear of dying alone in her own urine surrounded by malnourished cats.

Ideal date scenario for her
Couple of quick cocktails at some uptown designer bar, then off to party it up all night, clubbing with champagne and anything that goes nasal-ward.

Ideal dupe scenario for you
You convince her to bankroll a trip for two to an exotic island off the African coast to join the Hula-Hula tribe to detox and 'find yourselves' for three months while you write a self-help book.

Maintenance levels
Low to ultra-high: Thrill Seekers are the bipolar daters from potential Hell. They swing from magnificent highs, where you'll be dragged along on their every whim, to dark lows when their reality kicks in. You have to know when to be with them when they're spending – and to avoid them when they're spent.

Watch out for
The moment they fall for you (See Possible Psychoses below).

Possible psychoses
When this worm turns, all hell breaks loose. Bright-eyed and carefree turns to dead-eyed and nasty, as she realises that you are 'The One' – and she ain't gonna let you go nowhere! Prepare an escape plan immediately if this happens.

Best advice
Party with this madcap madam at your peril and beware the tipping point!

3. Virtual Vixen
Strapline
Existence is futile

Demographic
18 to 100-years-old

Personality traits
Cyber

Pixelated
Connected
Ethereal
Untouchable

More about her
Web 2.0: Online dating was made for the Virtual Vixen. She is too internet savvy to see dating as anything different from social networking, gaming, emailing, ordering a DVD online, and so on. To her, 'Second Life' is 'First Life'.

Denizen of cyberspace: This girl belongs firmly within the Net generation – high-tech, wired, and with a typing speed that's Warp Factor 12. This type is online 24/7.

Chosen path: Any job that involves stroking a keyboard all day is usually where these ladies feel safest.

What she's looking for
In her words: 'The one'

In reality: 'The cyber-one'

Ideal date scenario for her
Online, a bank of computer screens, her own server, a hyper-fast internet connection, and 400 men all ogling her onscreen persona while she IMs with each of them effortlessly.

Ideal dupe scenario for you
You get her to fall in love with you, but you're really a sixty-five-year old disabled transvestite on the run from a murder rap.

Maintenance levels
Nil to Low: Virtual Vixens like control. Hence, when she's in the mood for online flirtation, she's in the mood for online flirtation. And as she's cyber, she never appears online as being moody, jaded or irrational. Bonus. And, as you're never likely to meet her offline, there aren't going to be any expensive dinners or drink bills to pay.

Watch out for
Guilt deletion: Virtual Vixens disappear fast when they realise that showing their bits on a webcam in the name of steamy Cybersex is indeed a dirty, shameful pastime.

Possible psychoses
There's a whole host of virtual illnesses now – internet addiction, repetitive strain injury, cybersex addiction – take your pick.

Best advice
Don't expect anything more than an onscreen romance.

4. Power Monger

Strapline
Control their minds and the rest will follow.

Demographic
25 to 35-years-old

Personality traits
Driven
Ambitious
Go-getting
Hectic
Calculating

More about her
<u>Promoting efficiency</u>: Dates are like meetings. Interact, analyse and make decision. Next, reject 99% of potential mates as you attempt to 'seal the deal' with that special one.

<u>Hectic hearts</u>: With barefaced audacity she'll ask you: 'Can I fit you in after my last meeting at work and before my Yoga class?' Will you ever be able to get laid in her busy schedule?

<u>Over-achievers</u>: Lawyer, bankers, business woman. Power Mongers come from any background where it fits to crave success and competition. They love climbing to the top far more than climbing into bed.

What she's looking for
<u>In her words:</u> 'To hold the World Cup winning male'

<u>In reality:</u> 'A trophy boyfriend for the mantelpiece'

Ideal date scenario for her
A large bouquet of flowers arrives at her office with a card announcing your arrival. Your helicopter is hovering outside her office block and all her work colleagues gawp in envy as she gets in and flies off. She's wined and dined before switching to your Lear jet where you sweep her off to the Maldives for a long weekend.

Ideal dupe scenario for you
The above, but on **her** credit card.

Maintenance levels
<u>High to very high</u>: High class is all to the Power Monger. She has to be seen in the right places wearing the right clothes drinking the right drinks with the right guy at the right time.

Watch out for

The Power Monger is totally driven by her status in society. If she thinks that you are 'last season' or she spots a Bigger Better Deal, expect a rapid dumping.

Possible psychoses

<u>Medium</u>: The typical bunny-boiler type. The Power Monger is used to getting what she wants. When Shakespeare wrote, 'Hell hath no fury like a woman scorned', he must have just been dumped by a Power Monger. Cross this type at your peril. She plays hard ball at work and will do the same with you. Her wrath is likely to be vicious but brief, however, as she'll soon realise that she doesn't really have the time available to make your life a living hell for too long.

Best advice

Not for Novice Bastards. With her gold cards and company expense accounts, dating a Power Monger can be like having a winning lottery ticket. But, be warned, if you want out before she does, then things could get very messy. Know a good lawyer.

Using the Four Women Types

Four very different women, but each with their own delights and dangers. While in the dating game, you'll come across all of these types and part of the fun is trying to work out which of these four types the woman you're looking to date most closely resembles.

It is best to think of the 'Four Women Type' as a rule of thumb. If you can pinpoint a range of traits that best fits one type, you know what you're dealing with. You can then tailor your coping strategy accordingly.

Any coping strategy should aim to include much of the teaching, tips and techniques that this book provides. This will ensure that you get as much as you can out of your date. Plus, of course, the secret to being a Complete Bastard is not getting caught. Survival is paramount and you need to learn what you must **avoid** with each type too.

Understanding women is no easy task, but the 'Four Women Type' framework is a portable, useable and highly effective tool that will aid you in pigeonholing just who and what you are dealing with while dating.

Of course, as a framework it's not flawless. There aren't simply four types of women in the world. Instead, you should think that there's probably a little bit of each type in every woman that you meet online dating and beyond.

Part of the reason why dating is such an exciting experience is that **all** women are unique in character, personality, and attitude. But that doesn't stop the Complete Bastard making his life a whole lot easier by working with just these four basic stereotypes.

Also, no single type is necessarily the 'best' or the one that you should ultimately seek. Depending on your wants and needs, one type may be more conducive or susceptible to your *modus operandi* than the others. That's for you to work out and decide.

Sometimes, it will be immediately apparent which category a woman falls into from her online profile alone. Look carefully as to how she describes herself and what she's looking for together with other clues such as her job or interests.

Other times, however, you will need to start communicating with the woman in order to find out more about her personality. As you begin to 'frame' women through the 'Four Women Type' approach, it will surprise you how many women do fit into a particular category. And once you have successfully categorized them, it will be so much easier for you to construct your strategy as how best to move ahead with your seduction of them, and how to spot the warning signs that it's time to move on.

No single type is easier to manipulate or dupe than any of the others. All offer perks that you will see are within your grasp. And all threaten perils that may impede your getting these benefits.

However, with the right knowledge, applied in the correct way, comes the power to make sure the perks come to you and not to some other guy. You should now be starting to realise that you can begin to gain the upper-hand over women who, just several pages back ago, seemed almost impossible for you to even consider as an option.

If you still want to argue that all women are too individualistic to categorise, then that's fine. Let's agree to disagree. But many Complete Bastards have had great success and fun with the 'Four Women Type' approach already. Plus, successful Complete Bastards don't stick around long enough to discover the finite intricacies of every woman he meets and dates. He leaves it for her shrink or some Wimp Chimp to pick up the pieces after he's gone.

In conclusion, what is important for a Complete Bastard to understand about women is that they are fickle creatures who are themselves adept dating game players. They have their own social rules and best practices within their gender and they'll be damned if they want us men to know how they work.

The good news is that now you have an easy-to-use framework to begin taming women and understanding how they will behave under certain circumstances. It all takes time, commitment and lots of dates to finally see that women aren't as complex as you probably might once have thought.

The next Diary extract entitled 'The Date-athlon' tells of how the Complete Bastard planned a mammoth dating challenge – dating ten women in one week. He was able to use the 'Four Type Women' approach to work out what kind of women he was dealing with and how best to manipulate them for his selfish gain.

The Date-athlon

The Complete Bastard reveals a lusty fetish – dating ten women in one week and not getting caught.

As I began to reach my pinnacle of flirting online and setting up dates, my confidence began to soar – as did my ability to seduce all types of women and to hone the potential to dupe them.

One of the Complete Bastard's most common goals is building a harem of dupable lovers. As Papa Bastard says: 'If you're going to be a Complete Bastard to one, it's just as easy to be a Bastard to 'em all!'

Even he was impressed however, when I came up with the Date-athlon - a frenzied seven-day madcap marathon of ten first dates with ten different, unsuspecting chicks.

But where would my Date-athlon take me? What would I become by the climax of it all? Would there even be a climax? Or would there be lots and lots of climaxes screamed from rooms all over the city with me as the Casanova-style protagonist, leaping from bedroom to bedroom? And what was the point of it all? What would the Date-athlon achieve? A lover? A wife? Many wives? A hernia? More worryingly – would I get caught? And if I did, would I live to tell the tale?

Monday, 1p.m.: Met city banker 'Magpie29' in an upmarket eatery for a lunchtime flirt. Online dating Newbie and 100% Power Monger. Apart from her seeming more attentive to her Blackberry than to me on occasion, this charming chick and I clearly hit it off. We parted after a long kiss and she promised to squeeze me in her diary for a next date whenever she can.

Monday, 7p.m.: After a quick nap and a shower back at my pad, I'd invited 'Backflip09' for a few drinks at 'The Merry Jester' bar. This former gymnastics champion turned school teacher was a black, six-foot stunner and clearly on course to wind up as a Doomed Damsel. Luckily for her, I was on top form on this date – and she soon found herself back at my place, re-discovering her former acrobatic prowess and forgetting her mid-life woes.

Tuesday, 4p.m.: Even though feeling a little jaded after my romp with 'Backflip09', I still met 'V4Victory' – an online dating veteran and an ultimate Doomed Damsel. I chose a coffee shop for our date as she'd asked for a 'quiet, safe place to meet'. Clearly caffeine had no effect on her: this girl was dull, nervous and even her great cleavage wasn't going to stop me vowing to dump this chick pronto. She did pay for all I could cram into my mouth after I played my heartless, 'Oh, dear, I've maxed my credit card' trick. Looks like she'll be on the dating circuit for years to come.

Tuesday, 9p.m.: Hotel bar, city-centre. This was more like it! 'Kiss_Me' was gorgeous – 27 years old, working in media sales, from an Old Money family, and scintillating company. Something of a Thrill Seeker but with no obviously deep-rooted psychoses I could spy, 'Kiss_Me' giggled and flirted her way throughout our meeting. She even asked me to join her and her friends on a skiing holiday next month. If I can keep focused, she is a definite Dupe for the Duping.

Wednesday, 9a.m.: My bedroom. If there is one thing that Virtual Vixen, 'Dark_n_ dirty' likes to do before work, it's jack off. She's the ultimate cyber chick, who just loves to get her rocks off to phone or IM sex chat. She has a strict rule though that she will never meet offline. She looks good in her online pictures, has the sexiest of English voices, and screams like a banshee when she hits climax. For me, it's just another satisfied customer, no matter where she hides.

Wednesday, 10p.m.: Sometimes great dates come in the smallest sizes. Weighing in at only 120 pounds and 5-foot tall, South African property tycoon 'Reckless_ Roonie' was cute and curvaceous. From all of the women on my Date-athlon, she was the hardest to pigeonhole – part Thrill Seeker and part Power Monger. She was out to date for what she could get and this was a swift few drinks and back to hers. Mind-blowing sex and a definite see-again.

Thursday, 11p.m.: At the halfway point of the Date-athlon, I was beginning to flag. I figured 'Brooklyn_Babe', hair stylist to the stars, may have provided me with the lift I needed. This chick was certainly full of energy that defied her 40-years. I decided to meet her in a nightclub close to my apartment. Unfortunately, she was a Thrill Seeker of the worst variety, and she proceeded to drink herself silly before trying to straddle me in the club. I was tired and I figured a little rejection would make her all the keener when she sobered up.

Friday, 8p.m.: I had to travel out of the city for this date. 'Barbarella' was a foxy single mother. It was a shame, as she was hot. Luckily for me, she'd turned to online dating to inject a little oomph back in her life. Clearly, she enjoyed our date at her local wine bar as, after her third glass of Sauvignon, she was rubbing her heels against my leg and whispering some of the smuttiest lines I'd ever heard (and believe me – I've heard a **lot**!). I hope her kid never finds out what Mummy did in the alleyway behind the bar after last orders.

Saturday 3p.m.: It's an odd time for a date, but that's all I could get from Power Monger, 'Jenny_Jen'. Dressed in business suit and sadly more plain in the flesh than in her profile pics, she was manager of a staff of twenty men, and took great pride in telling me how stupid they all were. A strange theory in my opinion, as she was the one who left our date getting a false phone number from me, footing the bill, and showing how easily duped women can be. She may have thought she was smart and led a hectic life, but I'm too busy a Bastard to waste time on this petty dangler.

Sunday, 7p.m.: The Lord may have rested on the seventh day, but there was no such respite for this Hard Working Bastard. 'Eyeful_Tower' was a hot French babe from Paris who was now living and working in the city as a graphic designer. She was 29-years old, hot and haughty. As befits her Gallic heritage, she demanded some arty date traipsing off to some poetry reading in the city. However, I did demand booze straight afterwards to loosen her up. Sadly, although we made it back to her apartment for some Ooh-La-La, she was a definite husband-hunter (Doomed Damsel). I would maybe have to play this one a little cool – which was a shame, as she was one fanciful French femme.

And there you have it. Ten dates, ten very different women, and a hugely enjoyable experience, with lots of sex to boot. All were met as a result of meeting on internet dating sites and wooed towards a real life date via the art of flirting online. In the next chapter, it's time for you to see how creating your own Cyber Persona is the first step in getting your own set of dastardly dates.

Complete Bastards Online Dating Tools

Tools of the trade

As well as preparing yourself properly for the many dates that await you as you begin your online dating experience, you also need to prepare the necessary technology.

As mentioned in chapter one, your entire online dating experience doesn't necessarily have to cost you a dime. If you really wanted to, you could access the internet from a library for free, meet your dates only through the free sites, and take your dates for nothing more than a walk in the park. If you did take this approach though, you would be dramatically limiting your potential for meeting the large quantity and high quality of women that it's possible to meet by investing just a modest amount of cash.

To get the maximum amount from your online dating experiences, here's what you're going to need:

Internet connection

Chances are that you've already got this sorted so let's not dwell on it. Getting the most out of online dating requires your being online a lot of the time. You'll also want a good broadband connection if you are going to use webcams or voice chatting on a regular basis.

Anonymous email account

It's a good idea to keep your online dating emails completely separate from the rest of your life. Don't even think of using your work email address for online dating purposes – you're just asking for trouble.

It's best not to use your primary personal email address either (especially if you're already in a relationship!) It's possible to make a Google Search for any email address and you don't want any of your potential dates to do this and find that you have some skeletons in your cyber-closet that a quick search of your regular email address would uncover.

The Complete Bastard approach to online dating does involve your taking some risks and this could mean making some mistakes along the way. Having a dedicated email address just for dating is a damage limitation exercise. If it all goes wrong, then you just need to abandon the account and start up another.

You can set up a free anonymous account from many sites including:

www.gmail.com

www.yahoo.com

www.hotmail.com

Pick a fairly neutral email address or one that is going to match your screen name that you will use on the dating site itself (see chapter seven for more information).

Instant messenger account

Instant messaging (or IM) is a very useful tool in the Complete Bastard's online dating arsenal as it allows you to communicate instantly with people, making it the perfect tool for flirting.

The most popular instant messaging program today is Windows Live Messenger which you can download for free at:

messenger.live.com

Or, if you prefer Yahoo! to Microsoft, then download their messaging program at:

messenger.yahoo.com

Both programs are able to communicate with one another and so there no need to download both of them – either one will do.

Skype is now becoming more and more popular as an alternative, particularly in Europe, so you might want to download that one as well from:

www.skype.com

AIM and ICQ are two other instant messaging programs, but their popularity has waned over the past few years and so there's probably little need to download these as well.

Microphone

The instant messaging programs described above now have the facility to voice chat for free as well as chat by text and you can also use them to make cheap phone calls as well. Many laptops these days come with microphones built in, but the quality tends to be mediocre. It's worth getting a decent quality microphone if you fancy doing a fair bit of voice flirting. You can pick one up from any computer hardware store or online from stores like Amazon.

Webcam

Modern instant messaging technology not only allows you to speak with other users, but also to see them providing that they have a webcam. Women are probably not going to reveal themselves to you unless you reciprocate, however, and so you're going to need one too if this is something that you would like to take advantage of. Again many laptops these days come with them already included. If not, a trip to your local computer hardware store will allow you to pick one up without breaking the bank.

Be prepared to use some common sense if you are going to video chat using a webcam. Don't use one if you look like garbage or if the background is going to be of the filthy hovel that you live in. Do plenty of experimenting to see what you look like before you start broadcasting yourself to potential dates or else it could ruin your chances. Lighting can make all of the difference between you looking like an Adonis or a goblin on video chat.

Choosing the right site

There are countless numbers of different online dating sites out there to choose from, so it can be difficult to know where to start. Add to this other forms of online interaction including social networking sites such as 'Facebook' and 'MySpace' and it shows just how much of our time spent on the internet is social.

Online dating site operators are in a competitive marketplace today and, while many boast of the technical facilities they offer, all are only as good as the people that join them.

It is for that reason that internet dating sites are keen to boast that their site offers a unique portfolio of eligible single people who will be ideally suited to your needs.

But what are **your** needs? People join certain online sites because they want something or someone that fits their expectations. Think of online dating sites as huge whiteboards where we, the online daters, come up to that board one by one to scribble our messages and pin our pictures there. There would be many, many unique messages there, but there would also be a surprising amount of messages that were practically identical.

And this is an important fact. Although everyone is looking for 'someone different', we are all pretty much looking for similar things. This means that the site we choose is relatively finite in terms of the 'unique' services or variety of people it offers and that the advice this book offers can be applied to just about any site, irrelevant of its cultural focus.

Take a look on search engines or surf the Net and you'll see there is a huge variety of sites. Choosing a site means first deciding who and what you are looking for. These sites can be categorized as follows and you should consider each type relative to your needs when deciding where to join.

Orientation sites: Also called 'lifestyle' sites, they focus on attracting members through a single attribute, such as race, ethnicity, sexuality or religion.

Paid v free sites: Just because you pay for a service doesn't guarantee better results. On the flip side, fee-paying sites tend to be better regulated, have better back-end technology, and offer a higher end service. Although you might grumble at the thought of having to spend a few bucks to join a paid site, one of the advantages is that the payment involved serves as a screening process to weed out anyone that might not be serious about dating. If you use only free sites, expect to waste a fair bit of time communicating with flakes who only put up a profile for a laugh or are complete timewasters.

General v niche sites: General sites are open to anyone who is interested in the phenomenon of online dating, while niche sites are aimed at people in a particular location, those who share a particular hobby or pastime, or those who are part of a particular 'scene'.

Branded sites: Like choosing what newspaper you read, so daters may opt to affiliate themselves with brands they like and trust. This is why many newspapers actually run their own dating sites where people associate the daters with the type of people who make up that paper's readership.

Domestic v international sites: If you are after someone a little more exotic, then why not join a site based outside of your home country? There are many beautiful Russian or Asian girls who are looking for a handsome prince to provide them with a better life (or maybe just a green card) and so the opportunities there can be tempting if your ultimate goal is a long-term relationship. On the other hand, if long distance conjures up images of heartache and pain, perhaps looking local is your best bet. Choose whether a national or local site suits your needs.

Don't know where to start? Spoiled for choice? In that case, your best bet is probably to go for one of the bigger online sites rather than one of the more specialised ones. By joining one of the larger sites, you're likely to find more people in your local area and more people with whom you have similar interests.

In the world of internet dating, these are some of the most popular sites globally:

Match: Owned by Microsoft, match.com claims to have more than 15 million members and web sites serving 37 countries in 12 different languages. This general interest dating site definitely knows how to match – bringing together a reported 200,000 couples every year. www.match.com

Lava Life: Another big-hitter in the dating industry. The site boasts a similar membership figure to Match.com but Lava Life has the added feature that you can choose the type of encounter you want – 'Casual Date', 'Intimate Encounter' or 'Relationship'. No 'Bastard Dupe' as yet though. www.lavalife.com

Yahoo! Personals: Yahoo! is still the biggest website in the world and so you can be sure that there are going to be plenty of suitable dates on this site. It's free to join and while quality may not be the best, the quantity is certainly there. personals.yahoo.com

Plenty of Fish: This site has rapidly increased in popularity over the past few years due to the fact that it is completely free. Although this means that you are likely to come across more fake profiles than on the paid-for site, it's not a bad place to start while you are learning the ropes of internet dating. www.plentyoffish.com

But if it's sex, sex, sex you are after, then the following site is a good first booty call:

Adult Friend Finder: Unashamedly a sex hook-up site. Beware that many of the women on there are likely to just be prostitutes who have found a free advertising medium. www.adultfriendfinder.com

Finally, for the Complete Bastard seeking real perks, 'Millionaire dating' could be his next new sport. Here are some sites to get you started:

MillionaireMate: Packed full of site features, this upscale personals forum is where money and beauty meet to mate. Join an elite database from all over the world and help them spread their wealth your way. www.millionairemate.com

Sugar Daddie: You're meant to earn at least $100,000 to even join the site. Women get free membership which means that, if you make it as a Sugar Daddy, you're going to be inundated with gold diggers trying to dupe you. www.sugardaddie.com

Wealthy Men: Online since 2002, the site is for men and women looking for a better quality of date. Again, only men who are mega-rich can join but that's never stopped a Complete Bastard blagging entry to the elite. www.wealthymen.com

If you would rather start off with a niche instead, then all it takes is a little bit of Googling. Type in *internet dating <niche>* and you'll probably be surprised at how many options there are for dating sites in some very narrow fields. Beware though that, the narrower the niche, the smaller the number of people there are likely to be using the site. So, unless you live in a large city, you could end up with just a handful of potential partners within easy travelling distance.

Most of these sites allow you to search for free without needing to register on the site or pay a monthly subscription fee. Take advantage of this by seeing what kind of people are on the site already. If you can't find more than a few people who you think you'd like to date, just move on to the next one. If you find hundreds of gorgeous women in your area, you're probably at the right place.

Once you have chosen the site that's right for you, join up! As you register, you should start to feel a buzz of excitement. What happens next could very well change your life forever.

The Complete Bastard Goes Online

With his newly acquired Bastardly persona, the Complete Bastard returns to online dating with renewed spirit and frenzy.

'Son, online dating has the potential for you to find the women of your dreams. And if you don't find her there, why not at least get on in your career; get some sunshine holidays; free lodgings for a while, and a whole lot more? Anything is possible. You've just got to know where to look for it and what it is you're looking for.'

Papa Bastard explained all that and more to me. In the old days, I'd been using online dating sites regularly and knew how they worked inside out. In fact, I'd developed quite an unhealthy compunction for the new technology.

What I had discovered during my previous onscreen wooing sessions was that dating sites are social playgrounds. And, as with fitting in within society, you have to find your niche with online dating as well.

In those unenlightened days, I'd used a scattered approach. I'd pop in and out of sites – usually only the free ones that just required an email address to register. Here I lurked, looking for a profile picture that caught my eye or blitzed messages to all and sundry. I'd join a site and get bored of it after a few days, or even hours.

I met a good few girls this way but, really, this was just a pursuit for sex alone. The more I slunk around cyberspace, the more frustrated I got. The quality of women that I was meeting was poor and the journey towards getting an actual real world date was, at best erratic and, at worst, a complete dead-end.

The problem with online dating – as with a lot of Net-based pastimes – is that you really have to wade through lots of dross to find any quality. And, as the Net has grown, so has the amount of spammers, scammers, liars, dupers, timewasters and more.

This time around, I decided to choose a site that attracted the quality of women I was after. I opted for one of the major dating sites in the UK which was owned by a newspaper corporation.

My theory was that those who regularly read the newspaper would join the site. It was here that I would be able to flirt with a bunch of liberal, well-educated and wealthy women of all ages, but mostly in the 25 to 35 year old category, which is where I guessed that I would have the most success. Sure, it would cost me a little in monthly membership fees – but a lot less per month than I would have regularly spent on one unsuccessful date with entirely the wrong sort of woman in the past.

I also made the decision to stick with one site only – for three main reasons.

Firstly, most good sites have a regular intake of new members and fresh opportunities. This ensures you have access to a huge variety of profiles that are being constantly added to.

Secondly, actually networking a site and getting your profile visible – like joining any social club – gets you integrated among members. It's surprising how often a woman with a profile you've glanced over but never thought of writing to will one day get in touch and you'll connect.

Finally, getting to understand how a single site works and learning how to get the most from it takes time and persistence. This needs a bit more explanation.

All sites operate in slightly different ways. This includes everything from the software they use and how the user can interact with it, through how negative behaviour is regulated on the site (from no regulation to strict moderation), to the array of available site features. As a result, learning a site takes time and so I've learned that it's better to understand a few sites well rather than to dip in and out of lots of sites and not feel fully involved.

With the right site chosen, it's then time to get playing. Quite how you maximise your fun and opportunities online, you'll learn soon enough.

– 7 –

Creating Your Complete Bastard Online Profile

People differ on the Web

As an online dater, you don't exist. You're a blank canvas to do with as you will. Who you are in the eyes of other online daters may be very different from who you think or know you are. This is both the beauty and the bind of online dating.

In the society within which we live, we are defined by our identity: our job, our function, our attitudes, and our reputation. We also have a certain obligation (legally or of our own freewill) to be a part of society. We must attend school and then pay taxes. We must act lawfully and obey the legal code of where we live. We choose to follow moral codes or not. And so on.

In cyberspace, however, things are different. In terms of identity, we can choose to be whom or what we want (within reason). We can adopt a new name or nickname without having to go down complex legal channels. We can also redefine our jobs, sexuality, gender or even race if we wish.

This brings us to another key element of our Cyber Persona – that of suspension of disbelief. This ability to be whoever we want to be has been a tremendous creative and liberating force for many hundreds of thousands of internet users. The problem with a terrain of no boundaries is that some people can begin to confuse reality with fantasy.

How we participate in cyberspace is also a lot more fluid and undefined. We can use our shifting sense of identity to join groups and interact with other cyber citizens of the online community without the same elitist restrictions that exist in the real world. We can also play the part of voyeur or 'lurker' as it's sometimes called, staying in the background and simply watching others participate.

All in all, the internet is one of the most varied and democratic spaces that mankind has ever experienced. Your identity and how you participate within the online community are two key themes for you to understand. The good news is that, as you will soon realise, **you** can control both in order to profit in ways that you would never have believed possible before.

The online profile

On most, if not all online dating sites, there is a place for information about yourself. That information could be on display either to anyone just browsing the site, or to just those who are registered members.

Whether your profile is available for viewing by casual surfers or only paying members, one thing is clear: people read your profile and make very definite judgments about you from it. They interpret who you are based purely on that information. Though it's your profile, your words and your images, it is the viewers' perceptions of your profile that defines you.

For most online daters, their profile **is** who they are. It's an honest representation of themselves.

There are many versions of the 'Truth'. In fact, the actual entity that is the 'Truth' – a definitive, unarguable piece of knowledge – has been debated as non-existent for centuries by folk much wiser than us. In the end, 'Truth' is something framed by what we know and think culturally. For that reason, it's always open to new interpretation.

Now this Guide is not advising any would-be online dater to dare write a completely fake or fraudulent profile. That is a breach of the Complete Bastard Manifesto, Clause 7. Profiles that do contain misinformation are far more prevalent than you may imagine (See chapter eight, section on Bastard Heartbreakers). But we are stating this: your profile is your threshold to opportunity. Therefore it should represent you in the best possible light.

Approach writing your profile in the same way you would write your résumé. Would you dwell on those years spent languishing as a barfly out of work? Or would you instead exaggerate those three months working as a salesman when you got lucky and exceeded your targets? The answer is obvious: you play up your successes and play down your failures.

Before looking at **what** should go into a good profile, it's worth looking first at common mistakes people make when creating them.

Common profile mistakes

The ego has landed

Most of us have an ego problem. We honestly think our beliefs, aspirations, tastes, desires and opinions are the only ones that are 'right' and what everyone else should want, think, believe and feel. Perhaps we're victims of a consumerist 'We have the freedom to be anyone we want' society, or perhaps we drank too much breast milk as an infant. Nature or nurture? You figure it out.

With these swollen egos, we get into regular conflicts. Think of any date you've blown or any person you have fallen out with. Bad blood can usually be traced back to a mismatch of interests or a clash of opinions, right? Two people can't both be wrong – or maybe they can? If we take the assertion that a sole 'Truth' does not exist, then you're both right and you're both wrong. It's just that the two of you were too blind to realise that. Your egos had valid points and they wanted them made.

So, let's try and lose the ego, shall we? You're dating here - not debating. One critical step to becoming a Complete Bastard is realizing that telling people what **they** want to hear is the first step to getting what **you** want to experience.

There's a simple theory behind all this: people like people like themselves. What this basically means is that people tend to like those folk who share the same values, opinions and interests as themselves. So an online profile or a date who seeks to create conflict, challenge people and stir things up will certainly get the blood flowing and adrenaline pumping. But the only passion you'll be raising is the passion for the other person to delete you immediately or else to send you an angry message telling you what a complete argument-seeking loser they think you are.

Rule one: **Lose the ego and win some friends**

Your profile is not about you

Now that you've lost the ego, it's time to go one step further and that means losing the sense of yourself.

When people go online dating, they bring to the fore their dreams, their fantasies and their ideals. When they look at your profile, they don't ask: 'How does this person fit into society?' Rather it's more a case of: 'How can this person fit into **my life**?' This is an important difference.

Many online daters are out to find their unique 'soulmate'. They honestly believe there is someone out there who is a unique, magical fit and that finding that person, finally, will mean you both live happily ever after. Walt Disney built his empire on that schmaltz. But, then again, he also believed that mice talked and that dwarves could hold down regular jobs as woodcutters.

The Complete Bastard is far more pragmatic than Walt Disney. Successful online dating means dating more than one person at the same time. There is no search for that one 'soulmate'. Moreover, many women will fit your needs and wants. Many women will dazzle you with their beauty, charm and personality.

Your goal as a Complete Bastard is to aim for a situation where you can successfully and effortlessly arrange dates with many women simultaneously and enjoy the perks of each one individually.

The 'soulmate' myth is one of the main reasons why so many people are single today, despite it never being easier to meet compatible people. The ease with which it is possible to search through several thousand potential online partners on a dating site and dismiss each and every one of them because they're not '100% perfect' leads a massive amount of people to stay single and lonely in the mistaken belief that soon their 'soulmate' will one day miraculously materialize. It rarely does.

The Complete Bastard would never get taken in by such a myth. Perhaps there's a better match coming his way at some point in the future, but he'll be out having fun with what's available today rather than sitting at home waiting for 'The One'.

In conclusion, when you create an online profile, think about your viewers and not yourself. Your profile is not for you and it's not really even about you. It is a dream catcher for your admirers to see you as whatever they want you to be. You can be 'The One' for many people and the first step towards achieving that is having mass appeal.

Rule two: **Build your profile in your viewers' image, not your own.**

Clumsy clichés to avoid

Inventing your profile for the benefit of others may seem like odd advice, but it works. You are merely presenting your information in such a way that it appeals to many women and, in particular, the women that you want to attract.

The next fatal mistake many men make is misunderstanding what women want to see. Chapter three showed you how fickle the modern-day woman has become. Long gone are the days when the man was the dominant figure during a courtship. Things are now at the point where it is now quite the reverse.

The type of men that most women want to date tends to be confident and in balance across his personality. The secret is knowing how to temper your personality characteristics to create a profile more conducive to female tastes.

We'll go on to look at some tips and ideas which you can put on your profile to better appeal to women. For now though, let's look at some clumsy clichéd profile errors that men are making time and time again on dating sites:

Crotch pouting

If there's one thing that's highly annoying when checking out female pictures on an online dater's profile, it's coming across images of girls posing and pouting in front of the camera lens. We all put on our most beautiful face when the camera is pointed on us, but when you have folk who snap into a supermodel grimace whenever someone pulls a camera-phone out of their handbag, it makes you want to force-feed these vainglorious peacocks your fist.

Men are less prone to posing. Instead they have a more awful habit which involves tensing every one of their muscles into a taut Herculean pillar of muscular perfection for the camera – as though their physical prowess somehow shows a romantic readiness for all of life's possibilities.

And it gets worse ...

Vain sporty types

There is nothing wrong with attention to personal fitness or having an interest in active sports. But there is something highly unappealing about a man over thirty who has convinced himself that dressing up in a fluorescent rubber suit in some way makes him 'sexy' to women. Where did the link between sporting apparatus and Lycra come from? Dating sites contain profile after profile of men proudly squeezed into tight Lycra cycling shorts with a bicycle or surfboard propped against them, arms folded, grinning to camera. This 'artform' is 'Crotch Pouting'. It is to be avoided unless you want to court ridicule instead of romance. Lycra means laughter. Avoid! Avoid! Avoid!

Beta-Banes

In chapter four, we described some very simple and effective ways for masking any physical inadequacies or 'Beta Banes' that you might be afflicted with.

Perhaps, while reading through those handy tips, a lot of the advice was blindingly obvious to you. A look through the profile pictures of many male daters shows that this is far from the case. Here are just a few handy hints for some of the most common male problems:

1. Got a beer belly? Then don't make your profile picture a full body shot showing your gut crammed into a T-shirt that's two sizes too small for you. Just show your face.

2. So you're bald? Don't grow the bits you have left long and wispy like some wacky wizard or a soccer player from the 1970's. Shave your head and join the millions of men who look cool, manly and have accepted baldness with dignity.

3. Eyes better suited to a mole? Ditch the bottle-tops and either get yourself a pair of designer glasses or contact lenses.

4. Think fashion is for girls? Wrong! Dressing to impress is an essential part of seduction (see chapter four). It's time to start learning how to present yourself properly.

Rule three: **Showcase your good and hide what's bad.**

Creating the perfect profile

What woman want

Have a look at female users' profiles on dating sites. Consider in particular the traits that women are looking for in a man. Do that for long enough and you'll see a pattern emerge. It's not that every woman wants her 'soulmate' at all. Many women are simply looking for 'fun', 'friendship' and a 'f....'.

Likewise, there are a number of male character attributes that appeal to women time and time again. Below is a list of desired traits that come up regularly on women's profiles. Include references to them in your profile in some shape or form and you will begin to tick more boxes with the opposite sex. The more boxes you tick, the higher the chances of your interesting her. It's so obvious it hurts.

Women's desired traits from men

Self-belief

Caring

Amusing

Adventurous

Intelligent

Successful/talented

Physically attractive

Fun to be around

Sexual chemistry

Thoughtful

There is also a range of characteristics that woman are keen to avoid. Sadly, the Complete Bastard possesses more of these traits than positive ones, so the secret is to make sure that as few of the negative ones as possible become known to women. There is an added complication: women have excellent inbuilt radars for male bullshit. Watch out!

Undesired traits

Arrogance

Uncaring

Boring

Unadventurous

Stupid/crass

Lazy

Unattractive

Liars/cheats/love rats/etc.

No sexual chemistry

Thoughtless

So with a sense of 'what is' and 'what is not' wanted, let's now turn to writing a killer Complete Bastard online dating profile step-by-step:

Username

Your first, and most prominent, piece of information that is carried everywhere on your profile and across online dating sites is your Username. This is your online identity. It is usually a combination of words and numbers which tends to not be your actual name or to make any allusion to it. It offers users a cyber-identity and keeps people's true identities private.

While your username won't be the reason anyone falls in love with you, it is one of the most important pieces of information on your profile. This is because, like your Tagline (see below) and your main profile image, it is information that **every** viewer sees when they glance at your profile.

It would be impossible in the space here to tell you which name is best for you, but here are a few top tips that will help you come up with a compelling name and avoid any useless Usernames.

Avoid overtly sexual usernames: They will portray you as a pervert, a deviant or as someone sinister. Even though you may be such a type or indeed, the complete opposite, people will be put off by a name like 'DatingStud666' or 'BigCockAndy'. It just smacks of knuckle-dragging man-smut.

Avoid using your real name: e.g. 'JohnSmith25'. It just appears unimaginative and looks wrong in the virtual environment. Like, 'How creative are you with a billion possible name combinations to choose from?!' So stupid an error is this that many dating sites will refuse to allow you any username containing your real name anyway.

Avoid wordy or complicated spellings: This will go against you when a user comes to try to find you through the 'Search' facility that most sites have. Plus, who really wants to be called 'Supercalifragilistic99' anyway?!

Avoid anything too risqué: Proclaiming yourself as 'Love_Lothario2000' or 'SimplyTheBest01' may just be a joke but, for somebody that doesn't know you, you'll just come across as arrogant and conceited.

Avoid anything that is too 'hit or miss': For example, one male internet dater kept coming across girls who were called 'Marmite Lover' or 'Marmite_is_yummy'. He hated the stuff and the thought of a long-term relationship indirectly staring at the black goo was enough to make him not click.

And this final piece of advice is perhaps the most obvious:

Choose a name that is memorable: A Username that makes user's elicit an emotion (a smile or even a frown), and doesn't put them off you will always be remembered.

Tagline

Also known as a 'strapline' or 'headline', the Tagline is usually a 5 to 10 word description that reveals a little more about you. The Tagline can be changed and is often used to display recent thoughts, moods or status. More so than the Username, it displays your personality, point of view and intent.

You need to grab attention with your Tagline – but how can you do so with just a handful of words?

The secret here is to avoid sounding stupid, pervy, aggressive, arrogant or anything else that will cast you as negative in the user's mind. At this stage, sounding hyper-intelligent, overly philosophical, clichéd or trite won't work well either.

Here are a few examples of genuine Taglines that were definitely better than the rest. These users may have had problems in other areas of their profile, but there was nothing wrong with their tags.

Tagline	Meaning
Never been in prison. Never been in a fight	Funny, anti-hero stuff.
Fun loving, ambitious Northerner	Informative and says a lot in a few words.
Let's give this a go! Go on! I dare you... Love is in the air ... Take a deep breath!	Upbeat clichés work and depict you as having a similar personality.
Dynamite seeks fuse	You are looking for a partner after all.
Listed in the 'Good Man Guide 2009'	Witty, but and doesn't give too much away.
Fattie seeks feeder	Dark but amusing way to get that lunch date.
Wanna come and say hello?	Frank, friendly and flirtatious.
Idiot seeks informed debate	Making light of some 'Beta Banes'.

I just won the lottery	A playful fib, appealing to all gold diggers.
Wanna hear my great joke?	Teasers are great for curious clickers
I love Madagascar	The surreal or the random can work well.
Closet romantic seeks sturdy armoire	Post-modern taglines attract high brow clicking.
Violent alcoholic with bad breath	Shocking but witty can work well.
Hate the sin, love the sinner	Wise words can be bang on the money.
Sally still looking for Harry!!!	Cultural references connect.
Professional boxer with ballet shoes	The contradictory will arouse curiosity.
WARNING! This boy is loaded!	Attention grabbers like this will get noticed.

And here are some to avoid:

Tagline	Meaning
I'm new to this and I'm nervous	Insipid, weak and whimsical.
Blonde, blue-eyed girl	Informative but inane. Waste of wordage.
I'm the best – click here	Arrogant and unfunny doesn't get clicks.
GSOH required	And the reader's is being tested.
Wanna meet tonight?	Way too much!
I'm fat, bald and fifty	Is this funny or a cry for help?
Unique bilingual trysexual quadrophonic	When being too clever reads too obscure
Carpe diem	Clichéd doom more like!
Hello!	Goodbye!

It's a good idea to change your Tagline as often as you can think of something new and interesting to put there. If your first Tagline didn't attract much of a response, then maybe your second, third or fourth attempt will. All that a Tagline needs to achieve is to be sufficiently intriguing enough to make girls want to click on your profile.

Basics

This is the information that is called 'demographics' by marketers and people who conduct surveys.

'The Basics' consists of factual information that defines everything from your gender, age, location, job, through to your astrological sign, income and vices. Most of this information takes the form of options you select from drop-down menus or lists, or even just simple yes/no answers. For that reason, it reveals little of your personality, but it is nevertheless very important because many sites have options for screening potential matches by one or more of these criteria. Tick a 'yes' instead of a 'no' on one of the criteria that are important to women and you could wipe out 75% of your potential dates with the click of a mouse.

Your Basics are like your 'dating DNA'. It's what will determine which 'shelf in the supermarket' you best belong to.

Are you a recently retired and widowed ex-Colonel now living on a remote farm? Or are you a young, fit Porsche-driving high-flier who just wants a fling?

Your Basics convey a lot. For that reason, they need careful consideration when answering. Here are some examples why:

Your profile asks you to state if you're a smoker. You do smoke, but only a few while hanging out with friends in a bar. Ticking yourself as a smoker puts you in the same category as those who puff away on sixty-a-day. Your best option here is the white lie that you're a non-smoker. You don't want to alienate yourself from all the healthy chicks who don't want to kiss an ashtray.

Be careful how you portray yourself with vices in general. Some sites ask if you have ever taken drugs, have body art or piercings, enjoy erotica, etc. Unless it's an adult-orientated site, its best to not appear like some powder-crazy hedonist who lusts for nights out down in his local S&M dungeon with Miss Whiplash. This is what many women will assume even if you just once puffed on a joint and had some fun when you came across your Dad's stash of 'Playboys' when you were 14.

Never state your astrological sign. Instead, opt for, 'Tell you later' if you can. It's completely ridiculous, but some women reject men purely on account of their star signs. They've sworn never to date a Gemini again and blame the misalignment of Mars in relation to Uranus last month for all their bad luck ever since.

Do reveal what your job-type is providing it's not the type of career that many people dislike or have negative preconceptions of. If you are a traffic warden, a tax inspector, a pest exterminator or your job description involves your saying, 'And would you like fries with that?', then it's better to leave this section blank. Otherwise, your career can be a great ice-breaker. Its non-sexual, non-threatening and like attracts like after all. I've gotten free legal advice, found an accountant and met several people who work in my industry through online dating. They didn't become lovers, but it just goes to show some easy additional benefits that can come from online dating.

Blurb

After all the virtual 'paperwork', it's finally time to get to the juicier, albeit trickier, part. This is completing the 'Blurb' – or the bit where you can elaborate upon what a fun, great guy you are and explain why on Earth you could possibly still be single after all these years.

The Blurb usually asks you to state within it some background about yourself and who you're looking to meet. For most people, their blurb either reads like a chapter of their memoirs, or it is brief, uninteresting, and shows them lacking in effort. Remember that this is the Web and, while brevity is good, write a dull, clipped Blurb and people will quickly click on someone else's profile instead of yours.

Here are some tips and techniques here that should be of help:

Write in a conversational style and try to create a warm, friendly tone: This will instantly draw people in and make them think that you are a warm, friendly person.

Never reveal too much personal information: Leave your personal email address, mobile phone number, and work address for when you have met people that you know and trust. Most sites have moderators and will reject any profile with email addresses or phone numbers anyway.

A couple of paragraphs are ideal: Any more and people won't read or skim through. People tend to read around 50% less on screen than in print, so bear that in mind. Plus, your location, pictures and age carry more weight than your Blurb.

People do get messaged from others reading and enjoying their Blurb alone. It's the one place where a song line quoted or a pastime stated can really connect you to another. It provides an easy opener for people, i.e. 'Oh that song's one of my all-time favourites. What did you think of their last album?'

The best Blurb is one that communicates strong personality yet reveals little about you. This achieves two things. First, you attract attention and you make an impact. Second, you use the tactic as outlined earlier in this chapter: you aim for the middle ground, seeking to neither offend nor overpower people.

As a Complete Bastard, the Blurbs of others are fertile grounds to find tit-bits of info that you can use to get in touch with others. Showing that you've taken the time to read someone's Blurb goes a long way too, especially with girls who are getting hundreds of overly sexual or clichéd messages along the lines of, 'What's a pretty girl like you doing on a site like this?' So, use the Blurbs to find nuggets of interesting facts that you can turn into ice-breakers in your first message.

Interests

The 'Interests' section is where you list all of your favourite activities, hobbies, sports, interests and pastimes.

The secret here is to avoid seeming like a couch potato. Most dating sites give you a list of options to choose from. If you **are** a couch potato, it makes Complete Bastardly sense to choose a few sports and social activities to make you at least **appear** to have a full and rounded life. Don't go overboard though. Adding something like, 'I'm a keen scuba diver' could see you come a cropper when you are quizzed by your date who loved the thought of a hunky man in wet suit and flippers swimming among the tropical fish. But after she's glimpsed your non-aquatic pot belly and realized you've never been near your local swimming pool, never mind the ocean depths, you'll be a fish out of water for the rest of your date.

On the other hand, if you are a highly active and social type, you don't want potential admirers thinking you'll have no time for her in your busy schedule. Balance is key here. If you're a complete sports fanatic, for many women the thought of some testosterone-dripping bloke glued to the television shouting for his football team every weekend can be just as much as a turn-off.

One other thing to note is that people look for shared interests to connect. There is nothing wrong with you realizing that your life could do with a few extra-curricular activities. So take up that new sport or start to learn French. It can serve as a great talking point on a date and shows that you are open to embracing new interests and hobbies – and adult education courses can be a great place for locating new hot chicks to conquer – but that's a subject for another book.

If you're struggling to come up with a list of the 'right' Interests to put on your profile, one tip is to take a look through the profiles of the women on the site who you would most like to date. What interests on their profiles do you see coming up over and over again? These are the ones that you should be adding to your own profile as well where relevant and practical and not too 'girly'.

Images
There is simply not enough space in this book to begin to discuss what technically makes a good photograph. This sort of information can be found in good quality photography books at any good bookstore or online.

Everyone has a personal photograph in which they look great or they can buy or borrow a digital camera and try to take one in which they look great. This is not what this section will detail. This section is vital though, as it will first explain why images are so important for online dating sites, then illustrate what makes a great profile image. Finally, it will show you how to avoid some basic image composition errors.

Virtually all dating sites give you the option of uploading and displaying your image. After all, this is the game of attraction. Just how many people have fallen for a picture that they glanced at on a wet Thursday afternoon while at work and it became 'love at first click?'

The decision as to whether or not you put your photograph online is a simple one.

Without a picture, your odds of getting clicks on your profile become **drastically reduced**. Most people, coming across a profile without a picture immediately think, 'He or she must look so bad that they're scared to show their face', or 'He or she must have something to hide – maybe he or she is married?'

Many sites now offer the means to hide your images until you allow a member to view you. For women (and some men) this was a useful way to prevent unwanted attention from people only interested in looks. However, the same rule applies: no easy-to-access picture and your chances of getting that all-important first click are substantially reduced. Why go to the hassle of contacting someone first to get to see their pictures and risk the chance that they're hideous when there are plenty of other profiles with attractive pictures to choose from?

So the bottom line is – unless you look truly, truly hideous – always upload a picture to your profile.

You probably think that this section is rather pedestrian. You'll be advised to use one picture of you when sun-kissed on holiday and another one of you on a jet ski five years ago and the ladies will love it! However, there's a lot more to choosing the right image than you might think.

Over the years, I learned what the right photograph could do for getting reactions from people and today I can upload five images and generate lots of responses based on the photographs alone.

Very few of these people contact me to say, 'You're cute' or, 'I'm in love with you'. Instead, I get everyday responses asking some of the most ridiculous things:

'What brand of camera do you have in your photograph? I'm keen on photography and blah, blah, blah...'

'I recognise that guy standing beside you in your picture. Is he famous or have we met?'

'Where was that photo taken? It sure looks like Venice, my favourite place in the world!!' (The actual answer was Dubai!)

With images, it's all about setting up prompts. Holding an expensive camera in a photo depicts me as a keen photographer. A celebrity and I together and I'm fun to be around, have connections in high places, and it's almost as if a little bit of their fame has rubbed off on me too. The backdrop of a water lagoon and I'm an adventurer.

You see how easy it is to create your own myth? All of the images that I upload to dating sites are consciously designed to set up prompts to arouse curiosity and attract admiration for my lifestyle – and to make it as easy as possible for women to start a conversation with me.

There are a few more tips I can offer with regard to the type of photograph you should or should not include as follows:

Photos with you and celebrity/famous folk: They attract a great response from fans or just the curious, ('How did you meet Tom Hanks?') A great trick is to use photos of yourself with cult celebrities or unfashionable ones (like 'Big Bird' from 'Sesame Street'). This signifies irony and that's a good talking point too. They are also a lot easier to get close to than A-List stars well.

Be aware of background: The Complete Bastard is on the lookout for women of wealth and prosperity. You can tell a lot about where a person is from by what's in the background of their photographs. On the one hand, a couple of Ming vases in the foreground or a convertible Maserati looks fantastic. Conversely, a girl posing in a scruffy, bedsit-style room with a mangy pet dog beside her (or, even worse, a mangy child) can be a not-so-subtle clue to a lifestyle best avoided.

Arty shots: You know the kind – that grainy black-and-white shot so beloved of actors. They show every high cheekbone and rugged jaw-line and hide a thousand wrinkles and blemishes. What level of vanity drives a man to such an act of sheer egotism? Leave these for the women.

Hedonism shots: There is a fine line between wanting to be perceived as a 'fun-lovin' kinda guy' and having an alcohol problem. Why, in a small selection of photographs representing your adult years on Earth, would you include one of you lying half-naked and covered in your own vomit? Yet people do. Remember: women are looking to weed out the problem types as quickly as possible. So why invite rejection so stupidly?

True or false?

One of the questions asked the most by men looking to maximize their potential on online dating sites, is: 'Should I lie on my profile?' Earlier in this chapter, the ethics behind such a move were discussed.

In short, there is no one definitive answer. The Complete Bastard trick is to use your discretion. If a little white lie will get you that date, then go for it. If a big, dark filthy lie gets you up before a magistrate on a charge of deception, then you should have kept your mouth shut or your message unwritten.

Remember though that you are not on trial here. You have not sworn on the Bible, 'To tell the truth, the whole truth and nothing but the truth'. Particularly when it comes to the 'whole truth' bit. So you're incontinent? No need to shout it out to the world on your profile. Conversely though, if you are married and you ticked the box marked 'Single', then you have most definitely crossed the line by telling a big, fat, barefaced lie and that is wrong (unless you are really separated and there's no box for that option).

Always bear in mind that the whole reason that you are going through this entire online dating process is to get to meet women. Whenever you're tempted to tell a lie, ask yourself the question, 'Is it likely to be a deal breaker if or when the lie gets discovered?' If you've added or subtracted a few years to or from your age, added a couple of inches to your height or subtracted them from your waistline, your first date probably won't end in a matter of seconds with a slap in the face. But if you've been using a photo of a Calvin Klein underwear model as your profile picture when you in fact look like the Elephant Man, you've just wasted everyone's time and earned the undying hatred of one unlucky woman.

The Perfect Profile

How the Complete Bastard's profile saw him rise to prominence as become the Most Popular Man on his dating site and beyond.

If there was one profile that stood out for me as perfect in what it said and was extraordinary in the response it got, it was this one:

Why you should you get to know me?

Highly amusing, adventurous, artistic type – with particular penchant for travelling.

Keen to avoid girls who frequent karaoke bars, have grainy black-and-white, pouting profile pics, read self-help books/pulp fiction/chick lit, believe that spiritual contentment comes through shoe-shopping, and those that shriek. All else considered.

My ideal match is someone who has already vomited bile out of her eyeballs from reading all these other men's pseudo-intellectual, bluntly dull and clutching attempts at manliness. She probably feels like she wants to bang her exasperated, clenched fists in frenzied panic on the doors of her local nunnery. I offer late-night drinks and Hope of an impious kind.

I created this short profile in just twenty minutes and it would go on to get me countless dates and admirers. It illustrates what can be achieved with a few moments of easy-to-conjure inspiration and an understanding of how online daters' minds work.

What you say on your profile and how you say it transmits many messages that your viewers will interpret and give meaning to. Let me explain by showing you how and why the above profile was so effective across several areas:

Firstly, it is perfect in length (or 'copy weight' as it's more correctly known). Just a few hundred words across three short paragraphs are ideal for the Web reader. With several other parts of additional information on my profile too (About Me, Hobbies and Interests, Star Sign, etc.), this pithy personal statement was just enough to give an insight into my personality without deluging any reader with egocentric hogwash or information overload.

It is best to leave the reader wanting to know more about you than to have your life story already out there before you've even exchanged your first message.

Secondly, in terms of writing style, it hits the mark. It's written in a friendly, conversational, engaging tone. It comes with a little good humoured snarl too. Humour, if done well, always works.

The secret to writing an engaging profile piece is to write as you speak. Adding language that is a little out-of-the-ordinary, even archaic, makes your profile really stand out from the rest. In the profile above, look how words and phrases like, 'penchant', 'shriek', 'bluntly dull', 'frenzied panic' and 'impious', are very different from the usual language to be found on profiles. It affords the language an amusing, persuasive, exciting and even shocking resonance.

You also want your language to affect readers. I tried to use language that provoked ('Keen to avoid girls who'), entertained ('vomited bile out of her eyeballs'), and signalled mischief and a sense of adventure ('I offer late-night drinks and Hope of an impious kind.'). These were the personality traits that I possessed which I wanted girls to pick up on. Think of which traits you want to convey and find the words and phrases that best communicate them.

Language is a complex, fathomless beast. Play around with it and experiment as to what gets responses and reactions in what you write. Just make sure that you try to write something that is compelling and make sure readers leave your profile with your words jarring in their minds.

Another useful writing tip is to get the pace of your content right. Read and re-read what you've written. It should flow easily. This is not easy to get right, but you'll know it when you get it. A handy test is to read what you've written out loud. If you find yourself tongue-tied while reading a sentence, then you know it's in need of a tweak or a redraft.

The third aspect of a good profile is to give your reader an incentive to respond to you. Offering something creates the opportunity for female readers to have an easy opening to start initiating that first response or even a date. Meeting in the real world, after all, is why everyone has joined the site, and one of the most difficult issues is moving from, 'Hi, it's great to have met you online,' to, 'Hey, let's date!' My offer of, 'Drinks and Hope of an impious kind' offers a definite suggestion that I want to meet and the offer is there to any takers. An action prompt in a profile is highly recommended.

Next, my profile is candid in its message. It doesn't rattle on, bragging what a great guy or lover I would make for a woman. Instead, I wanted to differentiate myself from all the other guys who were gushing forth about how they loved skiing and white water rafting, wishing they could play the guitar just as good as Jimi Hendrix, or desiring a girl for quiet nights in, blah, blah, blah...

Instead, I took a step back and, with my cunning use of mockery, I achieved two things. Firstly, I created a bridge of empathy with women, showing them that, 'I feel their pain'. This is connecting with them. Secondly, I took on my rivals – men.

On the dating site I joined, few men carried such a scathing attack on their own gender and their failings. Perhaps they were too noble to betray their compatriots, but who cares!? It was I who won the attentions of women with my brash statements.

For many men, the understanding that competing with the **men** on the site is just as important as wooing the women, is a much overlooked aspect of the world of online dating.

Across the remainder of my profile, I did what I advised in this chapter: I avoided extremes. In selecting my interests, what I wanted in a partner, and all the other information about me, I steered away from any extreme that would classify me as a specific type of person, (e.g., a smoker; not sporty; vegetarian, etc.). Getting your profile read and getting people to express interest in you is about connecting with them.

In my experience, no one will reject you if you have not even one shared interest or hobby, but they will very often click away if you clash on something that's a more definite lifestyle choice, like smoking or that you're not looking for marriage. Why state either of these things on your profile? One can be given up and the other reconsidered if the situation or person is right.

Finally, which pictures did I use on my profile and why?

I normally go for about five or six pictures. A few with a smile are vital as 'smilers' draw clicks. Then it's one or two with me in exotic backdrops (the sand dunes of the Gobi Desert and on an icy peak in the Alps). I also included one of me grinning beside a minor British television personality. I caught the guy drunk at an Arts Festival one year and asked him politely for a quick picture. He was only too happy to have his ego fanned. Little did he know that all I wanted was a 'talking point' photo for my online dating profile!

So there we are. Writing the perfect profile doesn't seem too daunting now, does it? This profile swept the dating site like gold dust. I had a huge daily response rate with girls applauding the choices I had made on my profile by sending me their telephone numbers with their first messages. I quickly became the 'Most Popular Male' on the site's popularity chart and stayed there for an incredible three months.

Your profile is a sure-fire way to create an illusion that can convince women that you are perfect for them in every way too. Never backwards at coming forwards, I leave you with Papa Bastard's sweet words on my splendid achievement:

'Just goes to show how some deft tricks with language and a few good photos can disguise even the most slippery louse!'

– 8 –
How to Flirt Online Like A Complete Bastard

Online dating is great!

Isn't it just? You just write a message, send it and the woman of your dreams writes back declaring her undying love for you. Amazing that a few simple words sent online can elicit such heartfelt emotion from another.

Except it rarely works like that for most of us.

Becoming a successful online dater usually means you'll make a good few attempts at writing messages, sometimes getting replies but, more often than not, you'll be inexplicably ignored or receive terse replies simply stating: 'Not interested'.

As you may have already experienced, life for many online daters can be a disheartening and depressing journey that simply lowers your self-esteem.

But that's all about to change.

This chapter will show you how to get women interested in you from the very first message so that they can't help but reply to you.

Online dating is not like dating in the real world. There are some similarities, but you are playing Casanova in the cyberworld. That means there are different rules and parameters. Even more complicated is the fact that women behave differently online from offline. (See chapter five)

Yet, whether on the internet or in the real world, women are different from men. They do not think and behave like us when it comes to finding a partner – they're more cautious, deliberate and emotional. Sure they enjoy sex, adventures and can throw caution to the wind too, but in the early stages of online flirting, they aren't going to show that side of themselves to you.

Fortunately, even though the gentler sex would like to keep their dignity for as long as possible, the Complete Bastard has a few sneaky tricks up his sleeve to get them to open up to your devilish suggestion.

In the first section of this chapter, you'll learn how to maximise your success with women via dating sites. Revealed will be the key techniques on how to attract attention to yourself and win the attention of others. In the final section, you'll meet a number of online characters who you might encounter on dating sites. Depending on how you interact with them, they have the ability to make your online dating experience either heavenly or hellish.

Online v offline

Communicating online is not the same as communicating in the real world. There are a number of reasons for this:

Online communication tends to be text based.

The successful online dater must quickly learn to shift from a focus on conversation and pick up lines to becoming a witty, eloquent scribe. For handy advice on how to write killer online dating profiles, check out chapter seven.

Few visual cues affect online interaction.

With the exception of a small selection of photographs, there is little visual representation in the early stages of online dating. Even though websites are getting more sophisticated by adding audio and video communications into the mix, the written word is still the dominant first and main point of contact.

Interaction is not in real time.

If much of the communication is made using IMs, this can often give interaction between a courting couple a heightened sense of excitement and intensity. Alternatively, if two busy and cautious people are getting to know one another via email, the process can often appear to be going in slow motion.

People you meet online have little knowledge about you

This can be a blessing or a curse. On one hand, you can control every aspect of the impression that you will make on a person. From your profile to your first message, you are in total control of what you say and how you think it will be perceived. On the other hand, from your profile and messages, a person can make incorrect or unfair judgements about you that you cannot control. The art of online dating then becomes subjective, fickle and at the mercy of people's whims and fancies. For the Complete Bastard who reads, understands and uses all of the advice given here, this ability to invent a total persona gives him a definite advantage using online rather than conventional dating methods.

Online, people come and go

As you become better at online dating, you may end up being contacted by hundreds, maybe thousands, of girls. How many of them can you realistically maintain a long term relationship of any kind with? Hopefully, a lot, but nowhere near the first figure. Online, people get in touch and then disappear. Maybe they leave the site, find someone better than you, or are just too busy to find the time to write back. Whatever the reason, be prepared to put up with the ethereal nature of the Net in that it allows people the freedom to come and go as they please. As a Complete Bastard, the skill is to keep them baited to stay around.

In conclusion, online dating has its perks and perils. This is a radically different (but no less satisfying) new way to meet people compared with, say, picking up a girl in a bar or bumping into a hot chick in the tinned foods aisle of your local supermarket. For those who are shy or of a nervous disposition, online dating requires a lot less courage than approaching girls in the real world, as usually the worst result possible is simply that you will not to get any response back at all, making it a lot easier to simply move on to the next one on your list.

Understand the limitations and the potential of dating sites and you'll be prepared for anything.

Wooing, Cooing and Shooing.

Wooing, **Cooing** and **Shooing** are the three main forms of online dating interaction that people participate in. This section will look at each form in turn and give you tips and advice on how to perform at each stage.

Wooing

This is the art of proactively attempting to win the interest of another on an online dating site. It's the method of choice for the Complete Bastard as he gets to choose exactly who he wants to use it on and when.

The most obvious way to Woo online is to send a message of interest. This is the ultimate online dating hallmark – a few lines expressing why you had to get in touch with this girl, along with in a compliment or two plus a bit about why you're the greatest guy currently walking the planet. How can you possibly fail?

But people do. They either write too little or too much. They write their own clichéd account of what's been written in a million messages before. Some people pour their heart out to someone who they have never met. Others communicate nothing that reveals any sense of who they actually are.

Too light-hearted; too serious and stuffy; too deep; too stupid – how do you gauge the right tone for the first message to someone you want to impress deeply?

Additionally, as emotion grips a male's lower and less cerebral half, smut or overtly sexual connotations can creep into what he writes. This is probably the one faux-pas that has turned more women away from the potential enjoyment of online dating than any other.

Let's deal with these problems one by one:

How much to write?

It is the first message to someone whom you've never met or spoken with before. At the same time, after reading her profile, you know a good few things about her, from her age, through the fact that her favourite sport is skiing, to the characteristics of her ideal match.

There is no magic length to a 'first contact' message and, over the years, the Complete Bastard is best advised to send a variety of messages to a mix of people. A good length for a first message is a couple of introductory paragraphs while, on rare occasions, a witty one-liner in response to some aspect of a girl's profile can still be enough to get the ball moving.

The best advice is not to go all out and write your life story in the first message. Nor should you pack any message full of tragic events, like your messy divorce or how much you hate your boss or that you've just recovered from a bout of measles. Instead, compose a light, friendly message that is in some way personal to the individual woman you're trying to impress.

Avoiding saying what's been said by others

The Complete Bastard does not settle for sending a few, nice messages in the hope that he'll get a few, nice replies. No way. The Complete Bastard needs to write text that stands out in the crowd and gets his readers howling in laughter, mouth open in shock, or grinning in admiration. That's a whole different ball game.

Every great novelist had his or her own unique style and so it's the same with writing messages to online daters. Find the way of expressing yourself that comes most naturally to you and go for it. Be bold, be brazen. Write with confidence and panache. Be witty, be wicked. Do whatever it takes to startle your reader. Approach them in a style that they have not been approached with before.

As a Complete Bastard, your favourite writing recipe should be a handful of shock, a generous grating of black humour and a sprinkle of barefaced cheek. Sure you might offend a few folk, but overall, this approach will get you a high response rate and a reputation on the site for being someone out of the ordinary.

Here are some of this Complete Bastard's favourite examples of good messages. Remember: these were first point of contact messages to women and they worked a treat:

To 'Eagle_Eyes':

You seem quite Evil. That's a great thing. Let's do lunch! Who shall we eat??

Better still, let us just walk the streets roaringly drunk, spitting on passers-by. I love doing that. Or we could shoplift lots and then sell the stolen goods on eBay. I cannot believe I may have found my partner in crime! How cool. :)

To 'LaughterLines100':

I have nothing really gob-smackingly interesting to state right now. But that's my inimitable charm: to be able to create amusement and joy out of the emptiest of situations. I'm oft invited out to poorest Africa or war-torn Middle Eastern countries where I bring unity and riches to all. How we all laugh and laugh and laugh. I'm like Jesus Christ. But funnier.

If you have a funny bone in that rather delicious body of yours ('Oh, too creepy' she squeals) then write me. If you don't, then may your first born have the face of a goat. My mother's a Gypsy. As a family, we have supernatural powers.

Before you start copying out the conversations above and sending them out to every woman that has attracted your attention, however, bear in mind that the first message that you send to anyone is going to set the tone for all of your communications with the woman from there on in.

These examples may work for one particular Complete Bastard, but there is never a 'one size fits all' solution. Below are some examples of some other ideas that could be adapted to most styles of approaches.

Remember that the message should ideally be personal to the individual woman you are approaching. This could take the form of something that you have spotted in their picture, such as the example below:

To 'Chablis09':

I was looking at your profile pic (like a million other guys, I'm sure) and it looks like you have a pretty face. But your picture is just terrible! Who the hell took it for you, and where was his guide dog at the time?

I happen to be a budding photographer and would be only too willing to come round to see you to take some better ones. Nudity optional.

As in the previous examples, it's a very confident approach. It's quite a bit forward as well, but the humour in the message stops it from being coming over as being too sleazy.

Look for other ways in which you can comment on their pictures, but make sure that you can add humour to your initial approach message to let her know that you're going to be fun to communicate with.

If there's nothing that you can pick up on in her picture, then try the same tactic with the text that she uses on her profile. Find something there that you can gently tease her about, as in the next example:

To 'Shooting_Starrs':

I see from your profile that you love candlelit dinners for two. As I was not able to pay my electricity bill for the past three months, dining by candlelight is a regular event at my place. I also have no friends so you can be sure that there would only be the two of us.

Care to join me? Here's the number of my local takeaway.

This approach doesn't have the same smutty innuendo of the others, but the humour is still there. The fact that you are not bragging but are instead making you out to be impoverished should also set you out apart from every other first message that she has ever received, many of which will have been bragging about the guys' achievements.

Another source of humour can come from the shared experience of online dating – a common bond that unites everyone on the site who are in the same situation, the primary one being that you are still single.

Here's one that, at first glance comes over as being perhaps too arrogant. However, any woman with a sense of humour will immediately realise that you're actually simply making a joke about the fact that you're in exactly the same situation that she's in:

To 'IrishJenny':

So I see you're online on a Saturday night as well. I imagine that in your case it just means that you have no social life, whereas I had to turn down ten social invitations this evening because my favourite documentary is on the Discovery Channel later tonight and my TiVo is broken.

Hopefully, by now, you are starting to see how you can make a major impact in your first message to just about any girl based upon what you can find in her profile.

How much to reveal?

Too many men start their messages showering the women with compliments about her eyes, lips or anything worthwhile below the neck. At no point do they include anything about themselves. This is fatal as, even though everyone likes flattery, they also need a reason or two to get back in touch with you. You may be one of the lucky few whose pictures are irresistible, but **any** guy can get a response if he reveals something interesting about himself in the message.

The secret to this is to find common ground on the girl's profile – some nugget of information which you can excavate and use as fodder for an interesting message.

Another good tip is that, instead of going into your life history, talk about your present. People love reading a snapshot of someone's day, no matter how mundane it may seem. It's the stuff of soap operas, so why not turn your everyday moments into something more dramatic? Even a trip to the dentist can be an opportunity to woo a chick:

To 'AutumnLily':

Hey there, I've just come back from the dentist – where a nubile 25-year old female hygienist had to wrestle a man fitting my description back into his chair as he tried to make a run for the door on hearing the dentist turn on his drill. For comfort I decided to do some 'window shopping' on this dating site and found you! Care for some toothy chat??

Once you have been online for a while, you will be sure to have a few amusing anecdotes to speak about. And you can be sure that every half-decent woman will have had plenty of goofballs contacting her too and will be only too willing to share her ghastly experiences with anyone who wants to listen.

Here is an example as to how you can start off a conversation using this method:

To 'PinkPrincess23':

Last night I had a message back from a girl I fancied. She told me that she was looking for someone to 'entertain her'. So I just gave her the phone number for a bloke from the Yellow Pages who twists balloons into amusing shapes.

So what online horror stories have you had recently?

Gauging the right tone

You have one chance to make an impact, so don't blow it by sounding too cocky or arrogant. Also don't be all grovelling and pathetic either. There's nothing more off-putting for a woman than when there is no chase in a romantic encounter and the man lays his heart open. The woman, when she gets bored – and it's only a matter of time – will simply drop you in an instant and move on to someone with something more interesting to say.

Avoid being sexual

There are a hundred women all looking their best, showing cleavage or draped half-drunk in nightclubs, writing flirtatious profiles and here's me telling you not to start feeling horny! Online dating can often be an arousing process – it's just knowing that you can't translate what your loins are feeling into words in an initial message. It's sleazy.

Women are on high-alert for signs of sleazebags, so be smart. Let lesser men fall into the trap of getting deleted or booted off the site for smutty chat. You, conversely, are the perfect gentleman!

That being said, a new phenomena has been slowly percolating through online dating over the years, and that's cybersex. It splits camps as to whether it's seedy or just harmless fun. That's for you to decide. For more information on cybersex, see the last section in this chapter.

With the advice in this section and some sample messages, you should now have no problem coming up with great ideas of your own. Small things like spell-checking your messages while drafting and not bombarding girls with messages also avoid negative impressions of being sloppy or over-keen.

The mass message

There is one 'black hat' messaging technique that many site users employ while attempting to Woo the opposite sex. It is the act of sending out **mass email messages**.

This is the tactic where the Wooer composes a template message and sends that same one to every girl he is interested in. That often implies his sending it to tens, if not hundreds, of women.

You're probably thinking that the Complete Bastard would embrace any method where he could send out one well-scripted message to as many dupe-worthy girls as possible. By the law of averages, he knows he would receive a good few responses – maximum efficiency, for minimal effort. And, best of all, no girl would ever find out.

Wrong. Mass messaging is a total no-no.

There are a few reasons for this. Firstly, the key to making an impact at first contact is getting attention. That means appearing unique and finding an inroad to startle your reader's curiosity. Of course, there's a chance they'll just fall in love with your picture. For most people, however, that's not how it works.

Secondly, the mass message trick is usually easily exposed. This lazy piece of communication tends to be general in subject matter, bland in tone, and brief in length. If and when it is exposed, it is usually instantly deleted without a reply sent. It's the internet dating equivalent of spam. And when was the last time you did anything with a spam email other than being irritated by it and deleting it immediately?

Hopefully this should be enough to convince you that the mass message is a poor tactic and best left for dating charlatans and absolute beginners.

Aside from email, there are other ways to show interest in people you see online. Internet sites come with a range of extra 'flirting features' that can be used to good effect to attract and stir interest in others.

Favouriting (a.k.a. 'cyber-tagging' or 'winking') is one such feature. This is where the site allows you to prompt someone that you like without writing to them. Basically, they get a message or an online alert telling them that you are interested in them. From that small 'nudge' they can take the next step – and many do. To get a woman's interest from this method, you need to have a strong profile (see chapter seven for how to do this) in order to give her something to comment upon.

In general though, if there's someone you are particularly keen on, it's better to message her rather than just 'favouriting' her. To some women, 'favouriting', instead of messaging, can be a sign of shyness and fear of rejection, which are two completely non-Bastardly attributes that are major turn-offs.

Profile licking is a useful technique. It's a good way to register the fact that you are interested in someone. You don't message and you don't favourite (or you've messaged and 'favourited' and received no counter-interest so far). Instead, you take advantage of the feature that many dating sites have that allows users to see who has been checking out their profile.

Here's what you do: you regularly check her out. You know she's probably aware that you're her most active fan and, every time she looks, you've already had your daily fix of her. Everyone likes to be liked and, just maybe, this rather odd form of flattery will be enough to sway her to write. It's worked many times for me.

Cooing

If you have created a killer profile as per the instructions in chapter seven, chances are that it will pique the interest of several female members who will make the first move in contacting you rather than them waiting and hoping that you will contact them. This is called **Cooing**. You already know that the woman has some interest in you or else she wouldn't have taken the effort to get in contact.

Cooing makes your task of finding women a whole lot easier than the Wooing approach where the woman is probably on her guard after receiving your first message. You should respond with a message of your own shortly after receipt. Chapter nine will give full details as to how the conversation should proceed from here.

Shooing

One of the disadvantages of Cooing is that often you are going to receive approaches from women who are just not of interest to you.

It's up to you as to what you do about these unwanted approaches. Quite often, the best thing to do is to simply do nothing. This method has the advantages of not taking any effort at all on your part and perhaps saving the sender the pain of rejection because she might just think that you never received her message (although several dating sites now have features which allow you to check which messages have been read or not). The downside is that she might try contacting you again and again.

One other method of gently Shooing away any unwanted interest involves the telling of a little white lie or two. Thank her for her attention, but tell her that there is someone else that you are starting to become involved with – it's early days yet, but you want to see how it goes before starting anything new with anyone else at the present time. This keeps things nice and open and shouldn't get her suspicious as to why you haven't removed your profile.

Whatever approach you decide on for Shooing, remember that the Complete Bastard is always a charming fellow on the surface. Even though you rejected her in a split-second because she's too old/too fat/too flat-chested/too illiterate for your tastes, there's absolutely nothing to be gained by telling her this.

Sometimes, however, the above advice is easier said than done. After receiving many approaches from many totally unsuitable women, the temptation is always there for you to tell you exactly what you think of her – a temptation that I sometimes gave into, to my shame, as you will read in my next Diary extract at the end of this chapter.

Networking your profile

You have now seen how to flirt like a Complete Bastard online, but you also need to network like a Complete Bastard too.

Networking your profile means getting others to view it – and this means using many of your dating site's features to help you. All dating sites are different and there are various ways to get your profile 'rewarded' by getting the site itself to help promote you by keeping your profile among the most popular of the many thousands or millions that are often members of sites.

The first way to promote yourself is by **keeping your profile fresh**. This involves regularly updating the text and/or images on your profile. Many sites will flag up 'Recently Modified' profiles just as they do 'New Member' profiles. This will increase the number of viewers you will get. Furthermore, a new photo or a new angle on your profile text may attract some new interested viewers.

On the subject of fans, many sites have a 'Most Popular' list. This features the most clicked on men and women on that site. Dating sites have no idea which members get the most dates or sex in the real world, so they work on more rational, self-generated information. This means that the key point to consider when trying to boost your popularity is that sites reward its members according to who is most active on the site. So to boost your popularity, try the following cheats:

Be online regularly: The more you flirt online, the more people will view your profile because it is active – and users tend to want to write to someone that they know is logged in right now and not last logged in a month ago.

Send as many messages as you can: The more messages you're sending, the more sites tend to regard you as playing the online dating game. Active means popular.

Reply to as many messages as you can: It doesn't matter what you say or how much you say – to network your profile, sending any form of message will count as a reply. As stated above, dating sites reward those who interact with their members.

Add favourites: Many sites allow you to bookmark or 'favourite' the profiles that you like. The more profiles you tag in this way, the more people who will tag you back – and this will get you fans (see below).

Collect fans: Sites often show you through a bookmarking system, as described above, showing which members have expressed an interest in you. The more fans you get, the higher your popularity ranking. So encourage fans by sending out lots of messages to lots of people and don't forget to treat your fans well when they add you.

Get a membership: It sounds obvious, but many people register on a site as a lurker or just to browse. What dating site will seek to promote your profile if you aren't contributing to their revenue? Answer: not many.

The secret is to use all of these tactics (or as many as are available on the site you use). With popularity listings, most sites use an algorithm that is a measure of a range of the above variables to calculate who is 'Mr. or Miss Popular'. And if your profile begins to generate clicks, the site will increase your visibility – and that means even more clicks and potential admirers for you. So find the time to network yourself on the sites you use and you'll soon see just how vital a part of flirting online it is.

Complete Bastard Heartbreakers

The majority of women that you will come across during your online dating adventures are likely to be more or less who they say they are – but occasionally you run across some exceptions. You should be on the lookout for the following Complete Bastard Heartbreakers who have the potential to either waste your time or, at worst, completely ruin your entire online dating experience. They are as follows:

- Fakers
- Jugglers
- Teasers
- Chokers
- Moderators

Fakers

Fakers are online dating site users who lie about their age, physical size, job status or any other aspect of their professional or personal life that could influence your opinion of them. Their reason for faking is usually to make you like them. Chapter seven almost encourages you to inject a little fakery yourself into your online dating profile in an attempt to win the attention of others. However, it is important to note that, once exposed as a Faker, it does cast a negative impression of you. In conversations with other online daters, there are countless stories of the, 'I turned up and he was six inches shorter than he'd stated on his profile' variety.

As a male online dater, one of the things to look out for is female Fakers who have the annoying habit of lying about their body size. They tend to upload a couple of very flattering pictures, taken a few years back, and describe their body type as 'curvaceous'. You've flirted with them for weeks online, opened your heart and mind to her and vice versa; you really like this girl, and may even have dallied with a little cybersex together. Now it's time to meet for real and you excitedly await her arrival in her 'favourite little restaurant' that she recommended you both meet in (there was a clue there!).

As you sit, preening yourself nervously, a colossus ambles forth. With each thick-ankled, crashing footstep, the ground shudders and tables rattle. Your date is not only three times larger than you imagined her to be, she's a Faker to boot.

Avoiding Fat Fakers is not an easy task. Many women are very sensitive about their body shape. They inhabit a world in which the media constantly bemoans the big-boned lady and bows down to girls who have their rib cages showing and who consider a handful of blueberries and pine nuts as a Bacchanalian gorge-fest. But no Complete Bastard in his right mind wants to spend a date, never mind an entire relationship, with a bloater who has lied about how she looks.

Before you meet – while still at the stage of online flirting – ask to see some more photographs of her. Maybe send her some recent ones of yourself initially to lull her into a false sense of security that you're not subjecting her to a 'fat test'.

Warning signs to watch out for are if she uploads photographs showing only her face, or ones where she looks visibly younger across her pictures or different from one picture to the next. If she refuses to send you pictures (and some online daters just don't like to send out pictures for genuine privacy reasons), then carefully confront the issue with probing questions such as, 'Do you play much sport?' or, 'What's your favourite food?' Especially with the latter question, if she writes you an email as long as your arm, it might just suggest she has a more than healthy appetite.

Jugglers

Every competent Complete Bastard who follows the advice of this book will become a Juggler. To 'juggle', in the context of online dating, is the act of deceit whereby the dater tells others that they are the only person whom they are contacting. Unbeknown to these naïve daters, however, the reality is that they have a string of admirers with whom they are in regular contact and plan to seduce them all.

Many women are Jugglers too. In fact, women tend to be better and bigger Jugglers than men. The reason for this is, of course, that women get approached much more by men than is usually the reverse. There is also a growing backlash from women to men's historical behaviour as cads. Some women, motivated by an increasing groundswell of 'chick lit' books and popular TV shows like 'Sex and the City', have taken the initiative and now positively seek to have their own harem of gorgeous guys. How the pendulum has swung!

So, what if you have a message from a suspected Juggler in your inbox or find her sitting in front of you at a restaurant on a date? A good tip is to just simply confront her: 'So, what's it like having most of the guys on the dating site after you?' Cue raucous laughter on her part and then she'll respond with the sweetest of rhetorical questions: 'What do you mean?'

She's lying and you know she's lying – but what can either of you do?

The answer to that is: not a lot. For you to get all moody and put out will only serve for her to consider you as one less 'gorgeous guy' to worry about. You'll be out of her harem before the dessert menu arrives.

Sadly, to deal with a Juggler you just have to roll with it. The long-term strategy is that you should successfully Woo her, quickly seduce her, and finally have her under your spell and completely besotted with you – so much though that all the other guys she has been Juggling fall by the wayside. For now though, she hasn't made that commitment and so your strategy is to keep her attention and work on her. You have blown her cover as a Juggler though, and that is a critical step.

Teasers

Teasing is the act of time-wasting by someone you enjoy online flirting with. They respond to messages and become one of your favourite cyber-chums but they have no intention of ever actually meeting you in the real world. (See Virtual Vixens, chapter five).

Teasers are definitely a group to watch out for. Women are consummate at knowing how to flirt with guys. They know what buttons to press to get guys' attentions and, when they have it, they can dangle a carrot in front of them and flirt with true finesse. Men react because we are a lot more easily sexually aroused than women. This is not to say women have no sex drive – it's just that the male instinct to pursue a woman for sex is much stronger.

It becomes, therefore, imperative for any Complete Bastard to watch out for being teased. It can lead to anger, resentment and a feeling that you are owed something.

Teasers will scuttle off just as quickly as they appeared if confronted, so you need to either make the choice to enjoy the online flirtation, resigned to the fact you'll both never meet, or you get rid of her before she gets rid of you. This is one definite scenario when the old adage, 'Think with your head, not your dick' is apt. As every man knows though, it's easier said than done.

Chokers

To 'Choke' is the highly frustrating act when the person you have agreed to meet and date cancels at the 11th hour. They tend to use highly believable though suspiciously improbable excuses to cancel on you, like, 'Something at work came up', or an illness of a close family member. Chokers can be thought of as more complex, though far less organised, version of Teasers.

The Choke is usually not pre-planned. Chokers can defend themselves by saying that they had every intention of honouring your date originally but that, when it came to the live situation, the moment just didn't 'feel right'. Maybe they were tired, hungover, or simply forgot they had a date. Who knows? But Miss Choker's cancelling your date has caused you maximum inconvenience as well as being a huge letdown.

There are a number of strategies to deal with Chokers. The first is to have a, 'One strike and she's out' policy. It's brutal, but it puts you back in control of your dating destiny, and it will give her a taste of her own medicine. But maybe her excuse was genuine and/or maybe she is just too hot to dump at this stage?

The best advice here is that, if you have a Serial Choker, i.e. she is constantly shifting and/or cancelling your dates, the chances are is that she is just not that interested in you. It's time to walk away before you get too frustrated and begin to feel like choking her for real.

Moderators

Moderators are not online dating cyber-criminals like the others here that we have mentioned. Instead they're the site's 'cyber-cops' who are out there to try and stop many of these crimes from occurring.

Most online dating sites – especially the most reputable ones – have Moderators. These are folk who are usually paid (although they can also unpaid volunteers) to monitor and regulate any negative online behaviour which may cause distress, offence or harassment to site users.

There are a range of online misdemeanours that Moderators deal with and these include offensive, threatening, racist or lewd comments from site users, members sending personal contact details to non-registered members so as to avoid the non-member having to subscribe to the site, plus spammers, scammers, or anyone using the site to sell, research or promote services and/or products.

Moderators have a range of powers to deal with such misdemeanours. These include member profile removal, editing or censoring messages from members who are deemed to have written content that has infringed on the site's terms and conditions, and sending warning messages to misbehaving members.

For the Complete Bastard, it is advisable to be aware that Moderators are in the background and so it is wise to avoid behaviour that will infringe the terms and conditions of the dating website that you use. Providing that you follow the methods described in this book though, you shouldn't give anyone any reason to make a complaint about you.

So that's it. You've met a cast of characters who can really disrupt your online dating experience. This book has provided you with a few handy tips to counteract and survive these annoying types. Be vigilant of them, because every time you are a victim of their 'crimes', you'll have wasted time, emotion, money and energy – and all for no gain whatsoever. In short: watch out!

Not all special case members are bad news for the Complete Bastard dater, however. There is one type of member who provides some new and exciting opportunities:

Newbies

Every dating website has brand new members (or Newbies) joining the site on a daily basis. While most sites exaggerate just how many people are online at any one time, or the total membership numbers in terms of active daters, rest assured that, day-by-day, more and more people are getting hooked on the buzz of online dating.

The Newbie is a great target for Complete Bastards for several reasons:

First, they are new to the game and are, therefore, highly susceptible to receiving any form of positive attention. In their first few hours of online dating, they are often completely gobsmacked to find that online dating actually works!

Second, like joining any new club, everyone wants to fit in and be accepted. Thus, most Newbies will be over-friendly, tend to write back to most messages, and will generally be more personable than the online dating veterans who have found the 'Delete' key as their new 'best friend'.

Third, Newbies are fresh blood. They are to online daters what fresh virgin's blood was to Count Dracula. Newbies are *tabla rasa*; they have no bad stories or dodgy experiences. Yet.

For the seasoned online dater, most sites have an area of the site where you can see who has recently joined. It is here you will find wall-to-wall Newbie action and it's a great opportunity to, 'Get 'em while they're fresh'.

Cybersex

Growth in online dating has led to an explosion (no pun intended) in Cybersex activities. For all its negative images of being 'sick' or 'sordid', it is one way of enjoying the pleasures of sex and, to many people, it is a safe, fun and highly exciting way to achieve sexual arousal. It is proving more and more popular and commonplace between online daters across both adult and more general sites.

Conclusive statistics on the exact number of folk who are suspending their disbelief and getting into Cybersex is vague. This is in part because, for many, it's still a furtive pastime that they'd prefer to keep secret. It is also quite difficult to define the exact point at which online flirting stops and Cybersex begins.

One thing is clear however: there has also been a positive change in attitude towards Cybersex over the years. It has now become a commonplace and accepted form of social interaction and has increasingly begun to lose the stigma that it was given by the first wave of internet researchers and quacks, as this quote from 2000 shows:

> 'A specter is haunting the Internet. It is the menace of cybersex. And according to a small army of researchers and therapists, it's creating a legion of funk fiends.'

> – Richard Goldstein, Village Voice

'Funk fiends' or not, Cybersex's deviant nature continues to be partly responsible for its irresistible rise as an 'alternative reality' for horny internet users.

Online dating throws up the opportunity, if you want it, to participate in some form of Cybersex before you actually meet the girl in the real world. In situations where you may find yourself geographically separated or just want the convenience of the buzz when you are both at work or home, it can be a great experience and release from the frustrations of online flirting.

There are many girls out there who are already heavily into Cybersex and a good few who are keen to try it for the first time. As a Complete Bastard, there is no harm in spending some time looking out for these people who can transform your online experience into a way of exploring your deepest fantasies.

Cybersex uncovered

Although, in the majority of cases, the woman doesn't actually come out and say that she would like to indulge in Cybersex, there is often enough tongue-in-cheek humour, saucy talk and friendliness in many conversations to assume that this girl can be talked quickly into considering a little Cybering. Again, and because people like people like themselves, you need to seize your chance to respond with enough tongue-in-cheek humour, saucy talk and friendliness of your own to get her really interested.

The one key point to remember here and in all forms of Cybersex is to keep the tone playful and friendly. Sure, within the realms of Cybering, things may get steamy and downright outrageous but, at the end of the day, Cybersex should always be an enjoyable pastime between two people who are genuinely attracted to one another – or at least what little you know about one another at this stage. Come across as seedy and weird in your sexual appetite and watch your message trails run cold as women hit the 'Delete' button.

With a little care and focus on your manners, your online partner can be kept eager and willing to play. The trick here is to gently prod her into play, little by little. At all costs must you avoid making her look like a sex-depraved tramp.

Instead, tease her and titillate her by spicing up a few friendly messages with sexual innuendo, flirtatious jokes or some 'dare-you' challenges. Coming across as erudite over smutty is a winner here. A girl is far more likely to be attracted to a man who is intelligent with a streak of adventure, than one who is a complete sexual deviant showing just the occasional glimmer of intelligent conversation.

If your idea of cyber foreplay is something corny along the lines of, 'So what are you wearing, baby?' or else a typical Neanderthal approach such as, 'C'mon, love – show us yer tits!', your chances of getting much further than this is pretty remote.

Instead, below is a (condensed) example of an online chat which is more likely to gently tease her into action. Here you can clearly see the balance between a friendly, conversational tone fused with brewing, seductive desire:

> **Him:** Well, from your pictures you certainly look very attractive. Those legs of your must be able to get you quickly to a nearby bar to meet me?
>
> **Her:** You're not the first guy on this site to compliment me on my legs. Mind you, I think I have some other great features too …
>
> **Him:** Sounds verrryyyyy interesting! So, tell me, what may these 'great features' be?
>
> **Her:** Have a guess! ;-)
>
> **Him:** I'm very bad at guessing. Surely you've heard that men are more visual creatures and less perceptive than women!?
>
> **Her:** Well, why don't I switch on my webcam and I'll let you have a look?!

As for where the conversation goes from here, this is very much down to the two personalities involved. In general though, remember the saying that men fall in love with their eyes, whereas women fall in love with their ears.

For you, just watching her pleasure herself on webcam will probably be the ultimate

Cybersex experience. For her, however, just sitting there and watching you stroke yourself is going to be less of a turn on than you probably think it will be.

The market for erotic videos, magazine and online content is said to be worth around $10 billion per year. Nearly all of the consumers of these products are men. The only area of erotic entertainment where women make up a high proportion of buyers is in the area of erotic fiction. This is perhaps not surprising when you think that erotic novels are not too far removed from the romantic fiction that is such a popular genre amongst them.

So, if you would like to become an expert at the art of cyber seduction, you could do worse than to learn a few tricks from the writers of high quality erotic fiction, paying particular attention to the type of language that they use, as it is likely to be as much of a turn on for women as it is for men.

How Cybersex affects dating

Cybersex, once you've got a taste for it, can be highly addictive. You crave repeat adventures, enjoying the ease and convenience of existing in a private and erotically-charged world. You can lapse into becoming predatory as you prowl the internet for new and willing 'victims'.

During the time when I was at the height of my Cybersex participation, I flirted with married women and girls in relationships. I encountered some women who wished they had never begun what they ended up deeming a 'sordid' affair. And I lost a few relationships in the real world due to my cyber-dalliances.

For some people, Cybering can lead to feelings of disgust and regret after the event. But others just want the buzz of the cyber-orgasm and they're off with no intention of a real world date (See Virtual Vixens, chapter five). Therefore it becomes important to not confuse the boundaries between real and imagined lust.

Cybersex prior to a date can, in some cases, lead to a sense of disappointment upon actually meeting in the real world. This usually takes the malaise that the person you were imagining is physically nothing like the person now before you in a restaurant or bar. That can be a disheartening experience. If you have been using webcams during your Cybersex, it can lead to the girl feeling embarrassed that you've seen her naked on cam before you've even shaken her hand.

On a more positive note, Cybersex prior to a date can intensify feelings, heighten sexual tension and actually make the woman think that there is real passion in the relationship at such an early stage. Intense Cybersex sessions with girls based upon the theme of, 'What's going to happen on our first date?', can lead to very quick first-date bedroom action as you then go ahead and replay your cyber-fantasies in real life.

In short, the choice of whether to include Cybersex in a relationship is the choice of two consenting adults. How it affects the relationship later is very person-specific and should be treated with caution. As a rule of thumb though, ask yourself what your eventual goal is with a particular girl. If you're just looking for a quick fling before quickly moving on, then Cybersex before meeting could speed things along. If you are instead looking for a long term relationship though, maybe it's better not to take the risk of messing things up.

For the Complete Bastard, Cybersex is one outlet for enjoyment and the playful Wooing of women. Just don't let it take over your life. For there are plenty more ways for the Complete Bastard to enjoy the fruits of online dating.

DATING DIARY OF A COMPLETE BASTARD

Barbed Wired
A collection of some of the Complete Bastard's best email putdowns from his bile-stained outbox.

Though the best advice is to get women to like you on dating sites, sometimes the Complete Bastard can take it no more. Email after email of dull, boring, insipid messages from women that I was not interested in kept arriving in my inbox. This is simply one of the drawbacks of becoming adept at online dating.

Papa Bastard is never one for niceties. A lot of the 'nastiness' I adopted late in life came straight from that man's foul teachings. As the Old Dog used to tell me, 'Be bad and be liked. Be Bastardly and be adored.'

Unfortunately, the man must have been high on some unmentionable poison at the time because any internet dater that was at the receiving end of one of my rants or barbed replies, I never heard from again. That'll teach them for being too damn dull to date.

Here, in no particular order, are a selection of some of my most nasty, seething, and fury-laden messages that I sent to poor, unsuspecting women. Online dating: it is a game of emotion after all.

From '**Hypnotic75**':

'Hey there, fancy a coffee, a muffin and chat sometime?'

There was no way I was meeting this chick – seriously overweight with more chins than I'd had hot dates – and so I replied:

'Listen sweetheart, I see from your pictures you like the sweet snacks, but I think you got the wrong guy – I'm as sour as they come.'

Then there's dealing with those girls whose emails are so boring and toothless, your eyes have glazed over even before you've finished reading their messages. Here are just two such churning halfwits:

From '**Zena82**':

'Hello and how's the weather where you are today?'

I replied:

'Dull... like your message.'

From 'Doobie_Doobie_Do':

'Question – if you could have any super-power what would it be?'

Me: 'The ability to make you disappear.'

Some online dating sites are besieged with 'arty, creative' types only too eager to ram a gob-load of whimsical drivel into your head, if only to prove they are somehow in touch with their inner idiot. 'Hermione999' tried this to impress me:

'My imagination is flooded by my own reality, and that of the people around me. My art allows me to go beyond my perception of the world, unravelling as many layers as those which I form on canvas. With a visceral need to escape everyday sensations, I let the unconscious be my guide.

'The process is dichotomous: I need to find solace while revelling in the presence of form. These overlapping emotions adhere to both the real and the illusory. They find expression through work that is characterized by a strong palette and dynamic brush strokes. I want the viewer to live for a brief moment in the painting. I want my work to appear unfinished, to resonate with life, with a quality of simply existing.'

My reply was just as creative:

'Hermione, I was most impressed indeed with your artistic intensity. Like you, I too make art. Well, if you consider smearing my own excreta on walls while fusing this with some abstract Crayola Crayon scribblings. My work is on display every evening in my padded cell in the Bohemian wing of an East London asylum. Write soon, Marcus.'

Then there was this whimsical ditty from 'Crimson_Cheeks' after I'd fed her some balderdash that I'd toured Africa. She was recommending that I find spirituality in the Sinai sands:

'Because the night sky in the desert is a thing of wondrous beauty... stars between stars... I've never seen anywhere better. It's not touristy to see the places you travel to with an open mind and with your eyes open.'

My response was as scorching as the Serengeti sun:

'Cheers, love. But a couple of cold beers and a cheap hooker with her legs open is more my idea of enjoying exotic travel.'

At least arty types know how to slack off in life; devoting their souls to watching daytime TV, drinking copious amount of booze to 'inspire' them and skimping off State Benefits. With the Complete Bastard being notoriously lazy when it comes to work that is not for his direct gain, it's no surprise to learn that Corporate Whore types, no matter how hard they try, just don't impress:

From '**Emerald_city**':

'Well, hello. I shouldn't really be writing this at work but can't a girl have some fun?? I love my job – don't get me wrong. I'm busy, busy, busy with a Blackberry that's like an extension of my hand and it's always one email away from COMPLETE MELTDOWN. I've got meetings all day and all week and I've just had to cancel my skiing trip to France. Boo Hoo. NO!!!!! Positive thinking is what my gym trainer advises. Oh, that reminds me. I have a workout tonight. Reps, reps, reps and then its home for low-calorie salad and an early night. Is your life so hectic? I hope so!! Busy means end of year bonus! Regards, Maggie.'

Me: 'Hey, thanks for finding the time to write. I hate my job and I hate my life. I'm a husk of a man. I go home each evening to an empty fridge and have only the bedbugs for friends. I'd like to tear open my skull and spoon all my bad memories out. Fancy a drink? Might be fun.'

Finally, we come to my most hated of online dater types: the downright weird. Check out this email I received from some cyber-chick called 'Lana':

'Raised by a tribe of Siberian huskies, I travelled through Ukraine and, thanks to Chernobyl, I now glow in the dark (which is handy at raves). This is my main sales point! I lived in Moscow – billed as "That Glowing Ukrainian Girl" at the State Circus. I am used to fame.

'Since then not much has changed. I have developed a soft spot for stuff like unicorns, Kleizmer music, regional dishes, flying carpets, home sewn folk print dresses, death, fleamarkets, orange lipstick, 1920s, the smell of wet dogs, bric-a-brac, Victorian porn and other things I might discover with you.'

There can be but one Bastardly retort:

Me: 'MAD C***!'

– 9 –
Moving Towards A Date

Interest – now what?

Congratulations! Whether as a result of you Wooing her or her Cooing you, you've found yourself a girl who's interested in making contact with you. So now what do you do with her?

This chapter deals with that awkward stage between meeting someone new on a dating site, and shifting the relationship offline by arranging to meet them in the real world.

It will teach you how to select the women who will be best suited to your needs and desires from the many initial exchanges of messages that you should be getting if you have been following the Complete Bastard plan. Then with her (or them) in mind, it's time to show you how to connect more deeply with them online through the messages that you send.

And there's more to Wooing a girl than just writing her love letters. We focus on the next tricky stage, which is how you move the situation away from messaging through getting to know her better, then towards a real world first meeting. You did, after all, join online dating to improve your real life.

Selecting a date from a dud

Most people, when they crack how to write a good online dating profile and have learned how to write initial messages that spark girls' attention, get responses. With responses come opportunities. As this book outlines, the Complete Bastard is able to use online dating as a means to achieve his own selfish goals and agenda. Remember: he seeks not only quality of women but also **quantity**.

The type of woman and quantity are at the discretion of every Complete Bastard. However, what is vital and separates this guide from any other is that it educates you in ways of remorselessly using women for a variety of needs and purposes beyond simply making contact online with them.

If that translates as, 'We recommend you go online and get as many virtual buddies as possible,' then you've certainly missed a trick. Every cyber flirtation, every message and every date you go on consumes your time and cash. From maximising your time as a paid-up member of a dating site to preserving your bank balance from gold diggers, it is imperative that you minimise wasteful dates by rooting out the wrong women as early as possible. This is not as easy as it sounds.

This is because, as has been already touched upon before and will be revisited later in this chapter, many people give the best possible impression of themselves both pictorially and in their profile text. But not everyone is telling the complete truth. Furthermore, as we learned in chapter eight, there are a host of totally fake profiles that are designed to attract the male gaze and, in some cases, his credit card details.

However, the most important first task after receiving some responses and Wooing some would-be dates, is determining **who** you would like to meet and **why**?

You can't date everyone who contacts you. A Complete Bastard will try, but even he knows the merits of screening his interested parties before getting involved in a conversation which will hopefully result in a date. So what are the factors that should separate a date from a dud?

Attractiveness and sexiness
This is an obvious and easy rule of thumb. If she's hot, the date is on. Nothing is better for a man's self-esteem and public image than some gorgeous eye-candy on his arm. As if you are pondering whether or not to date the most stunning girl on the site who, straight out of the blue, messaged you and asked you out?! Chances are you'll be booking a candlelit table for two as quick as a flash. And quite right too!

Wealth
And they say the Class System does not exist any more? It does for the Complete Bastard. A monied madame with a successful job or wealthy parents is a delicious catch. Money makes the Complete Bastard's world go round and who better a source than some rich Rita who'll open your world to new adventures every time she opens her purse? But beware: all that glitters is not gold. It's vital to spot the difference between a genuinely, disgustingly rich woman and simply a kind one (i.e., a girl who buys you things because she likes you and is, for now, so blinkered that she's driving herself to financial ruin for you). Even Complete Bastards should try and have some compassion.

Lifestyle or career
Girls with high status jobs, memberships at elite clubs, or any other trappings of a lavish lifestyle can be great targets. They can become tickets into an illustrious, privileged world that no Complete Bastard could enter on his own merits. Important here though is knowing what is worthy of your efforts: own apartment (but with

negative equity), membership of a gym or a job 'with prospects' isn't really what you're aiming for. Think big: corporate high fliers, illustrious sports club members, a great address book of business and social life contacts – these are the types of benefits that the Complete Bastard should seek to sink his devilish claws into.

Getting into regular conversation

Sometimes you will be able to work out which girls are worthy of your best efforts from the first exchange of messages alone. More often though, you will need to drop a few subtle questions into your early exchange of messages to discover the information you need to decide whether she's worth continuing to Woo, or whether you need to Shoo.

Men tend to send messages that fall into two categories – either, 'I'm a sweet fellow, really,' or, 'I'm the greatest thing since sliced bread!' **Pandering** and **Proclamation** are two conversational strategies that should be avoided at all costs. Women, or at least those women who you are looking to meet and eventually manipulate, are very rarely attracted to weak or arrogant men.

The irony of this, however, is that, to convince the women that you are a worthwhile catch, you need to persuade her that you are, 'A sweet fellow, really' and, 'The greatest thing since sliced bread.'

So, how do you do that?

Focus on a single profile detail and don't let go

This is an easy way to steer the conversation from the start. It involves your going down a focused, definite route, ensuring that what comes across most is your energy, wit and bravado. This will override the fact that you may be jobless, have a drug habit, or be fresh out of jail.

Let me give you an example. 'Greenfingers' was a tree surgeon from London. She was also in her early thirties, single and had just joined the dating site I was a member of. A couple of pictures on her profile showed her up trees in the course of her job. A tree surgeon is certainly an interesting and unusual job, but think how many men began their first Wooing message with something like, 'Wow, so you're a tree surgeon! Great job! Tell me all about it!'

'Greenfingers' was a highly attractive woman who loved travel, literature and photography. I figured she'd be a great steal for any guy and so would be inundated with eligible bachelors bombarding her inbox. So, I took the tree theme and decided to 'monkey around' with it:

'Hi Greenfingers, from your pics it seems you hang out in tree houses all day?

This so? Or are you really a monkey, swinging from branch to branch?'

It worked. Within a few hours she replied:

'Pretty much ... occasionally I stop to pick off fleas x'

I quickly answered back:

'Strange ... that shouldn't float my boat ... but it does!! :)'

Now, with the exchange of just three one-liners between us, here I was: (a) chatting with one of the site's best-looking chicks and (b) chatting her up with wit and sexual innuendo. Note: nothing I've said so far is smutty.

So what did she say next?

'Well, maybe you should be looking on Pri-mates.com! x'

The monkey metaphor continued for a few more exchanges until it was 'Greenfingers' who suggested:

'Wanna meet me at the zoo?'

My reply was enthusiastic – if a little cute:

'Haha Actually a great place for a date! Educational too. When u wanna SWING BY and we can MONKEY around for a while? '

Here's an important point: 'Greenfingers' and I showed how a simple, disposable bit of conversational banter can be the perfect foreplay to setting up a date. Luckily for me, 'Greenfingers' was as good an online date player as I was at that stage. And so our date with the animals was hastily arranged.

Tell a random story

Another tip for tempting the opposite sex to start chatting with you is to send out an amusing if a little random story. Everyone loves a tale and, in my view, the bawdier the better! Here are some ideas for you and types of tales that I've used in the past as ice-breakers:

Happy tales: A light-hearted, cheery story can lift the spirit of your reader and will make you appear likeable and entertaining.

Heroic tales: Any story where you can 'modestly' show her that you did something brave or manly.

Humorous tales: If you can make her laugh with an amusing anecdote then you'll get her smiling and liking you.

Humdrum tales: You hate your boss. Your car needs a service. You don't know what to cook for dinner tonight. Talking about the most mundane things can have a surprising effect on building rapport between two people.

Heart-rending tales: From the death of your pet goldfish when you were a boy, to sharing a truly tragic tale, a real tear jerker can build bonds and show your alleged tender side.

Horrific tales: A master tale teller can shock, startle and even scare his audience, winning their complete attention. Rather than put them off you, a compelling tale laced with some digestible macabre will make you intriguing.

In short, the point is that an interesting, concise, well-told story can be an excellent ice breaker and also a great way to use your first few messages to inject some humour and energy into getting to know someone. Furthermore, it's a prompt to encourage them to swap similar tales or write back with a reaction.

Be bold and get into role

Nothing gets a girl's attention like a good, old posture-arresting bit of brash overstatement. Providing that you avoid sounding arrogant, a swaggering confidence from the first message will create a manly impression of yourself, as well as firmly putting your fussy female firmly on the back foot.

Though this tactic does work on most occasions and comes highly recommended, the secret of its success is sustaining the mystique of bold machismo.

Everyone is prone to moments of self-doubt and low self-esteem but, if you go down the bold route, you have to be bold all the time. Show one glimmer of a confidence quiver and she'll become mistrustful and disappointed that her brave Prince has turned back into a frog.

A solid piece of advice here is to do what professional writers and actors do: get into role. Imagine that you are that bold, brash, swaggering hero of online dating and let the words flow from your imagination as if they were written by Casanova himself...

> Good evening, my fine lady,
>
> On my quest to find the perfect women, I have been traversing this lowly internet dating site for a woman of infinite beauty. I stumbled by sheer chance upon your exquisite profile and was bowled over in astonished glee!
>
> I am currently getting my page to saddle my steed, whereupon I shall race at a thrilling gallop towards you as you powder your ample bosom in anticipation for my arrival. I am of the belief that this is the beginning of a truly amorous union.
>
> Yours,

If that's a little bit too foppish, self-indulgent and not really your style, then there are plenty of other methods that you can use to stand out from the crowd. Why not avoid the waffle of introductory emails and give her a flavour of yourself with a witty tale:

> Hi,
>
> Do you believe in Karma?
>
> I 'borrowed' a luxury cotton dressing gown from a five-star hotel last week. While sitting in it this evening, scoffing on a homemade curry, I leaned across from some nan bread and the sumptuous white cotton of my gown dipped into my curry, staining it terribly.
>
> That's the Lord at work here. Or maybe the Devil? Or maybe it was just a case of 'Bad Korma'.
>
> I don't know which of these entities brought us together – only time will tell. :)
>
> Write soon,

Or perhaps something more bold and direct is suitable:

> Hey there,
>
> Couldn't help but write you. You've got one of THE best profiles on this site. We could send each other 1001 emails but why not let's just think about a real date. After all, we're real people living in the real world and we could have a REAL good time together.
>
> Let me know what you think if interested.
>
> Bye,

The above are all conversations that got the merry crackle of online chat started. Once she has responded, your next goal should be to keep the conversation moving forwards constantly, which means giving her more of what you gave her in your original opening message. You can't afford to come up with one good opening message and then think that the battle is won and that you can continue with a more mundane level of conversation.

Think about each subsequent message that you send her after the first – don't just bash out a quick response and send it. You need to make sure that your style is consistent throughout your entire conversation.

Avoid becoming too egocentric in your conversations so as not to come over as appearing arrogant. Although you might have Wooed her with your initial approach, you need to involve her in the conversation or else she could very well get bored of it quickly. One easy way to do this is by ensuring that you ask at least one question in each message that you send her. In this way, she will have some reason to write back to you, even if she can't think of much else to say.

The overall lesson that the novice Complete Bastard must learn is that it can really pay when you find a writing 'voice' that suits your personality. And before we leave this section, here are six things to avoid in any correspondence:

1. **Avoid one liners**: They show lack of effort and rarely connect.

2. **Avoid smut**: Sleazy lines with a strong sexual focus never get what they're after.

3. **Avoid essays**: Lengthy emails telling your life story are overkill in early stages.

4. **Avoid conceit:** Arrogance and bragging is a big turn off.

5. **Avoid mentioning past relationships:** Unless she brings up the subject first, don't mention anything about previous lovers – either good or bad. She doesn't want to hear about it.

6. **Avoid the obvious:** That girl with the 'Marmite_is_yummy' screenname must have really regretted coming up with it after she received her 100th message from guys saying how much they hated it or loved it too.

Dealing with the Slow Burn

So you've decided that your online girl is definitely a Wooer rather than a Shooer. Your goal now should be to try and get a date with her as quickly as possible. As much fun as internet dating can be, it's nothing compared to the amount of fun that you can have with her on the first or subsequent dates.

The speed at which you can move from an initial exchange of messages to a first date varies tremendously from girl to girl. At one end of the scale, I've had girls who, in their second messages, have said, 'I don't much like chatting by email – let's meet – here's my number'. This makes matters very simple as you just need to give her a call to set up the time and the place.

More often than not, however, you need to go through a 'pre-courtship' routine via email to get her to a stage where she's initially comfortable with you and attracted to you in order to want to meet. There are some girls who really like the long courtship.

It is this sort of girl who needs a careful rethinking of the strategy. Little bawdy tales and shock tactics won't work on her. She is a Slow Burner who wants to take her time to scope you out and make sure that you're a worthwhile investment of her emotional life. Often this type is just out of a relationship or has been hurt by a man before. She's wary, cautious and doesn't want to rush into anything.

She reminds me of 'Pixie' who was a hot chick on a site I was a member of. You will learn more about her and the long courting process that it took until she eventually agreed to meet with me in the Diary extract at the end of this chapter. Once you have read through it, you will see that I took her through six distinct stages before we eventually met; a process that you should use whenever trying to Woo such Slow Burners:

1. **Get their attention:** Write nothing too shocking or alarming.

2. **Focus on building a friendship:** Begin to send frequent emails that include compliments, upbeat tales and interesting facts about yourself.

3. **Play it cool:** Stop writing for a few hours or days from time to time.

4. **Re-engage:** Return to regular correspondence to show her what she has missed.

5. **Shift to the everyday:** Move to the stage where she comes home and tells you how boring her night out was, what she ate for dinner, what she is wearing, etc. – dull but significant details that show that she is now totally relaxed with you.

6. **Shouldn't we meet?:** Your question is almost rhetorical now, it should slip out so effortlessly that you've hardly realized you've asked her.

Email to IM or phone?

Before moving to the actual date, online daters often set up 'half-way meets'. These are where they extend the form of communication and interaction from purely exchange of messages or emails to either phone conversation or IM.

Both are safe, convenient and virtual means of further getting to know one another. For the Complete Bastard, both can be opportunities to affirm or scupper a budding relationship.

I'm personally a big fan of using IM rather than the telephone for a number of reasons. Firstly, IM is a fast and exciting way to chat and flirt. It's further enhanced by the ability to add emoticons, send files or images, and chat while having the full power of the internet constantly on hand as a tool of reference.

The drawback of IM is that sometimes things cannot be expressed so well due to the textual nature of communication. As we mentioned earlier in chapter four, communicating by words alone makes for a very poor level of communication. In fact, a study by UCLA showed that only 7% of effective communication came from the words, 38% from voice quality and 55% from body language and other non-verbal communication. So, on the phone, 45% of what you are trying to express is getting across – with text based communication, less than a sixth of that is getting through

To make matters worse, sometimes meaning can be lost in the concise, slang-driven expression of IM. Irony and sarcasm, for example, have to be treated with care as they can easily be totally misinterpreted. IM also encourages a looser form of communication – it takes effort to type compared to chatting on the phone. Hence people think more about what they write than say and, in my opinion, this makes for a more thought-through level of interaction.

The telephone can be a deal maker or breaker. A sexy accent or a stimulating conversationalist can really win over a woman here. Then there are the deviants who know how to use the telephone to titillate.

For many men though – perhaps the majority – talking on the phone is a nightmare. What to say? What happens if the conversation dries up? Am I talking too much? Talking too little? Speaking on the telephone is fraught with dangers for the dater who has so far lurked safely in his cyber world where he was able to take all communications in his own time and pace so he could think about what it is that he wants to say in order to make a perfect impression each time.

Once again, having confidence is key here. Pick up that phone a nervous wreck and your voice will be trembling like you've just come out of an ice cold shower when she picks up and hears your first words. It's only a call and you have to believe that she's already shown that she is pretty keen on you for her to give you her number, so the hardest part is done already.

But you don't want to screw up on the phone and here are a few tips that may just keep her hanging on the line:

Listen to her and let her speak

Women are expert communicators. This means that, not only do they talk a lot, but they listen a lot too. This is an important part of bonding and it's important that you take the time to just say nothing and listen to what she is telling you. This also means you can let her lead the conversation and react to her conversation topics. Easy.

Avoid waffling

When people get nervous, they talk faster and that can often lead to waffling, an annoying habit when you know you are talking, but have no real clue as to what incoherent stream of irrelevance will spill forth from your mouth next. It's dull to listen to, hard to join in with from the listener's point of view and can make you look a little mad. If you know you're waffling, try and stop yourself. At worst use the 'emergency brakes' line, 'I've started waffling so I think I'll stop now.' She'll thank you for it.

Avoid chat debris

Listen to yourself speak on the phone. Record a conversation and play it back if necessary. It's amazing how eloquent we all think we talk when, in reality, we often interject those annoying little 'ums' and 'ahs'. These little space fillers are signs of low-power talkers. With practice, you can learn to remove them from your speech and can achieve a more fluid, powerful and authoritative tone. Just try speaking slower if you're struggling – that will give your brain more time to keep up with your mouth.

Avoid ranting

Men love a good rant – the weather, parking tickets, airplane food, bad reception with your cell phone – we gripe about it all. During a telephone call with someone you've just met, however, this can come across as highly negative and make you look as if you're nothing but a grumbling, moaning old man. Instead, talk positively and hide your dark thoughts until she knows you better.

Whether you opt for IM or telephone chat, remember that your ultimate goal is to fix up a date. This may be a short, sweet, 'Hello, let's arrange a meet, shall we?' call to a series of long-drawn, in-depth conversations with a Slow Burner type. You'll invest the time if the girl is worth it.

In conclusion, to become a highly proficient Complete Bastard at online dating, it pays to start gaining confidence by enjoying flirting with your new Bastard personality. You'll be amazed at the results.

How and when to ask for that date

This chapter has showed you many techniques for getting the conversation flowing, for obtaining a reaction from your subject, and getting her interested in you. If you use these techniques effectively, you **will** get results. This means that you will get girls to begin to like you, to enjoy talking with you and they will feel relaxed around you. So why would they turn down your request for a date?

Your request can be declined though and this never feels good. But put it into perspective: you should be flirting with a good few others so you may not have been putting in as much effort as this girl desires.

The best advice in this situation is to take the knockback on the chin and stick in there. Maybe it's time to shift things down a gear or two and go back to the 'Getting to know you' stage once again in order to raise her comfort level a little higher. Leave it a while and try again – there's always the chance she'll come around. If not, and you can find no obvious reason for her not wanting to meet with you, chances are that she's just a Virtual Vixen who never had any intention of moving from the online level at all. So don't dwell on it – there was nothing wrong with you or your tactics – she was just being dishonest about her motives for online dating all along.

Avoiding pre-date nerves

For many daters, reaching the stage of getting a girl to agree to a date represents a dramatic shift away from their comfort zone. What started with exchanging some heartfelt, humorous or flirtatious emails ends up as a complete waste of time for both of you if you're unable to deliver on the perceived image that the other person has of you in their mind. It can be, for many people, a daunting prospect.

Why should any dater feel bad about moving towards a meeting with the person that they may have only dreamed about before joining the site?

Well, there are a number of reasons as to why, as follows:

Liar backfire

As we discussed earlier in chapter seven, lying either on your profile or in your initial messages can come back to haunt you at a later stage in the dating process.

Flirting online allows people to enhance their self image to impress the woman. This can take many forms. For men, it can be a case of exaggerating their job status or uploading their most flattering pictures from a few years back before their six-pack morphed into a beer barrel. It could be telling a few fibs during interaction about your alleged jet-ski hobby, your noble work for charity, or 'accidentally forgetting' to mention your three previous divorces, that you're the father of eight illegitimate kids and that you're currently on parole for armed robbery.

I once told a woman who I was Wooing that I had shot a lion on safari. For her, it cast me as a rugged adventurer. To this day, she still believes I did it. Sadly, the truth is that the closest I have ever been to shooting a wild beast was when I used to fire air rifle pellets at my neighbour's Persian cat from my bedroom window as a teenager.

As previously warned, you take your chances with lying and, if ever caught, you will be exposed as a sinister character and could very well lose her interest in you unless you have managed to charm her so successfully that she is willing to overlook a little 'massaging' of the truth.

Also as we mentioned earlier, women use the fibbing trick too. The temptation is there for everyone to play about with their reality while online dating. With the pressure on to find and keep a 'soulmate', you can see why the temptation is irresistible for many.

Keeping up with the Cyber-Joneses

The second confidence-dampener as to why people fear real world dating is that people are intimidated by others' 'perfect' lives. Everyone seems to have a bigger car than you, a bigger house than you, more money than you and to go to the gym more often than you. This malaise of consumer society goes on in the workplace, around tables at dinner parties and is no stranger to online dating sites too. It's an online form of, 'Keeping up with the Joneses'.

People deem every aspect of their life as a success or a source of happiness in order to cast themselves as a worthy catch. Avoid this. It might seem curmudgeonly, but there is something mistrustful about anyone who's too happy or too successful.

Online dating exists to fill a need in people, so why bullshit that you're on the dating site as a fully-actualised, joyous, 100% contented person? We all get lonely, we all crave love and affection and we all find it harder and harder to meet new people. There is nothing unattractive about being frank with others that your life lacks a special someone. That's not creepy or weak. In fact, most women will strike an instant accord as long as you don't come over as feeling sorry for yourself and harping on about it, *ad nauseam*.

The Complete Bastard's own preference is to cut the crap about pretending that his life is perfect and without flaws. Such a life doesn't exist. Instead, focus on furnishing your profile with a few life cracks and crises. There's nothing people like – and trust – more than feeling that they can relate to someone or be of help to them. (If only they knew that, as a Complete Bastard, you've been helping yourself for years!)

Hating dating

The third reason for fearing a meeting is fear of the act of dating itself. It's perfectly understandable too, because anyone's first blind (or semi-blind) date can be a daunting experience, especially when it is with a girl who you'd really like to connect with. This is one of the reasons why, if you are still quite new to the dating scene, it can be a good idea to go out on a few 'practice dates' with girls who you are not overly interested in where there is going to be less pressure. The more dates you go on, the easier and less nerve-wracking the experience gets. You'll quickly grow to love dating and will actually get a buzz off the nervous excitement that a first date generates.

Dating is about beating your nerves and not beating yourself up. It's a great experience that can be a real confidence booster. Think about it: somebody out there has selected you from all the many thousands of people she sees online, brushes shoulders with and crosses paths with every day. Somebody has shown real interest and intrigue in who you are, what you do and where you want to go in life. There's more than likely a sexual attraction too. So, someone out there has been thinking some naughty thoughts about you as well.

But maybe, on the cusp of going on a date, you are still unsure. Chapter eleven shows you how you read the signs and adapt your strategy to suit those signs. Nothing is set in stone. With the right know-how, you will learn how to swing any date around in your favour. And the Complete Bastard should know. He's sat with solemn-faced, defensive, monosyllabic women at the start of dates, and left with giggling, chatty, slightly tipsy (alcohol helps!) ladies, with both of them looking for a late night bar or a more secluded night spot afterwards.

With the right advice, you can move towards making a date an enjoyable experience and one to be embraced – not feared.

DATING DIARY OF A COMPLETE BASTARD

Wooing A Slow Burner

Occasionally online dating means having to use every trick from the Complete Bastards' toolkit to succeed. 'Pixie' was one such case.

'Pixie' was the site's most clicked on female profile when I came across her. Long blonde hair, beautiful green eyes, and a mischievous smile, she was certainly one hot online property.

And like a two-bedroom penthouse apartment with a sea-view, 'Pixie' was on the free market and available to the highest bidder. I figured that she'd be inundated with messages from men wooing her with date requests and elated compliments to her devilish beauty. If I was to win her attention, I had to do something out of the ordinary.

I composed a short message and sent it to 'Pixie'. My rationale was that 100 clumsy words with a bit of wit would be better received than 1000 eloquent words trying to dazzle her. The average Web reader is a skim-reader and, anyway, her inbox was probably stuffed with messages she just didn't have the time to read.

'Pixie' had stated on her profile that she loved fashion and worked as manageress at a famous clothes boutique in London. Going with her interests, not mine, should work, I thought – and so I wrote:

> 'Hey Pixie, I'm sitting here in fluorescent flares, a jumper my Gran knitted me for Christmas 17 years ago and a bowler hat such as a Victorian English gent would wear. Dapper or fashion disaster? Please advise.'

I waited hours, days – but when no reply came after one week, I figured the lady was not for cyber-flirting. I could have left it there, but I was now intoxicated by 'Pixie'. I'd been 'Profile Licking' her all week and she'd know I was highly interested in her. Perhaps she liked the tease?

I decided to give it another go. Perhaps something a little more roguish was in order. Message number two went as follows:

> 'Hi again, Pixie. I see you ignored my last email. Clearly you're not the sort of a girl who enjoys an ill-behaved night out – on my gentleman's account of course. Debauchery is guaranteed. It's a damn shame. Of note, I have been known to swing naked from chandeliers while singing our National Anthem. You game?'

That day, a reply came back from 'Pixie'. Cleary, this was a woman who enjoyed mischief – or a free night out at my expense. Either way, I was happy.

> 'Hi, Thanks for your email. I have to tell you, I've been getting loads of sweet replies from guys but NOONE has been quite so insulting about our fine nation's anthem. Do you know they still behead for such a crime? :)'

Breakthrough! As any Complete Bastard will tell you: 'Give us an inch and we'll take a mile'. 'Pixie' was in the game. My next message was critical, however. I had to keep my Bastardly poise at all costs. Lapse now back into compliments and pandering to her and I'd be back with the other boy-rejects in Inbox No Man's Land. My reply went:

> 'Most amusing' Miss 'Pixie' of our Queen's realm. I'll have you know I'm a staunch Royalist and my swinging and singing is a CELEBRATION of our great ruler and not ridicule. Although I do admit, the nakedness is a problem my therapist is currently analysing. Let us make a pact to form an alliance and celebrate our Sovereign State. Champagne and caviar this week?'

What came back from 'Pixie' was a shock, but I should have seen the signs.

> 'Hi, I'm not ready to meet anyone yet. Sorry if that's a problem but I'm just being honest. Hope you understand.'

What had originally shown signs of a frothy bit of flirtation had now grinded to a halt. At the first sign of date pressure, 'Pixie' had put the brakes on. Sure, she was up for some light-hearted banter, but she simply wasn't ready to date at this stage. Frustrating, but fair play. I could have dumped her there and then – and the purist Complete Bastard may well have done so. However, I was a little smitten with 'Pixie' by now and determined to win that date. After all, as Papa Bastard says: 'If a woman's worth the catch, then the pursuit is all.'

My pursuit needed re-starting and my next email was critical. In light of her last email, I played Pixie's game and went all sober and serious. I was chewing one fist as I wrote it, but it was time to temper my playful side:

> 'Hi Pixie, I got your email and fully understand that you're not ready to date yet. A lot of women on the site are put under pressure by guys and I'm sure you just want to separate the 'chap from the chaff'.'

And so began 50 odd messages that went to and fro between 'Pixie' and I, from the mind-numbing bland to the Beige Bastard ridiculous. I'd fallen for this chick and this was my penance if I was to Woo her sufficiently for her to trust me and agree to date me:

Pixie: 'I'm just back from visiting my parents. Goodness, I feel stuffed after my Sunday lunch. How are you? Had a great day?'

Me: 'Yes, Pixie. My day's been fantastic! A bit of gardening [lie!], the Sunday newspapers [lie!] and I'm just cooking a huge meal for all my friends who are coming over this evening! [lie!]'

The weeks passed by and we continued to email. I actually began to enjoy the regular messages between us for some strange reason. We'd even started talking on the phone and built up a strong rapport. Either I was losing my Bastard Touch or I was going mad. Finally, just as I'd nearly started shopping for brown cardigans and thinking about taking up gardening as a hobby for real, came the message I'd been waiting for all along:

'I think it's time we had that date, don't you? Yours, Pixie xxx'

I couldn't get my clothes off and up on that chandelier fast enough!

Winning my date with 'Pixie' was a great coup and shows that persistence and 'good' behaviour was the only way to Woo over this particular Slow Burner.

On the date, 'Pixie' was charming company, plus as delectable in the flesh as she was in her photos. We drank, we danced and at the end of the night we slipped back to my apartment.

It was a great night of sex but the following day I'd lost my desire for 'Pixie'. Perhaps I'd blown my romantic fires out during the long online courting routine.

If only the poor 'Pixie' had learned that the secret of making a man wait also continues in the real world. In truth, I think the pursuit had been the best part. The Catch simply wasn't my type.

– 10 –
Location, Location, Location

Where to meet your date?

Where you arrange to meet your date can tell you a lot about how the date is set up to go. Setting can dictate the tempo and mood of a date. Choosing where to meet is important. Choosing what to do to arouse the passion and set the mood also needs to be considered in advance.

The meal out at a restaurant or drinks at a bar are the most obvious and popular ways to share a first date. For many, the drinking/eating scenario is a great way to satisfy your pleasure centres while hopefully leaving a little space for 'dessert'. The downsides to such dates are that experienced daters can consider them a little predictable and unimaginative. Such dates can also be expensive and, for many Complete Bastards who will date many women – some of which will have very expensive tastes – it is financially a strain.

Going against the norm and looking for ways to really impress your date can work well. There are plenty of distractions in every city from going to see a movie, the theatre, live comedy shows, book/poetry readings through to music gigs and festivals. There is something for every taste – even a Complete Bastard's!

Maybe it's also time to consider more active ways to dazzle your date? From taking her shopping, through going to visit an exhibition at an art gallery, to both of you taking part in a shared hobby or sport. Active dates can be a great way to gel and enjoy each other as opposed to the usual 'chat and chomp' of a meal-for-two.

Finally, why not set yourself the challenge of **really** stretching your scope for a location to have your date? Try somewhere exotic, extraordinary, or just downright unusual. Suggestions that fit these categories will definitely intrigue your date and make you stand head and shoulders above the other men who suggested a BYOB restaurant and a slushy romantic movie before the last bus home.

When it comes to dating, one essential tool for the Complete Bastard is a copy of the current 'What's On' or 'City Guide' type publication for his city, whether it's in printed or Web format. Depending on the size of your city, there should be plenty of interesting events or activities listed there that can provide a good venue for a date. By keeping abreast of what's happening in your city, you will also come over as something of a clued-in socialite – the composite man-about-town – rather than someone who spends most evenings simply mooching around his apartment in front of his television.

Let's now look at some actual places where you could take your date. Some of them are popular choices, while the rest show you how a little imagination can really impress.

Coffee shops

A humble coffee house in the high street is hardly an illustrious backdrop for a Complete Bastard – a character dedicated to wringing every luxury out of life. But coffee houses still rank as one of the best and most popular places to date.

The rationale behind going to a coffee house is that they are relaxed, everyday spaces. Women feel safe and comfortable there. They are convenient, public, and highly social places set up to give people privacy and comfort to meet and talk. Also, there is usually minimal background noise, they're well lit and no alcohol tends to be served. So coffee shops act as a sober environment (on all levels), conducive to a one-on-one, distraction-free date.

Coffee shops also offer an inexpensive alternative to fine dining or getting drunk with your date in a bar. For only a handful of pocket change for a couple of coffees, you can both while away an hour or two. Perfect for the Budget Bastard.

Another advantage of arranging to meet for a coffee is that there is not the expectation on either side that a date is going to last all evening. This makes them a very flexible date location choice. If the date is heading towards disaster, you can drain your latte in a matter of minutes and then tell her that you only had time for coffee before another engagement. If things are going well, then you can always move on to another venue together afterwards. For this reason, have a few ideas in your pocket for what to do afterwards to make a whole evening of it. There are only so many cups of coffee you can drink in one session.

Best suited to: Dates that follow a hangover; nice girls that you don't mind chatting with sober for hours; when you are out of cash; dates with girls you are unsure of and might need a quick exit strategy to get away from.

Bars

Bars serve alcohol. Alcohol makes people relax and talk more. Relaxed talk leads to flirtation. And flirtation can lead to great sex.

The bar is a 'must-do' venue for the Complete Bastard. It is here he should be in

120

his element – showing his generosity by buying rounds of drink, getting free drinks bought for him, and ogling other girls while enjoying the company of his date. This is a great 'playground' for fun and frolics.

Bars are not 100% perfect, however. Firstly, bars have other people in them and annoyingly, many if not most of them will be men. Men, as you know, go to bars to hit on girls and this means that, if you are with a hot girl, she could get hit on by other men. This can be both a distraction and a danger to your success while on a date.

If your date is hot, you may need to consider somewhere more conducive to privacy and away from the leers and chat of other men. See: 'Coffee shops', 'Arty dates', 'Restaurants', or 'Somewhere extraordinary'.

The word 'bar' covers an extraordinary wide variety of venues – anything from grungy biker fleapits up to exclusive champagne salons. This means that choosing the right bar becomes critical.

Bars can be mellow or noisy, filled with middle aged folk or young students. Bars can have DJs, karaoke or live bands. They can be hang-outs for the rich, the poor or just places where old men go to forget their day. Selecting the right bar for your date is something worth spending some time thinking about and probably worth scouting out in advance so you know exactly what to expect.

The best advice is to try to find an upmarket yet not too pretentious bar or two where much, if not most, of the clientele is female. This will put both you and your date at ease that you are not in some testosterone-fuelled hole where a brawl could break out at any moment. You will also be in a much less male-predatory environment, so your date can focus on you and not spend the evening fending off the advances of other males. (And it doesn't hurt you if there is plenty of eye-candy on display as well!)

A good bar is also one where you can have the privacy to chat one-on-one if you need it and to join the fun with others if that's what you need also. There is nothing wrong with meeting other folk and chatting while on a date. As long as you don't try and seduce another girl in front of your date (or at least don't get caught!), then you will be viewed by her as sociable, likeable by others and a lot of fun.

Best suited to: Evening dates; dates with Thrill Seekers or party girls; dates where there's a good choice of heading back to her place for 'coffee' afterwards.

Night Clubs

Night Clubs are basically bars on steroids. All of the disadvantages of bars are apparent in night clubs, magnified many times.

Night clubs are also glorified pick up joints. Maybe you have read some books written by members of the 'pick up community'. This is their hunting ground – not the

Complete Bastard's. The Complete Bastard's method works on his talents for quick thinking and quick talking. It's not about how he looks or how many 'party tricks' he has learned to woo women. These Bastardly skills are next to useless when the music is so loud that you have to bellow in her ear just to get yourself heard.

The chances of a first date ending in disaster can be high if it takes place in a night club. Pop out to the men's room and, if you entered with a hot chick, you could find her with some pea-brained muscleman by the time you get back. And if you just happen to be both a muscleman and a Complete Bastard, you could well find yourself with company of your own when she returns from the rest room. That isn't going to go down to well with your date.

Night clubs also tend to be expensive places to entertain a girl as well – no good for the Budget Bastard with shallow pockets.

In general then, night clubs are not the best venue for a first date. They can make it easy to undo all of the good work that you've done during the online dating experience. If you have the desire and the ability to pick up women at clubs, go there alone or with a male friend or two (Wing Men – see chapter fourteen) and you could go home lucky. But if you're that much of a stud, chances are that you wouldn't be reading this book anyway.

Night clubs do have a few advantages though, the main one being that they stay open late, which means that the obvious next stop afterwards is either her place or yours. Night clubs are also renowned as 'places to pull' as well, which can make for an inevitable dash to the bedroom together when the night ends.

Best suited to: Late night dates; dates for guys that are used to the night club scene and are good dancers and or in good physical shape; dates with girls you're confident of taking to bed within a couple of hours of meeting.

Movies, shows and gigs

This covers a multitude of entertainment options, most of them having disadvantages that outweigh the advantages.

I've never understood why taking a girl to a movie is often considered to be a good idea for a first date. What sort of a great first impression can you make if you just sit side-by-side in silence, gawping at a screen together for ninety minutes? The 'movie first date' is one best left to amateurs who have nothing of interest to say to their dates, hoping that the stars of the silver screen can provide some entertainment for the evening because they are incapable of doing it for themselves. It's not place for the Complete Bastard to charm his girl with his natural wit and personality.

Same goes for the theatre, ballet, opera, musicals, concerts, and so on. Try to avoid such locations. Not only is taking your dates to such high-calibre events going to make a serious dent in your wallet, but they also give you very little time to talk and flirt with her.

Comedy clubs are a cheaper alternative and have the advantage that you should get your date laughing and 'warmed up' – potentially useful if you think that she might not be relaxed. The potential downside to this type of a date though is that, if much of your date consists of spending time being entertained by professional comedians, your attempts at humouring her during the rest of it could end up looking a little lame in comparison. So take care – unless you genuinely are a very funny guy.

So far, so bad. Do these types of events have any place in a Complete Bastard's dating arsenal at all? Perhaps.

If you are a Rich Bastard, for whom the kind of money you're looking at laying out for a night like this is of little consequence, trips to shows can be useful date locations. If the girl of your dreams is a bit of a gold digger, the offer of a ticket to a special event might just be the key to getting her interested in meeting you. The same goes for a girl who is still unsure as to whether she wants to meet with you or not – such as one of the dating site's most popular 'princesses', who finds ten offers of a free gourmet dinner waiting for her whenever she checks her inbox. If you have learned her likes and dislikes during your correspondence, the offer of a chance to see her favourite band when they come to your city on tour, or a rare showing of a French art house movie at the local arts centre might be just the ticket (literally) to incentivise her to meet with you.

If this method works, you should try and 'top and tail' the event with opportunities for the pair of you to be able to have a proper conversation – perhaps having an early dinner before the event, and late drinks afterwards. Conversation should be easier as you have 'the event' to chat about.

Best suited to: Dates with gold diggers; dates with 'hard to get' girls who are hard to impress with standard date venues; culture lovers.

Restaurants

Similar to bars but far more restrained, restaurants are places where the relaxed environment and access to food and alcohol allows easy conversation and the chance to really get to know one another. This probably explains why the restaurant date is the most popular first date venues for most people around the world.

If the restaurant is your preferred option, then – like bars – it is important to select one that is conducive to the mood and ambience you seek. Also make sure it serves food that you both like and can eat, and at a price that is within your budget.

Once again, your local 'City Guide' website or 'What's On' magazine should be good reference material to assist you in choosing the right restaurant. Try to check out the venue beforehand. If the restaurant is a popular one, make reservations in advance (you might even want to specify a particular table to make a really special impression – one that will give you privacy or one with a great view). Having to apologise to your date for the fact that your plans to go to a restaurant are cancelled because it is full is going to make you look sloppy. Also, long debates as to an alternative eatery are not going to get your date off to an impressive start. She'll just find you indecisive. So, even if your favourite place is booked out, Man Up, be decisive and tell her about 'another great little place' you know nearby.

The point I made regarding budget raises a big date conundrum: while on a date, who should pay? There is the traditional argument that it is the gentleman who should always pay. However, in today's world, women earn as much, if not more, than many men. They can easily afford to pay half or share the cost of a meal out. Many women are only too willing to do so.

On a first date, I usually haggle to go half on the bill. This is not because I am mean at heart, but it is because it gives a woman the opportunity to buy her way out of feeling indebted to me. She owes me nothing in return if she splits the bill. Trust me, if a woman doesn't want to see you again, she'll happily foot the whole bill if only to escape you.

The best time to broach the subject of dealing with the bill is actually not on your first date, but during online flirting (chapter eight) or moving towards a date (chapter nine). A great line that will save you 'forking out' cash needlessly over and over again goes along the lines of: 'I've been stung by many women just using me for my money. So I now have a rule: first dates pay their own way and we go halves on everything.' On hearing that little invented sob story, what woman would want to be labelled as a potential gold digger?

Hopefully things will work out well and your date will want to see you again. A pleasant dinner-date is one where both parties contribute to the final bill without any friction and without either party feeling bad about the other.

I have actually heard of situations where the man has paid the bill, gone to steal a kiss, been knocked back, and then asked her to refund him half of the bill outside the restaurant. He is someone far lower than a Complete Bastard will ever be. Avoid this type of weak behaviour at all costs.

One final point: if she is a true babe and you don't want to risk making a negative impression, then gladly pay the bill in full. This will always show you in a generous light, no matter what anyone says to the contrary. You can't lose.

Best suited to: Just about any type of woman.

Shopping dates

These are dates for romantic consumers. You both meet with a shared purpose in mind that forms a precursor to your meeting. For instance, you've been chatting to a hot chick online and you tell her that you need to buy a new jacket but you're not the best at choosing stylish clothes. If there's one thing that most women love, it's shopping and so you might find it surprisingly easy to get her to agree to this one.

It's a neat idea. If she isn't for you, well at least you've got her services as a personal shopper for the day. Whereas, if she's as hot as her pictures online show her to be, then you and her can enjoy a great day in the high street or at the mall. You can also impress her with your love of high-end gadgets and designer home furnishings. She'll also like the fact you don't mind coming with her shoe shopping (even if she hasn't realised it is only so you can check out other hot chicks while she tries on shoes!)

Best suited to: Daytime dates; dates that need a distraction; gold diggers

Arty places

Why not receive an honorary Bastard of Arts and take your date on a trip to a local museum or art exhibition.

It's perhaps not the Complete Bastard's idea of the most thrilling of dates, strolling around some stuffy cultural centre gawping at relics of the Chinese pre-Ming Dynasty in locked glass cases. However, spare a thought for your date who is a culture vulture.

Many women have a strong interest in the arts and culture. A suggested meet at a museum, gallery or art exhibition does make an impressive statement about what sort of an intelligent and urbane fellow you are. Also, it gives her the chance to show that she's just as up for being seen as high brow and debonair as you are.

One word of warning – if you do suggest an arty date, then make sure you have some knowledge and interest about where you are going. There is nothing more obvious than a man who is kicking his heels from boredom and who doesn't know his Monet from his Matisse.

Bullshitting that you are an 'art expert' can also be a fruitless yarn. This is especially true if the girl has a strong interest in and knowledge of an artist or the place that you're planning on visiting.

The best strategy is to come clean about your lack of knowledge, but pretend that you would love to learn. Chances are that her ego will be massaged by your perceiving her as an expert in the field and she will be delighted to teach you lots of interesting facts.

Another useful point of going on an arty date is that many museums and art venues are free or very cheap to get into. This presents an ideal opportunity to save cash while still appearing highly civilized. Now that's real Complete Bastard culture at work!

To put aside any final fears you may have about the arty date, after ten minutes around such cultural hogwash, she'll be just as bored as you are, hopefully. Early evening drinks at a nearby bar will go down a treat. This is a good thing as it's going to be a hard transition to go straight from the museum to the bedroom.

Best suited to: Culture lovers; Slow-Burners.

Action dates

An activity date is where you and your date agree to spend your time together doing something. This can range from a sporting activity, such as a game of golf, to something more daring, like a hot-air balloon ride.

These are great ways to enjoy a shared interest or introduce her to one of yours. They also get the adrenaline flowing and this heightened arousal state can transfer into passion for another 'shared interest' after the activity. Clearly, the more active the activity, the more this phenomenon works. Going to a pottery class together will have less of an effect than speedboat racing, for example.

There are a couple of rules for the action date. Obviously, make sure the desire for the activity is shared. Convincing her to parachute from 10,000 feet out of a plane may show you as a daredevil but, if she's afraid of heights and breaks both her ankles on landing, it's going to be memorable for all the wrong reasons.

Action dates also give you both less time to talk and bond – although this is not always so. Lack of conversational opportunity isn't necessarily a problem as you are both enjoying time together on some level. It's also great with foreign chicks whose English is not perfect. It removes some of the strain of the intense conversation that dating usually demands. Actions, in this case, really do speak louder than words.

Just remember though that you are there to date and eventually Dupe her. You don't want to have to re-arrange another date and do it all again because you had no time on your activity date to tell her that you liked her!

Best suited to: Daytime dates; dates that need a distraction; foreign chicks; jaded women who are bored with the usual dating clichés.

Extraordinary dates

This section may come across as unfeasible or unheard of by many men, but this is the type of date that you should ideally be aiming for. Why? Because it will position you in the tiny percentage of men who have the pluck and the imagination to really know how to Woo women.

When accepting a date, a woman is preparing herself to be swept off her feet (or at least hoping). Most women settle for the bottle of wine and steak dinner, yet there's a whole world of better experiences that you can use to entice and enthral your dates by giving them an experience that they are going to remember for the rest of their lives.

First, there's the exotic. Why not arrange to meet for your date in a new city or foreign place? For many men and women this is a step too far in terms of cost and perceived safety for a first date. But I've done it before on several occasions – and all thanks to some of the incredible deals that you can get on the budget airlines these days.

What woman could fail to be swooned if she received an email saying, 'Meet me at the airport at nine o'clock in the morning this Saturday. Bring your passport.' She will be sure to think you a dashing international man of mystery, even if a couple of budget airline tickets cost you less than a meal for two at an upmarket restaurant.

Then there is the erotic. For many, dating is about the pleasure of getting sex. For some, sex **is** dating. Such people do not want a relationship or emotional ties. During the stage of online dating, it's possible to get a surprisingly high amount of women into such a state of sexual desire that there is no need for a traditional 'first date' at all. Often there is scope to arrange dates that are purely meetings to explore mutual sexual fantasies. Over the years I've met such dates at sex clubs, hotel rooms, and even graveyards (read the Dating Diary of a Complete Bastard at the end of this chapter for more on the latter!)

Finally, one highly amusing way to 'impress' your date with your uniqueness and sense of humour is to suggest a meeting somewhere completely ridiculous. This could be somewhere odd and bizarre. I once met a girl at a taxidermist as she had a fear of stuffed animals and I thought I could cure her. I couldn't – but she let me 'stuff her' that night in thanks for my efforts anyway!

Or what about somewhere that you both detest (a karaoke bar; a working man's club; or going to see a band whose music you really hate)? The bonding that you will both attain from back-biting your way through the horrid event can be better than sitting all jacketed and sophisticate at the opera, politely applauding or remarking 'How wonderful this venison is, darling!' while eating in the most exclusive restaurant in town.

Other dates I fondly recall were ones where we accidentally ended up in situations or places that we had no liking for at all. This may be a bar that was filled with dirty old men or a restaurant where the service was awful. There is no need to seek out such places but, if you do end up in one, revel in and make light of the moment rather than worry that it's a date gone wrong – just think of it as a shared experience and milk the comedy value out of the situation for all it's worth.

Best suited to: Dates with Thrill Seekers; veteran daters that have done all of the usual dating venues; girls looking for casual sex.

Final words

In summary, the Complete Bastard has the imagination and creativity to consider **anywhere** as a potential date location. From the obvious choices, like coffee shops and restaurants, to hang-gliding for two naked.

You have seen that where you go to date can really alter the mood and tempo of a date and also how certain locations are better for certain date types.

The Complete Bastard needs to also remember that where he takes a woman is a further representation of his levels of style, taste and an insight into his status. For example, if you always take girls to your favourite greasy spoon café, then don't be surprised if you don't date many aristocratic daughters of Earls (unless you are deliberately trying to be ironic in the process). Later in this book, when you go on to learn the art of Duping, you'll see how raising your social status – knowing great locations to seduce women – can swing you the most unbelievable perks.

Let your imagination go wild and your date will follow.

Slurping Milkshakes with Porno Baby & Other Tales
The Complete Bastard shows that getting the date location right can make or break a date.

The question as to where to take your date is a common mind-screw for men. Should you go all out and book a helicopter ride over the French Riviera or keep it low-key and relaxed at your favourite bar? The Complete Bastard knows that picking the place is a prime consideration of dating.

Papa Bastard – the Master of Manipulation – has this to say: 'Don't be a half-assed half-wit. Dating, especially on a first meet, is an easy kill to dazzle and delight with a truly memorable location.'

'Memorable' locations can mean big bucks. But, as my next selection of stories will show, variety really is the spice of life and I didn't have to spend a fortune in the process.

Slurping Milkshake with Porno-Baby

Eva was 23-years old, Icelandic and, from her online dating profile pictures, an absolute babe. Just about every Icelandic chick is hot stuff. There must be something in the air there and Eva, with her full lips, soft skin, high cheekbones and big, blue eyes was no exception.

She was a lot younger than me and had a bunch of interests I knew nothing about, so I was struggling to conjure up an interesting place where we could meet for our first date. It was actually Eva who solved the problem.

'The Diner' was a milkshake bar in one of the city's coolest districts - somewhere neutral where we could chill and drink milkshakes. It was a quirky step away from the humdrum circuit of chic bars and plush restaurants that I was used to.

We met outside the bar in the early evening. Eva was certainly a fox in the flesh, though I couldn't help being amused that she had a face like an adult baby. It was cute, though kind of funny too. In tribute, I nicknamed her, 'Porno-Baby'. Luckily, for this Complete Bastard, Scandinavians have an open mind and a spot-on sense of mischief. She liked it.

Eva was great to chat with and so we instantly hit it off, covering all manner of topics as we slurped on our milkshakes through straws. In time, it was Eva who brought the conversation around to sex and so started a rather steamy chat that began to get both of us frothier than our 'shakes. This chick was clearly in the mood for something more than just flavoured milk.

'Want to try my 'shake?' Eva asked innocently.

'Sure. I like to taste everything in life at least once,' I replied with a wink.

With that, she took a huge fistful from her drink and slipped a couple of milkshakey covered fingers inside my mouth. I could hardly speak for the mouthful of banana-and-peanut-butter-milk-goo that was now running out my mouth and down my chin. In quick retort, I grabbed my own fistful of 'shake and did the same back to her.

We were sat in a secluded corner of the diner. This was just as well, as the young nymph proceeded to then chuck the remaining contents of her 'shake over my face and neck. This was swiftly followed by her grabbing me and kissing me with the passionate frenzy of an exploding geyser. So, I sat there being smooched, covered in milkshake and the voracious affections of Porno-Baby.

All this, from a tame milkshake diner date at tea-time.

Putting off the Ritz

As I became better at selecting women of a certain lifestyle through dating sites, I began to require an increasingly higher class of place to entertain them. One of London's most famous and revered haunts is 'The Ritz', one of the city's most ultra-posh and expensive hotels.

I'd arranged to meet 'Wilma_72' in the hotel's restaurant. Another online dating fanatic, 'Wilma_72' had been using dating sites for years and was looking for, in her own words, 'that Special One'.

She clearly hadn't figured that she'd be dating the ultimate Sneaky One, but then that's all part of the 'risky business' that is online dating.

I turned up looking justly dapper and befitting my lavish surroundings. I was early and so quickly unfolded a broadsheet newspaper and turned to the Business section. No one around me in the restaurant would suspect that this struggling, broke writer wasn't some 'city slicker' with his fingers on the money-making 'pulse'. First impressions, as you are rapidly learning, can be deceiving.

'Wilma_72' arrived late and in a fluster. She worked as a nurse and had been held up at the hospital and then in traffic.

'Oh, I'm so sorry,' she whispered, glancing around in awe at where she now found herself.

Poor girl. She could barely make eye contact with me. She seemed nervous. It was up to me to put her at ease.

'Don't worry about a small thing like good manners and punctuality,' I teased. 'Sit down and relax. I'm glad you're here now.'

Poor 'Wilma_72' – she completely missed my good-intentioned joke and blushed crimson in shame.

The waiter came with menus. 'Wilma_72' was now struggling to make conversation and spent a good few minutes hiding behind her menu.

'Oh my Lord, would you look at these prices!' she gasped. 'I'll have to work overtime just to afford an appetizer!'

This girl was clearly out of her depth. Everything, including me, was intimidating her. In the elegant splendour of her surroundings, around the formally dressed business people and hotel guests, 'Wilma_72', who dressed drably and was far plainer than her flattering profile pictures, was like a trembling dormouse.

Clearly, this was a case where a grand location was badly suited to such an ordinary girl. We made a hasty exit from 'The Ritz' and went to grab some coffees at a little café nearby.

The date was now feeling strained and uncomfortable for both of us and we parted company early in the evening.

Many months later I got an email from 'Wilma_72'. It said that she leaving the site as she'd found herself a husband – some doctor at work. Within three months, he'd proposed and they were quickly married soon after.

Wonder if they honeymooned at The Ritz?

Salsa with the Latino chick

Patzi was a Brazilian beauty who had been working in the city as some hot-shot lawyer's secretary for the past two years. I'd met her online and we quickly progressed from messaging to arranging a date.

I asked Patzi to choose where and what we should do on our first meet. It's a simple technique I use that shows just how interesting/creative/romantic a woman is at conjuring up a date; it gives them a sense that I'm not the 'controlling male' type, and, most Bastardly of all, it saves me the hassle.

The technique had backfired though. I now found myself standing outside a dancing school in the north of the city, waiting for my date to join me and take me on a cheek-to-cheek salsa dance. The bad news for her and me was that I hated dancing, possessed the proverbial 'two left feet', and thought salsa was something you put on tacos.

For many men, a nightmare scenario might be brewing. Not so for a Complete Bastard though.

Over the years, I have learned that the worst date scenarios can often work out in your favour. In a few hours' time, I'd be stepping on toes, flapping my arms all about me, and clumsily banging my forehead against hers. In terms of that all important date ice-breaker, this slapstick 'comedy routine' would go down a treat. Trust me - if there's one thing I've learned that helps your confidence on a date, it's not taking yourself too seriously.

Patzi arrived, finally – an 'exotic' twenty-five minutes late, mumbling in broken English about a delayed train. She looked more elegant and made-up than in her pictures, though still carried a panther-like athleticism. Her dark hazel eyes merged with their pupils, making her eyes seem almost like hypnotic black holes. Her full lips parted to reveal a dazzling set of white teeth. I then began to panic – Patzi towered a good three inches above me in her heels. And she looked so damn bronzed and healthy.

Patzi grabbed my hand and with a playful laugh dragged me through the doors of the club and into the salsa room. This Latino babe had instantly started a Rumba beat-a-beating in my heart.

In the class, I could see the wide-eyed stares of the people around me: a) staring at the Brazilian's beauty in wonderment, and; b) quizzically wondering why Patzi had picked a putz like me to hang out with.

The music began to play. Patzi seized me and held me tightly to her body. She flashed another huge, gorgeous smile and the beat began to quicken. We began to swirl and move to the salsa beat.

Predictably, I was an absolute oaf on the dance floor but I laughed it all off. I even had a few other girls giggling at my antics and asking to dance with me. What girl in her right mind would dance with the class's Worst Dancer? The sort of girl who much prefers a guy who is confident in his failures, than insecure in his strengths.

The salsa class was the perfect way to get my date with Patzi really moving. As locations go, an action date – such as salsa dancing – is a great way to get to know your date in a relaxed and fun manner.

And how did things with Patzi go after the dance class? Well, we had a few weeks of passion and, although things were to fade romantically over the following few months, we kept in touch, still remain friends, and I've even enjoyed a trip to Brazil to visit her family and friends. Not bad work for a man with 'two left feet'. Cha, cha, cha!

Date with the Devil

'Angel_of_Darkness' met me dressed all in black (including satin corset), wearing a gloomy expression, and towering above me like the Grim Reaper in heels. This seemed apt as we were in a graveyard on a bitingly cold and foggy autumn night.

'Angel_of_Darkness' (as if the name wasn't a giveaway!) was a fetishist who I'd met on one of the more adult dating sites a few years back. Her 'thing' was dishonouring the dead by screwing men in graveyards, probably for some horrendous pact she'd made with Satan. He was no doubt pimping her out to spread Damnation among the souls of 'good' men like I.

Unfortunately for Hell's 'Bad Boy', I wasn't a good man. And I was only too happy to embrace the Dark Side for a night if it meant getting my fill with this curiously sexy lady.

A graveyard was certainly one of the weirdest places I've ever met for a date, but there was something highly arousing about the macabre backdrop and my date, with her Dominatrix-cum-devil-worshipping ways.

Before I had time to scream a redemptive 'Hail Mary', she'd pinned me down on a tombstone and started having her wicked way with me. This was one bonkers chick. As she howled under the full moon in demonic pleasure, I began to see that there's something to be said for the date that contains a little devilish danger.

Date Her, Dupe Her, Dump Her

– 11 –
The First Date

Regaining your manhood

During my dating experiences offline, I was surprised when I began to learn as much about other men as I did about myself or the many women I met.

I love the thrill of the dating experience; the conversation with like-minded company; the crackle of sexual tension building throughout the evening; the possibility that you have met that 'Special One' (or 'Two' or 'Three'...). It was in this relaxed company of women that I was to learn the full horrors of what they had endured in the company of other men.

I heard story after story about how men sat in front of their dates trembling with nerves; how poor social skills let many guys down; how weak conversation bored and ruined many girls' chances of having fun on their dates; and how some men were even breaking down in tear-drenched angst as they related past relationship woes to the one person who least wanted to hear such drivel.

Hearing these tales of men and their disastrous attempts at dating, I realised that this placed me, a date lover, in a very enviable and authoritative position. The consistent theme of this book is how so many men today are suffering from some sort of confidence and identity crisis with women. They have lost their poise, their masculinity, their natural wit and their charm.

This chapter will show you how to get your confidence on a high for dating, how best to play a date, and how to regain your poise.

Understanding dating

If you think too much about what dating actually is and what it involves, you could easily turn your brain to a quivering jelly. You've met a girl online, you like her, or at least you think you do. She could potentially like you back, but she has given you all the signs that she suspects that you are some sweaty-palmed pervert who she wouldn't trust to water her pot plant for a day, never mind involving you together with her in the art of making babies. With more tension between the pair of you than penalty shootout time at the World Cup final, you guys chose not to meet in the safety of a nuclear bunker, but instead opted for a high class and very public restaurant where some of the city's leading doyens will gawp in horror as your spaghetti is tipped over your head if you say the wrong thing.

Dating, in the above context, is a horror show – fraught with dangers at every step.

So why do we date? Humans (and Complete Bastards in particular) are always looking for an easy path and dating isn't it. Dating is an adrenaline-pumping, heart-pounding, dry-throated rollercoaster ride, prone to derailment at any second. But it is the only option unless you want to spend the rest of your life single. Sure, this book has shown you an insight into a Bastard New World of online dating, but real world dating is where you take your first step back into cold reality, by hanging up your cyber persona and embracing the real you and her.

The move from cyber to real world can be a huge step. There is a lot to prepare for yourself and prepare yourself for. These are two very different things.

Preparing for your first date

'Preparing yourself' means to best present yourself so that you are what your potential partner is expecting or wants. 'Preparing yourself for' means to get yourself ready for some shocks and surprises that an offline meeting could bring. This chapter will show you how to deal with both and it looks at five ways to make sure that you are ready to romance:

Refresh your memory

She's the girl of your dreams, you think about her every minute of the day. She replied to your well-crafted first message and now you are totally smitten by her. How could you possibly forget the date of her birthday or her favourite author or the fact she loves French food or even her name?!

The reason that you could forget any of her minor details is that you are on the Path to Bastardom and she is but one of many women you are currently Juggling.

I've done it. I've sat right in front of girls on a date and clean forgotten their names. Beyond that, there are heaps of information she'll have dropped into messages and conversations with you. Your remembering the details is her test to see how much you care.

Rest assured, it's useful to take a little time before the date to read over old messages and brush up on all of her minor details. It will stand you in good stead. More importantly, the Complete Bastard is a notorious exaggerator of truth and that boast about you 'loving dogs because you are a vet' may trip you up if you can't even remember saying it in the first place or don't have plenty more related lies to back the tall tale up with.

Dress to impress

There are hundreds of self-help books out there telling guys how to dress. If you are serious about dating the Complete Bastard way, then looking the part is crucial. I discussed this back in chapter four, telling you that you should have started to take care of your image as soon as you began your first forays into the world of online dating. If you took my advice, by now you should be looking sufficiently stylish, have masked any obvious physical inadequacies you may have had, and may also have dropped a few pounds as well if you needed to. If you didn't, then it's time to plan a quick shopping trip now to get yourself suitably suited before the big day arrives.

There are some dating books that advise guys to dress to stand out – 'peacocking' as some 'gurus' call it. This is an outlandish technique where men who haven't had much luck dating in the past, find themselves strutting into bars wearing cowboy hats, nose piercings, and/or fluorescent pants.

This is 'geek chic' at its worst. You're supposedly draped in a 'conversation piece', but this technique hits cringe factor 10 with me. The point of dating is to keep attention on you. This means variables like your clothing should not stand out above you.

In any case, 'peacocking' is designed only to start a conversation with a girl you've never met before. You've already been speaking with the girl online for a while now and so you don't need such props to grab her attention. You've already got it.

So, in terms of clothing, smart-casual is usually the best bet here (although there are exceptions to the rule if the girl you're meeting is of a particular type (rock chick, hippy, biker babe), or the location of your date comes with a certain dress code (i.e. the opera or a very fancy restaurant). But usually, the more expensive, the better – but understated as a rule. A good quality pair of shoes and a decent cologne are especially recommended. Women note such minutiae.

Your aim is to get her thinking that, if she invited you to her boss's drinks party at his mansion next week, then you wouldn't be dressed like a clown, but rather a normal human being.

Too much male preening can also come across as a negative. Facial furniture (goatees, styled sideburns, elaborate moustaches, etc.), body jewellery and that 'too perfectly' groomed hair style all smacks of a 'metrosexual' who spends more time licking his own reflection in the bathroom mirror than going out playing sports, drinking with his workmates or just enjoying life in a traditionally masculine fashion.

No need for tricks

There's been a glut of dating advice books by 'gurus' which tell men how to bedazzle women with all sorts of attention-grabbing hocus-pocus. This has taken the form of anything from using magic tricks to rehearsed chat-up lines. It's all aimed at getting the girl's attention and winning her over.

The problem here is that many of these 'gurus' are former geeks who claim they have found the 'Elixir of Life' or the 'Da Vinci Code' for getting into a woman's heart and pants by turning up at a club with a pack of playing cards, some pre-programmed pick-up lines, and a crash course in hypnotism.

Use any of these manipulative techniques and you'll come across as nothing more than a nerd trying to punch outside his weight using some of the most crazy pick-up tricks imaginable. Sure, girls might genuinely like your effort at seducing them. They may even find you fun and interesting and, dare I say it, intriguing. But will they settle down and seriously introduce some overgrown Harry Potter into their life? Unlikely.

If you're reading any of these nonsense books, ditch them now. They are deeply odd, limited in getting beyond a 'quick smooch' with a girl in a bar, and not what Complete Bastards are striving to attain at all. Complete Bastards crave and can have so much more than this.

Bury your demons

Every guy has a sob story or an ex-girlfriend who messed with his head. Such negative experiences are just a part of growing up and Manning Up. Many women I have spoken with, have talked of men they dated who 'dumped' on them. Not 'Dumping' as in getting rid of them – but 'dumping' as in off-loading their worldly troubles onto a girl over a candlelit dinner or a drink in a bar.

Why bring this emotional 'debris' to a date? Even worse, why sit there sobbing like a lost school boy with a crush on his teacher that will never be requited? And, worst of all, why tell your **date** all this?!

Gloomy conversations are best left at home alone or, if you need to burden someone with them, then unload them onto a male friend over a beer or two. But keep them far, far away from your first date experience. They lower the mood, lower your manliness, and lower her eyeballs towards her gin and tonic. She'll quickly wish she was one thousand miles away and on a date with anyone else apart from you. Instead, you want to focus on bringing a little colour into the room...

Pump up your personality

Getting into the right frame of mind for a date is crucial. You want to come across as interesting, charming, and amusing. You want to avoid appearing arrogant, smug and crass.

No one ever gets the balance perfect. You'll always say a sentence that you wished you'd kept inside your head, perhaps something clumsy or stupid. Don't fret – a few misplaced statements are part and parcel of first date nerves. Dates are simply about trying to make sure your good moments outweigh the bad ones. Unless you say something really offensive or hurtful, nine times out of ten, you'll be forgiven and the conversation will carry on regardless.

One of the problems most people take with them when dating is the idea that they must go out of their way to amaze and appear 'perfect' on a date. Seeking to amaze your date is a brave and valiant goal but, unfortunately, most of us are not that fascinating in real life or that in control of our poise.

Another problem is that men seek to convince women that they are nice guys really. Behind that Neanderthal façade is a big softie who loves the poems of Byron and romantic nights curled up in front of the television set watching movies.

This is perhaps one of the hardest facets of personality that the Complete Bastard needs to master and adopt. For a ruthless, reckless character such as he, 'niceness' doesn't come easy. Yet to be liked by his date, the Complete Bastards must learn the art of gaining trust and liking.

During your first date just remember that Rome wasn't built in a day – women tend to be more cautious when it comes to relationships than men. Although you might have decided before you've finished your appetizer that she truly is the woman of your dreams and the future mother of your children, chances are that she will need a fair bit more convincing that this is the role that she was put on Earth to fulfil. Sure, you might get lucky and see from the wistful look in her eye that she can't wait for the meal to be over so that you can whisk her away to your apartment or hers to consummate your new relationship. But just treat this as an added bonus – your primary goal from a first date is just to make sure that she wants to go out on a second.

Bring your cyber persona to life

So you're now at the moment of truth. You're at the start of your first date with one of the women that you've selected from the many, many possibilities that were available to you when you joined that dating site. You're well on the path towards achieving your goals now, but all of the hard work that you have put in so far is for nothing if you blow it over the next hour or so.

So, how do you make sure that you don't mess it up?

Generally speaking, the answer is simple – you just need to continue to be the same person that you were while you were Wooing her online – namely confident, witty, direct, and entertaining.

You should already have your cyber persona worked out by now from all of the emails and maybe IMs that you've sent her (and probably a dozen other girls) before you got to this first date. Now your virtual personality needs to become flesh and blood.

If most of the elements of being a Complete Bastard come naturally to you, this will probably not be so difficult. If, however, you have been 'faking it' online and have embellished many of the details of your life and personality (or told a pack of complete lies) you will have more of a challenge ahead of you.

To do so, you need to continue with your online strategy – you need to hide the elements of your personality that are less than desirable and pretend to be that 'perfect partner'.

You've probably heard about 'method acting', the style of acting employed by such greats as Marlon Brando and Robert De Niro. It's where they try to actually 'become' their characters. This is also a good method for you to employ during dating as well. Forget about your own flawed personality – you need to act as if you really **are** the person that she expects you to be – the Complete Bastard inside you should take over during the date to such an extent that you don't have to be constantly thinking, 'What would a Complete Bastard be saying now?'. If you are sufficiently into your role, your Bastardly personality will be running the show to such an extent that, once the date is over and you are running it back in your head afterwards, you can scarcely believe that it was actually **you** saying all those witty, confident statements.

Conversational strategies

Chances are that the girl in front of you is as nervous as you are – maybe more so. People show their nervousness in different ways and conversation is the one place that confidence and nerves battle for the floor. Some just babble on and on whereas others freeze up and find themselves incapable of thinking of a single thing to say. Let's look at these two very different date-types, the Babbler and the Freezer, and look at how best to deal with them during conversation on a date.

The Babbler

If you find yourself in front of a Babbler, conversation will be a lot easier (although can also often be frustrating or a little dull for you if she's yakking on about nothing at all). Let her talk as much as she wants. One advantage of this is that it gives you plenty of time to think of how to contribute to the conversation when she finally takes a breath of air or has to shut up in order to take a mouthful of her dinner at least. You should be thinking of some witty and amusing anecdotes to drop into the conversation, stories along the lines of, 'Oh, that reminds me of when...'

If your anecdotes are witty, amusing and show yourself in a good light and just happen to be true as well, that makes things very easy. If you don't have anything that's completely relevant, then by all means embellish and exaggerate what you have. It's a lot easier to take a grain of truth and grow it into a fascinating tale than it is to come up with a complete work of fiction (although, as your Bastard skills become sharper and sharper, you'll find it easier and easier to do this).

Another great advantage of dropping anecdotes into the conversation is that it helps you to **empathise** with her. Empathy is a very important part of the dating process. In general, people tend to get on better with people who have similar views, interests and pasts to themselves, so the more you can demonstrate that you have a lot in common with her, the better your chances will be.

Anecdotes achieve this result a lot better than coming out with simple statements, like, 'So you like dogs? That's cool. So do I.' Instead, come out with an anecdote about the funniest or most embarrassing thing your dog or your parents' dog did and you're well on your way to making a deep connection with her.

The Freezer

Much harder to work with than a Babbler is a Freezer. This is a girl who just sits there in front of you with a frozen grin (or worse, frown), expecting you to do all of the talking and to keep the conversation flowing.

Unfortunately there is no way of knowing in advance if you're going to end up facing a Freezer on your first date. Just because she was the type who chatted away merrily online doesn't mean she is going to do the same on the first date, so the secret is to be prepared in advance for such an eventuality.

As I explained earlier in this chapter, you should always read through your previous email and IM correspondence with a girl before setting out on a date. Another advantage of doing so – in addition to the primary one of not forgetting what lies you've told her – is to think of a number of questions to ask her during the date. It will also remind you of what questions you've asked her before but have forgotten all about since then (which is very easy to do when you've been chatting with a dozen different women simultaneously). You will definitely lose points if you go over old ground with her.

If there's still not a lot of material to chat about based on filling in gaps from your online conversations, try and question her about some generic subjects in order to try and get the ball rolling. Some safe areas are:

1. Careers
2. Travel/Holidays
3. School/College days
4. Family
5. Pets
6. Music

7. Movies
8. TV (but avoid coming over as a couch potato)
9. Sports (participation sports rather than those you watch on TV)
10. Current events (but avoid religion, politics or anything controversial)

Pursue your questioning in a light and conversational manner – you don't want to come over like you're interrogating a terrorist at Guantanamo Bay. Ask open-ended questions that can't be answered with a simple yes/no answer to get her talking a bit, (i.e. 'What did you like best about Mexico?' rather than, 'Did you like it in Mexico?').

If she has any social skills at all, she will at least finish answering each question with a, 'How about you?' If even this is beyond her conversational abilities, feel free to answer the question for her. Some people define a 'bore' as someone who continually talks about himself or herself when you just want to talk about yourself, but if you've given her ample opportunity to talk and she refuses to take it, then you can hardly be accused of being egocentric if you're the one who ends up doing the majority of the talking.

If you don't have a lot of experience of dating, you might find your conversations suffering from a few awkward silences in the early stages. But it's like everything else in life – practice makes perfect. After you have a few dates under your belt, you should have a good repertoire of questions to use, plus a large number of proven anecdotes to entertain her with.

Being a good conversationalist is very similar to being a good DJ. Whereas he has a box of CDs or vinyl at his disposal, so you have a wide assortment of questions and anecdotes to provide the ultimate conversational mix for the encounter. You won't use them all in every date, and you won't always use them in the same order. Be responsive to the feedback you're getting from your audience and keep amending your 'set' in response. Monitor the response you get to your 'material'. Scrap those elements that don't get the desired response; reuse regularly those that go down favourably with the other person.

Occasionally, however, you can sometimes be on top form with a set of witty and charming banter that would get you your own late-night TV chat show – yet she still is not responding. In this case, it's not you, it's her. It happens. And when it does, the only thing to do is to quickly come up with a Bastardly excuse as to why you need to cut the meeting short and just put it down to experience.

More often though, if you've put all of the advice that I've given here into effect, she should soon be practically wetting herself with laughter at your outrageous adventures, hanging on your every word as she falls deeper and deeper for your charms, and giving off little signals such as toying with her hair. All signs that she is inviting you to take things to the next level and towards making a move.

....

DATING DIARY OF A COMPLETE BASTARD

....

Russian Maria

A first date with an exotic dancer turns as frosty as a Siberian winter. Can the Complete Bastard warm the moment?

I encountered 'Russian Maria' by chance. It was on a stag night with some male friends where, after some drinks around town, we ended the night in some glitzy pole-dancing club south of the city.

We all sat in schoolboy-glee as the long limbs and muscular arms of the dancer bent and contorted up and around the pole as Madonna's 'Like A Virgin' played out and the swirl of dry ice filled the stage.

This was my first sight of Maria – a 21-year old 'exotic dancer' from Moscow who'd toured the world's club circuits, plying her acrobatic skills.

After her dance, she came over to our table and joined us for a drink. I admired the way she coolly played each and every one of the guys for drinks. I could learn something from this girl.

Luckily I met Maria at the pinnacle of my success with women. I quickly dodged her drink request and instead succeeded in persuading her to meet me later that week for a date. She agreed.

***

'Russian Maria' sat before me sipping a cocktail in the trendy 'Essensual' bar in Soho. She was dressed in a gold, figure-hugging top, black leggings and ankle-boots. She looked ball-breakingly hot.

Her English was not bad, but everything she said was uttered in a slow, husky, Moskovian drawl. It sent shivers down my spine as we talked.

For our first date, however, things were not going well. Everything I said seemed to agitate her and send waves of sneers and scowls across her face.

'Breeteeesh men bores me,' she said at one point. 'Like cheeeldren. So frightened. So verrry, verrrry nerrrvoos.'

Was it any wonder men melted around her? Even at her young age, she had an air of mature sexual authority. I was struggling to keep my voice from quivering with excitement.

I answered her: 'I see myself as someone more... international. Like James Bond.'

On all dates, you will usually utter at least one complete dickhead line and that was mine. Here I was sitting there trying to convince a girl who could have her pick of just about any man in a bar or club that I was James Bond. I braced myself for her reaction.

'Hahahahahahahahahahahaha!'

Her mocking laughter was like a volley of AK-47 fire to my ear drums. I was dying here. It was time to reach deep into the Complete Bastard Box of First Date Tricks.

Maria was a Freezer – and her icy expression needed thawing. I also had the added problem that her English was not good. So I began to tell her some funny anecdotes, but added to this a lot of comic gestures. This began to work nicely. It helped her understand me better and made her relax and smile more. Suddenly, it was her and not me who was averting eye contact and blushing as my tales worked their magic.

She began to really open up to me. I had achieved a critical breakthrough and gained both her trust and her liking of me. Soon the Freezer became a Babbler, as she told me outrageous story after story about her work life, her views on men, and even that she was conceived during a 'verrry, verry, verry angreee' electrical storm in Moscow one night. This storm, she fervently believed, was what made her so feisty and capricious when she was born.

I began to like 'Russian Maria' and I thought she'd taken a shine to me. It just goes to show that even the most difficult date can be won around with some deft Bastardly masterstrokes. The bar we were in was now calling last orders, so it was time to now ask if I could see her again.

So I did – bluntly, confidently and ready for rejection in a worst case scenario.

She looked at me sternly.

'Perrrhaps. I will theeenk about thisss. But one theeeng you must understand is thisss...'

From here she took one of her long, sharp, manicured fingernails and pressed it hard to my windpipe:

'Eeef I everrr catch you weeeth anotherrr girrrl – I will keeeeeel you!'

I began to shuffle nervously in my Bastard shoes as an imagined scenario flashed into my head. It was of me running around my apartment, dodging flying crockery and saucepans as Maria furiously cursed and screamed at me in a patois of broken English and Russian. Then she had me, my face being squeezed tight between her powerful inner thighs as I gasped for air and begged for mercy. But Maria knew no mercy. She'd uncovered my deceitful ways and found out about my other lovers and now she was going to 'keeeeeeeeel' me.

I snapped back to the reality of the date. This girl was no bauble to be toyed with.

Days later, I sought advice from Papa Bastard about Maria. Should I risk everything to pursue this intoxicating creature? His advice was simple: 'Play with this firebrand, Son, and you'll bring the whole fucking house down.'

Papa Bastard was right. There are some first dates that you just know should be left not to go any further. Maria was one such date.

So sadly, I never did see that pole dancer born in a storm again.

Date Her, Dupe Her, Dump Her

– 12 –
Making Your Move

The next step

This chapter will show you how to end your first date on a high and move it towards the next stage – getting your date to fall head over heels in love with you.

On all first dates, there's a fine line between success and failure. The Complete Bastard tends not to fail through his know-how of seducing women. Hopefully you've been picking up all his cunning techniques so far in this book.

It's now time to look at the stage where a lot of men are unsure about how best to play the situation. When and how to make 'the move'. This is simply figuring out if she likes you or not and knowing where to go from there.

With the woman safely on your side and raring to date you more, you can begin the real Complete Bastard tactic of getting her infatuated with you (next chapter) before starting to Dupe her (chapters fourteen and fifteen). It is the emotional state of infatuation that will make her easily susceptible when you start taking her for everything you can get your devious little claws into.

But let us begin this chapter as the first date draws to a close. You think it went rather well, but you're still on the Path to Bastardom and unsure. Read the next few sections and it will all become a whole lot clearer.

Ending the first date

It's a first date. An hour or two has passed since you first met and now it's getting late. The waiter has cleared away your finished plates and both your wine glasses are empty. What happens next?

So far the Complete Bastard's dating process has been fairly linear as you have been the one calling all the shots. But what happens from now on and in what order depends very much on how successful you have been in following the process and also the personality of the women you are pursuing.

At the end of a first date, you are in one of three scenarios:

Date Disaster: The worst case scenario is that the date was a washout and both of you know it. You're beckoning madly for the waiter's attention so that you can pay your bill (or your half of it) and put this hideous event out of its misery, pronto.

Just accept it. It happens from time to time. The best remedy is to learn from the experience and see if you can pinpoint anything you could have done to have changed the result. Then log straight back on to your dating site of choice where there are hopefully many other equally, if not more, interesting women with whom you can start all over again.

Date Dynamite: At the opposite end of the scale, perhaps you've made such a great impression on your date that you can tell by the look on her face and the feel of her hand squeezing your knee beneath the tablecloth that the only decision you need to make now is to whether to head straight back to her place or yours.

Date Disorder: More often than not though, the situation you will find yourself in is usually somewhere between the two above extremes: that uncomfortable 'no man's land' where you're wondering just how interested she is in you and how far you're able to push it without undoing all your good work so far. You like her, but a fear of rejection begins to creep into your head. What's a Complete Bastard to do?

Understand her body language

One definite way to judge how she feels towards you is by reading her body language. This is the visual cues that she gives off that portray accurate signals as to whether she wants to be with you, or without you. With 55% of a person's total communication is given by facial and body cues, that means there's a lot to look out for.

Interpreting body language is a very sophisticated social science when done professionally, but for you and your portable Complete Bastard toolkit, here are some handy hints that you can use to tell on the spot whether she is interested in you or not.

9 signs she likes you
Preening: She plays play with her hair, swirls it around her finger, or tosses it over her shoulder. She's flirting with you and wants your attention.

Mimicking: When you're talking to a girl, if she copies your body position and actions, it means that she is comfortable around you and is most likely interested in you and what you are saying. This is mimicking.

Eye contact: Prolonged direct eye contact means she likes and trusts you and is herself honest with what she is saying. Either that or you have something stuck to your face.

Dilating pupils: The eyes offer big clues. If her pupils are dilated, this can indicate that she is interested in what you are saying. Unless she's off her head on narcotics!

Open hands: Look out for open palms. This means that the girl is relaxed and comfortable. Also, rubbing her hands together is a sign of expectancy. Look out for that as the first kiss moment nears.

Touch: The more you see her touching her body, the more she wants to draw your attention to her. Also, she may touch you briefly in a safe area, such as your back or your arm. This will usually be quick and innocent, but conveys a sense that she wants to touch you more.

Smile: A smiling girl is a genuinely happy and relaxed date, enjoying you and your company. A false smile moves only the lips and mouth; a genuine smile involves the eyes too.

Proximity: The closer she gets to you, the more she likes you. Leaning means liking. Look out for her shoulders pointing towards you.

Stroking chin: This is a sign of evaluation and is a neutral signal. It probably means she's still weighing you up in her mind.

6 signs she doesn't like you

No eye contact: A lack of direct eye contact could mean she is losing her attention with you or feels uncomfortable. Catch her looking around you and you'll need to win back her interest.

Crossed arms: Arms crossed over her chest can be a sign that she is closed off and doesn't feel at ease opening up to your attention. This can be a tricky sign though, because it can also be a sign that she is slightly uncomfortable with herself, not a signal for you to back off.

Leaning back: If she is sat upright, leaning back, and looking as if she is not focused on you, chances are that you're right. Her body language says she wants to be somewhere else.

Neck touching: This is a sign that she feels threatened or uncomfortable. She may play with a necklace or rub her neck indicating anxiety.

Kicking foot: A jiggling or kicking foot when she is seated can indicate that she is nervous and the repetitive motion is a sign that she is trying to calm herself down.

Fidgeting: Foot and/or finger tapping usually indicates stress, impatience or boredom.

Reading her body language on a first or subsequent date will give you a useful gauge as to how things are going. Begin to learn how your words and actions affect how relaxed she feels and how much she likes you.

Dealing with mixed signals

So now you know how she is feeling by her body language, you can more confidently move in for that first kiss or, if things don't look good, reach for your wallet, pay the bill and order a lone taxi ride back to your bachelor pad.

First dates are rarely that black or white though – even to an expert in the art of understanding body language. Often people give off mixed signals. It's not something they do intentionally or even consciously, it's just that during a stressful event like a date, you can expect conflicting signals. This is because you and your date have probably passed through a variety of emotional states from nervousness, through possible confusion while evaluating the other person, to perhaps feeling highly relaxed.

If your attempts to read her body language have come to nothing and she has not let out any verbal clues as to how interested she might be by the time the bill arrives at the table or the movie credits roll at the cinema, then you need to either try and positively draw the date to a close and suggest a next date (see 'Last Words' section below) or just move in for the kiss.

In for the kiss

It's the traditional 'seal of approval' on a date: the moment where two people collide in a passionately-charged moment and their worlds merge as one. The kiss is that unspoken gesture that ends a perfect date and can often be the beginning of a naughty night ahead.

The kiss – that simple gesture where you pucker your lips and smack them on top of your date's – is one of the biggest stumbling blocks during the dating process. It is the poor seducer who never knows when is the right moment to make his move.

The reasons for all this confusion are multiple and include:

Fear of rejection

You should by now be bolder and braver as a dater than you've ever been. Your online flirting has become more direct and devilish, you can carry yourself through a first date with gusto, and now it's time to convince you that you deserve your first reward on the Path to Bastardom: a kiss.

Again there is no other advice to give here other than this difficult moment must be handled with courage. If the signs are there, just go forward and kiss her. You are the pursuer after all.

And don't utter the immortal passion killing line: 'Do you mind if I kiss you?' It's a proper romance ruiner and crushes the atmosphere of sexual tension. Instead seize the moment, seize her, and let your manly urges burst through. (Note: we are talking about only a kiss here and not full-blown intercourse on the restaurant table!)

She doesn't like me

Maybe you were an anti-climax on the date and the guy she met online just didn't match up to the shadow of a man shuffling nervously before her now. The plus side of online dating is that, before you both met, you should have established a rapport and a good sense of what you both knew you were getting as date partners.

If you are convinced that she just doesn't like you upon meeting you in the flesh, first take a step back. Ask yourself what signs (or lack of them) she has given you for you to come to that conclusion? Sure, maybe her body language is negative. But then there is the phenomenon of mixed signalling and you could have misread some of her cues.

The conversation may have been awkward too. Again, all conversations suffer from the curse of the Awkward Silence or pedestrian moments when you are both making small talk for small talk's sake. This is the mundane aspect of getting to know someone.

Then again maybe you've not given yourself nearly enough credit for that witty anecdote that made her laugh or never saw her impressed expression when you ordered the most expensive bottle from the wine menu.

Maybe she did look you up and down when you first met and then stared at your double chin or bald head which made you squirm. But you noticed too that she was a little heavier than her profile pictures and that she was a little over-zealous on the make-up. Everyone scrutinises their partner on a date and checking you out, warts and all, is part of that process. It certainly doesn't mean 'game over'.

The only way you will ever put your racing mind to rest is to make the move and kiss her. Which leads on to the next worry: how?

How should I kiss her

The simple answer to this is: kiss her how you feel you would like to kiss her. You are, after all, training to be a master seducer of women and a dating maverick with more than one woman on the go. Everyone has their own style of kissing and preferences as to how they like to be kissed. There is no 'best way' of kissing. People will tell you otherwise, but what they really mean is that they used to be kissed one way that they remember and have liked ever since. That way has now become their blueprint for a 'great kiss'. Unfortunately for you, they don't have a section where they explain the details of their 'perfect kiss' on their dating profile.

There are a few kiss credentials you should perhaps heed before you go rushing in there like Casanova on heat though. The first is that some men have a nasty habit of going in with a tongue like a lance. Imagine you're the gentler sex and you've been lip-glossing all night and chewing gum to keep your breath clean and some guy, after four beers and a cigarette, comes lunging towards your mouth, tongue a-waggling. It feels like you're going for her tonsils and not her heart. She's repulsed.

On that subject (and as chapter four went into in more detail), a clean, sweet-smelling mouth for you is paramount. You don't want your first kiss to be remembered every time she goes to slice an onion for weeks after. Take care of your mouth during your date and avoid 'Dater's Death by Breath'.

Too drunk to kiss

Booze can be a godsend for many dates. It helps relax you both and gives the night a sense of adventure and mischief. Often two people on a date – usually due to nerves and not to seem dull – drink far too much.

A drunken smooch while feeling like you're going to vomit is never on a par with a kiss when you feel fully in control and sober. Sometimes though the drunken kiss is the easiest way to break the ice and it can really make the uncomfortable move to a first kiss much, much easier.

Another problem with the drunken kiss is that it can often lead to renewed doubts and fears once you've sobered up. Insecurities creep in, such as: 'Because we were both drunk, was that kiss meaningless?' Both sexes can often regret things they did when drunk – it's part of the fun of drinking after all. A drunken kiss, therefore, may need to be followed up with some statement of clarity afterwards. Perhaps an email is best here: something along the lines of:

> 'Last night was great and you looked stunning! I seem to remember a kiss at the taxi stand... or was I just dreaming?'

Or, if you're feeling a bit more mischievous, maybe this:

> 'Wow, we sure were drunk last night! All I remember is waking up this morning with lipstick all over me. What did you do to me?!'

Shouldn't she be kissing me?

There is no reason why in this day and age women shouldn't seize the initiative – especially as most men are now so poor at it.

If she does – great! You've certainly found yourself the strong, confident type. But don't wait until she makes the first move. As has already been stated: men are the pursuers in the game of seduction and so they should be the ones making the first move to kiss.

Women tend to make the first move for two reasons: (a) she knows the guy likes her but he is shy, or; (b) she can see that this date is going nowhere in her future, but she likes him enough to take him to bed.

Both of these reasons are in direct conflict with the motives of a Complete Bastard. He should be viewed as forward and highly confident in his behaviour, plus he doesn't waste time on simple displays of public affection if there is no future in it. He is the consummate dater, duper and dumper after all.

Asking for a second date

If you don't get the kiss at the end of the date it doesn't mean that your date was a failure. Sometimes not getting that kiss keeps the romance and the anticipation much more alive for future dates. There is also the fact that some women just don't believe in kissing on a first date and want to continue getting to know you at a slower pace than you might. More likely still if you held your first date in a public place such as an upmarket restaurant or at the movies, is that she thought that smooching just wasn't very dignified.

What you need to do then is move towards getting some clarity that you are both mutually agreed that you want to meet again and keep in touch. Again this means taking the initiative.

The more vaguely you present your own desires, the coyer she will be in return. No one wants to beg for a second date, but at the same time women do like to be asked. So tell her:

'I'd really like to see you again. When are you next free to meet?'

'My boss gave me tickets for a rock concert. You interested in coming along?'

'This date went well in my opinion and we seem a good match. You agree?'

In all of the above, you need to assert a positive and then qualify it with a fresh opportunity for the next meeting.

There is the possibility that your date may agree to a second meeting but backs out when it comes to agreeing to a specific time and place. There's little you can do about this. Most people, when offered an invite to their face, rarely turn it down. Manners tend to overrides malice.

Following up

One of most asked questions on dating forums is: 'How long should I wait after a first date before contacting her again?'

Some dating 'gurus' believe that contacting a girl too quickly after a first date smacks of desperation and makes the woman think that she has 'got you' already. They advise

153

to leave it several days before following up with a phone call, email or text message.

Date Delaying should be avoided though as it is contrary to the next strand of the Complete Bastard's strategy: 'Making her infatuated with you' (see chapter thirteen). Infatuation focuses on your trying to build fast rapport and that means keeping in touch and quickly becoming an integral part of her life.

Setting up a next date as soon as possible after the first does not weaken your control on the situation or expose you as over-keen. Moreover, building 'buffer zones' between dates increases the fear that she is not that keen and not interested in seeing you again. It takes away the momentum from the first date and means that you almost need to go back to square one again for the next meet.

You also need to sustain the freshness of where you date (see chapter ten) and how you date. Dressing to impress (chapter four) and keeping your confidence high (chapter three) are again vital. The next two or three dates are still pitted with danger and she could go off you if you don't put in just as much planning and pay just as much attention to her as you did on the first date. You've come this far. Why blow it now?

Build a fast
Rapport *

DATING DIARY OF A COMPLETE BASTARD

The Language of Loathe
What happens if that first date is a disaster? The Complete Bastard shows you how best to get rid of unwanted amorous attentions.

Online dating sites give you access to a huge variety of girls, but until you actually meet them in the real world, you take your chances with every single one of them.

'Nu_Romancer' was no exception to this rule. Pretty in her pictures and with a profile that said 'Seeking my partner in crime', she certainly seemed a promising date. She also held down a well-paid job as a doctor. Maybe she would be the one to cure my Bastardly propensity for shagging and Duping everything that moves.

Anyway, cut to 'Joe's', an awful greasy-spoon café, east of the City. 'Nu_Romancer' had wanted to meet me here. 'It's so charming and bohemian,' she'd written.

I was just lighting up my umpteenth cigarette of the day to take away the taste of the dishwater coffee I'd been served, when in she walked. I stood up to greet her, as my eyes met with one of the dowdiest girls I'd ever laid my Bastard gaze upon.

'Nu_Romancer' was not only plainer than plain – she was positively grotesque. A shapeless, pasty-skinned frump, she had one googly eye that rolled around its socket like a stray pinball. Worst of all was her vile, brown, protruding teeth that smiled back at me like a busted rib cage.

Within seconds, a Bastard rage had engulfed my usually placid state. Here I was, stuck with the 'Date from Hell'. There was but one option: 'Nu_Romancer' must face the Instant Dump – a process of Dumping whereby I plant enough bile about me into her that she has no other reaction than to wish me dead.

I sat in stony silence and continued to drag on my cigarette. I was hoping that date killer, the Awkward Silence, would swallow her whole.

I glanced up to see her shifting uncomfortably in her chair. She flashed me a pandering smile with those god-awful gnashers. I almost puked.

'Oh, tsk, tsk. You never quite stated on your profile you were a naughty smoker, now did you?'

'100-a-day. And I love every deep, tar-filled lung-bash of it!'

Silence descended once again.

'So tell me' she went on. 'How did a guy like you end up single? You seem so nice. So what brought you to the zany world of online dating?'

Nice? **Nice!?** Was this chick born in the sun? I was a Complete Bastard! My blood coursed black; my heart pumped to the tune of the Funeral March; and if she was Father Christmas, I was the Bastard Child of the Grinch and Ebenezer Scrooge.

'Well, after I was caught hanging around fairgrounds with a pocketful of lollipops, it was only a matter of time before a life behind bars awaited me. My parole officer thought online dating would be a great way for me to meet people and integrate myself back into society.'

'Nu_Romancer' ran her fingers through her lank, mousey-brown hair and let out a high-pitched shrieking giggle.

'Oh, you are a card!' she squealed between guffaws.

And on it went. Barb after barb I threw at her. I recoiled in horror as she sat there, her one good eye dilating with infatuated lust; hunched, little shoulders leaning towards me in rapt attention; smiling flirtatiously as she stroked her lack of chin. And as she talked – dull story after dull story – her gnarled, little hands wildly gesticulated with excitement. The horrible reality of the situation hit me full on as I realized that all the signs were there: this chick adored me.

An hour passed and, no matter what indifference I threw her way, she just painted it girlie pink and seemed to like me all the more. There was nothing to be done – this girl was like a cockroach in a nuclear aftermath. She could tolerate anything. This was just going to have to be a good old-fashioned dump. I lit another cigarette, looked up at the clock on the wall, and smiled the falsest of smiles at 'Nu_Romancer'. She was getting her date's-worth, I'll give her that.

This was a dictum I was once told by Papa Bastard: 'There was once a man who swallowed a toad every morning. His reason was that the rest of the day could only get better from there.'

How the Old Man would have chuckled now if he could have seen me now, sitting with my own veritable amphibian. I had no intention of swallowing her though, although it was patently obvious that she would love the chance of swallowing me.

Finally, I managed to call time on the date. I went to bid 'Nu_Romancer' a permanent farewell. The audacious hag leaned in, opened her revolting gob to receive me, eyes squeezed tightly shut.

I seized her hand and give it a firm business-like handshake.

'It's been... interesting,' I said turning and hurrying out of the café.

The date had been a disaster.

For the next month, 'Nu_Romancer' bombarded me with emails and text messages declaring her yearning for me. I ignored every single one of them, befuddled as to how this girl could have not gotten the fact that I wasn't in the slightest bit interested in her. Sometimes online dating can lead to the strangest of mismatches. Some people don't even see the signs.

– 13 –
Getting Her Infatuated

Making her fall for you

In this chapter, we assume that either the first meeting with your online conquest has been Date Dynamite in the real world, or else you've managed to finally win her around on the second, third, fourth or subsequent dates. The next step is to now keep her attentions firmly focused on delivering every one of your Complete Bastard needs. This means getting her to fall for you.

Getting women infatuated with you is not as hard as it appears, especially if this has been something that you have not been good at in the past. The theory in this chapter is an extension of what you learned in chapter three about forging your Inner Bastard and being confident with women.

I'm now going to show you an utterly Bastardly way for doing just that, by getting her infatuated through Flooding and then keeping her in that state with the Magic-Mud technique:

Flooding

This is an effective means to starting to get a girl infatuated with you. Flooding is where, after a successful first or couple of dates, you accelerate the odds of a girl falling for you completely. It basically involves your bombarding the new object of your affections with Communication Overload and Proximity Overload.

Communication Overload

This is the strategic effort to open up as many 'communication channels' as you can to your new date and overload her with daily contact. The frequency of contact depends very much on her receptivity and the amount of effort you are willing to expend.

There are a number of mini-strategies to Communication Overload that depend on which stage you are at with the woman you are attempting to seduce.

For example, say you and her are still back at the online flirting stage. You have started communicating by email as is the norm. You now want to increase the regularity of your emails so that her everyday existence starts to become entwined with yours.

That will mean a change in the content and frequency of your emails.

When online daters first engage, their messages tend to be general: 'So, what brings you to online dating?'; 'How long have you used this site?'; 'Any interesting stories from your past dates?'; 'Are you looking for a fling or marriage?' and so on. As you begin to communicate more regularly, you want to give more of yourself away and involve yourself in her everyday life.

Good examples of that process in action include:

> 'How was your day at work? You told me you had a really horrible boss – is he still giving you stress?'

> 'What are you up to this evening? Another gig or a meal out with a friend? Where do you find the energy!?'

It's all an intoxicating mix of deeper interest, more attention to detail and lots and lots more questions than was the case with your initial emails. You put the focus on her and she tells you everything about her and her life. Soon you are like her inner voice and new best friend, easing her worries and spurring her through her daily challenges.

But why stop at emailing? You want to, as quickly as she will allow, open up faster and more personal modes of communication. Things such as: 'Hey, this emailing is sure a slow way to chat – do you use Instant Messaging?' or, 'Is it too early to swap telephone numbers? I would feel easier talking with you about this stuff if I could hear your voice.'

Beyond online communication, maybe the pair of you have already met in the real world, or are moving towards that first date but haven't actually met yet. The same advice as before applies: you want to engage with her more by using as many channels of communication as she is comfortable with.

By the time the two of you have got your first date out of the way and you are aiming to infatuate, you both should have opened up all possible communication channels (online, telephone, face to face meeting). You now have access to her from all directions and pure Communication Overload is now within your grasp.

You have to be careful though. Most people love to chat and be distracted, even at work. But if you start annoying them when they are busy or stressed, the tactic can backfire on you. Try to avoid Communication Overload at such times as:

- When she has just arrived at work, or has just returned home. She will be tired and more resistant to being interrupted.

- Anti-social times (i.e. when she is asleep)

- When she is at formal or private events (i.e. funerals, family gatherings, business meetings).

- If she is studying and you know she's in class.

- If her responses are unusually terse, it's a sign that you're probably over-contacting her.

Proximity Overload

So you've overloaded her mind and thoughts with your barrage of regular contact and she's now thinking about you every day. You also need to add to this good work by maintaining a strong physical presence around her.

As with Communication Overload, Proximity Overload is a highly successful tactic because it trains her to quickly accept your constant physical presence around her as normal. Instead of the typical cautious approach of getting to know someone, you're accelerating the time it takes for you both to become comfortable in each other's presence. By increasing the amount of physical/sexual time you spend together, as well as making her form a strong attachment to you, this will serve you well as you can quickly start to move on to the Duping process that will be dealt with later in this book.

Why Flooding works

The method of Flooding runs totally contrary to most dating advice you will find in other seduction books or websites. They tend to suggest that relationships should be slow to begin and taken at a mature, steady pace.

However, after winning her over with your confident personality and well-dressed image, the woman will be so dizzied with excitement and the thrill of a new relationship adventure stretching before her, that she will be highly susceptible to Flooding.

Flooding shows her that you care about her. Your level of attention – even if it seems perhaps a little over-zealous – is actually what she's always wanted from a lover. That is someone who is always there for her, willing to talk to her about her day and to listen to her problems.

Also, the fact that you mix in an overload of communication with being there (Proximity), shows her that the two of you are fast gaining a natural emotional and physical connection. This will increase her trust and liking of you no end.

Flooding also means that she has little or no time for other men in her life. This is particularly of importance when she has been online dating and may have stockpiled quite a few interested men (see Jugglers in chapter eight). Suddenly she has no need or desire to go online to flirt and collect other men's telephone numbers. How could she anyway when she's way too busy messaging, IMing and talking on the phone to you all day at work, or before you're both socialising together again in the evening?

Finally, through constantly either being around her, or in her mind because of Flooding her, you will have become the most important element of her life. You leave her no say in the matter of whether you are going to become her new boyfriend or not because, before she asks herself the question, she'll realize that you're her boyfriend already.

The results of Flooding can be remarkable to people who have always taken the cautious approach to dating. On many occasions in the past, I have gone from first date to actually moving in with a girl in under two weeks.

Another advantage of Flooding is that the relationship moves forwards at a lightning pace. What's the point in spending six months with a girl, seeing her just once a week or so and then finding out that she's of no use to you? Better to make the discovery after just a few weeks of being in constant close contact with her so that, if you realize that the relationship is not going the way you want it to go, you can quickly Dump her (see chapter sixteen) and move on to the next one.

The Magic-Mud technique

While Flooding is a very effective and powerful tactic for quickly becoming one of the most important elements in a woman's life, it's not enough by itself to get her truly and totally infatuated. To achieve this, you will need to back up your Flooding strategy with the Magic-Mud technique.

The Complete Bastard knows the secret to keeping a woman's attention on him: make her **your** centre of attention. Any woman of merit will seek this focus upon her. She wants to feel that she's been Wooed (amused, entertained, seduced, and more) because she's desired for more than **just** sex. As a Complete Bastard, that suits your agenda perfectly – as you also are looking for far more than sex from her.

Women are slightly more complex creatures than simply being 'egos with breasts' who crave a spotlight shone upon them. Women have raw needs that must be fulfilled too. The requirements that they seek from men include: loyalty, trust, emotional connection, friendship, intimacy and love. A woman ultimately needs to feel comfortable and earthed in her relationship before she will fall deeply in love with you.

So here we have a dichotomy. As a Complete Bastard you have to be two people: the entertainer and the earthy. Or, as it's called in this chapter: Magic and Mud.

The Magic-Mud technique is a great way to create intrigue with your date. Most women have heard it all before: the sleazy come-ons; the pandering half-man attempts at romance; the promises that are always broken; and so on.

No man is perfect, especially not you – a Complete Bastard in the making. Give a woman even the faintest glimmer of doubt that you are a rogue and, especially in the early stages of dating, she'll blow you out faster than a candle in a hurricane.

The secret to not exposing your Complete Bastard tendencies is to hover between two extremes. On the one hand, you are the swaggering, ultra-confident, intelligent cad. You're bold, you're brash and you'll play upon her emotions like a concert pianist on a Steinway. (Strangely, she'll like that because suddenly she finds herself, against her better judgement, compelled to be the 'chaser' and not the 'chased').

Then, just when she thinks you're borderline sociopathic, arrogant and no future father for her kids, you swing like Tarzan on his vine. Suddenly you're philosophical, open, serious-minded, and maybe even a touch melancholic. You have your flaws and crises, and here you are wearing them on your sleeve. We've all got our insecurities and here's you sharing them out like candy.

It's knowing **when** to play these subtle extremes that is key. You can't simply sway from swagger to whimsy in one conversational sentence. That **would** be sociopathic. Instead be subtle. As one side of your personality begins to dominate, be aware that, if you give her too much of one extreme she'll get bored, she'll get scared and, at worst, she'll get lost. To keep her stimulated and constantly compelled, swing your personality like a pendulum.

You've probably seen many times before on police shows how they use a 'good cop/bad cop' routine in order to get suspects to break down and confess. The 'bad cop' is screaming and shouting at the suspect, throwing chairs around and telling the suspect that he's going to end up getting gang-raped in jail if he doesn't spill the beans. Then he leaves the room and the 'good cop' takes over, offering the suspect a nice refreshing cup of tea and telling him that everything is going to be fine as long as he just signs a confession.

The Magic-Mud technique uses the completely opposite technique to the Good Cop/ Bad Cop routine. It doesn't focus on a push-pull method but a pull-pull approach. That is to say that though you undulate from two very different personalities, both types attract her and don't confuse her. This is a far more powerful technique than most other dating advice books offer.

Now you need to find out how to make Magic and Mud:

Making Magic

This section will give you a few tips as to how you can create an aura of Magic about yourself. Complete Bastards effortlessly create momentum and excitement within the build up to a date and the actual date itself. With some practice, you'll be casting your own 'spells' over women in no time.

Sweet indulgence

If there is one sure-fire way to impress a date, it is to show your extravagant side. A few gestures of excess go a long way to creating a buzz of excitement in the early stages of your relationship. Picking up a big tab at the restaurant or lavishing a gift or two may seem wasteful, but the girl will be both confused at your reckless spending and flattered that you've chosen her over everyone else to shower with your generosity.

Sure this will hit your credit card or bank balance hard. Either you've got some money spare or you'll be working overtime next month. But see this as a worthwhile investment. The sooner you ensnare her in your web of deceit, the quicker you can get your grubby paws on all the perks she has to offer you. Indulge her now and you'll encourage her to indulge you later.

Power of pomp

Create some spectacle and she will be mesmerised. Seeming larger than life in her eyes is a swift means to getting her audience. There is a multitude of ways to do this.

How you behave around others is something she will be keen to see. Once again, confidence here is all. On dates, it is often considered by many dating 'gurus' as taboo to talk to other people and take the focus away from your one-on-one romantic encounter. However, unless you are hanging on each other's every word in deep, meaningful chat, then there is nothing wrong with talking to other people and even flirting (though never too full on) with other girls around you.

Best practice here is to get chatting with a mixed group of male and females. For a time you focus on the group, then pull back and whisper some remarks in your date's ear – just so she knows that she's still your main confidante, e.g.: 'Jeez, that guy sure has dull chat, I wish I'd never spoken to these bunch of dead-heads now.'

This tactic is called 'Growing the Experience' and it shows how you can have a private date but can also use the chance meeting with others to heighten the experience. It also displays the fact that you are more confident than most guys and easy, likeable company around others. This behaviour works best in highly social places such as, bars, clubs or on action dates. In more intimate places (movies, restaurant), this tactic can be rather hit or miss.

Sex sells

The first few days and weeks of an intimate and passionate sexual encounter can really get a girl smitten. Providing she feels at ease with you and there is a physical attraction, she will happily succumb to your advances. This is the biggest factor in making both a physical and emotional bond with someone.

For the Complete Bastard, moving from bonding to bonking should be an effortless transition. With the confidence to talk, touch and tantalise her at dating level, moving to the bedroom is the next easy step. It feels natural because you have won her trust and liking and she feels happy to go along with you and be seduced.

For you on your Path to Bastardom, perhaps this is an area in which you still feel uncomfortable. After all, sex is one of the key perks of the Complete Bastard's Dupe. You're keen to have some too – preferably as quickly as possible.

Prowess and confidence in the bedroom is a sure way to infatuate her and give you seemingly supernatural qualities. This book will give you no help as to what to do during the actual act (there are more than enough books on that subject already), but it does advise you to adopt the same confidence and initiative when it comes to seducing her as you saw in the section of chapter twelve entitled, 'In for the Kiss'.

There is, however, a need to point out that moving to sex has far deeper consequences than the first kiss. Her being comfortable enough to have sex with you means that she feels so comfortable with you that, apart from offering you her most intimate self, she will feel at ease being alone with you at her apartment or even a hotel room. She may even come to your apartment, so make sure it's tidy and shows no signs of a lonely slob whose main pastime is surfing the porn channels on his television. Pay particular attention to your bed. Make sure that there are clean sheets on it, especially if you were romping with a different girl in there the previous night. Never forget that many women have a sense of smell that would put a Bloodhound to shame.

The Complete Bastard now finds himself in the position where his everyday life is under scrutiny. You need to look at every aspect of yourself that casts an impression upon her and ensure that all of these represent you in the best and most attractive light. Key areas to think about that will make more Magic are:

Conversation: As she spends more time around you, you have to talk a lot more and keep entertaining and stimulating her. As she is now feeling relaxed around you, she will begin to really open up. Listening to her becomes one way to shift attention away from your constantly having to Woo her as the focus now will be upon having to keep her.

Affection: With more time alone in her company, you are now being given the green light to show your affectionate side. Increase your proximity to her, move closer to her more often, and touch her more. Not sexually, but in her 'safe zones' (upper arms, shoulders, hand holding). You will both kiss more too. The kiss now has shifted in its intensity from being that first nervous, passionate seal of approval to affirmation that you both like each other and desire increased intimacy.

Impression: How you dress and present yourself are still highly critical parts of this ongoing seduction. From your first date, a significant drop in your attention to your clothing, hygiene, and general appearance will create disappointment and maybe even rejection from her. She will continue to look good for you and you must do the same. Now, as things get more intimate, everything from your toe nails to your body hair will be on show. Attention to detail here is paramount.

Seduction: Perhaps things are now so intensely passionate that ripping each others' clothes off is little more than a formality. For most guys, things don't move so fast. Women are way more cautious than us. They are big emotional bonders during and after sex. Plus, there is also the added threat for them of falling pregnant. So you play it cool. You use Magic to seduce and Mud (see next section) to generate her trust and assurance in you. Restrain from unleashing your Dirty Bastard on her at this early stage. It will smack of desperation and look like there is only one thing on your filthy mind.

Lure of travel

Another means of Magic is to try to build rapport over the possibilities for travel together as a couple. This means finding a favourite destination that you both would love to visit. Perhaps the mercurial delights of a long weekend in Venice or a spontaneous shopping trip to New York appeal to you both? You then plant a seed in your online or offline conversations that this fantasy is a definite reality for the future. Set the trip somewhere in the imagined future and let it become a central theme in your conversations. This 'travel teaser' does a number of things:

Firstly, it paints you as wild, extravagant and flamboyant of character – somebody who is imaginative, with a strong adventurous spirit, and the strength of character to carry out your ideas. Secondly, it shows her that you 'think outside the box' – that dating is a jaunt around the world and not merely a night out at the local bar. Thirdly, it's an exciting development in a conversation. You are both building a fresh new adventure together which will, in turn, generate excitement, passion and interest in your already blossoming relationship. Finally, and most Dupe-worthily, it might just get you a free holiday that she'll pay for. You'll learn more about how to achieve this in chapter fifteen.

At this stage and for now, choose your dream destination and imagine a holiday. After all, you're a Complete Bastard – you deserve it.

Making Mud

It's not going to be simple for a Complete Bastard to convince anyone that he's a stable catch or long-term boyfriend material – you signed up for the maverick approach to online dating and beyond and that means **lots** of women for **your** needs and gains. By showing your Magical side, your date might begin to worry that she is dealing with a larger than life character and a potential Player.

Realize now that, without some signs that you have earthy qualities (ability to commit, trustworthy, devoted), she will begin to develop a serious mistrust of you and may decide that you are not the one for her. By making Mud, you can avoid this.

Here are some ideas for ways to impress upon her that your name is 'Mud'.

Share your fears

During your conversations with her, be open about your fears and insecurities about relationships and life in general. This may seem in conflict to earlier advice in this book to Man Up and avoid Wimp Chimp, but it's not really.

By showing her that you are emotionally open yet strong with it, she will develop a deeper empathy with your male perspective. Also, with your opening up to her, you offer her empathy for her own fears and worries in return. For women, this emotional bond is linked to her feeling more comfortable with you during sex. What greater incentive is there for you to share your fears than to have the reward of her sharing her bed with you?

Show you care

Showing her affection, whether on a first date or later, when in the context of priming her to like you or to become infatuated with you, is not Wimp Chimp behaviour.

Most men have a difficult time being affectionate but, saying the right words, giving her that surprise gift, or touching her on the 'safe zones' of her body (back or arms) will leave the impression that you are a nice guy, plus make her prime seduction fodder.

Learn to find the right words and the right actions at the right time, in your own unique style, suited to your personality and you will make Mud without her even knowing that you're playing the dirtiest of games with her. Who knows? You may even be genuine in your affections.

Show you like her

One of the best ways to make your date feel special is through complimenting her – and often. Complimenting is a tricky business. Do it wrong, and it can sound false and insincere – the very definition of Wimp Chimp behaviour. Get it right, however, and she will lap up your every word, grow in her own confidence, and reward this guy who really appreciates and understands her with his every fibre.

Women are likely to be most flattered if you compliment them on something that only you have noticed. Perhaps her taste in clothing has always been assumed by others to be impeccable. It's no crime to tell her too that you love the way she dresses. But go further than the others: tell her that they way she moves with her clothes is 'sexy and alluring'.

And it's not just her beauty that needs complimenting. What about her sense of humour, her intelligence, or her talents as a cook? Look for her hidden talents and

167

make sure she knows that you admire them. It all goes to making her think that you have that extra depth behind your showman's image.

When infatuation goes wrong

There are a number of potential problems that can come with getting a girl infatuated at such a fast pace. This section shows you what these negative reactions could be and how to deal with them:

Too much, too soon

The high intensity of your attentions, mixed with her quickly having a man around her may, after a short time, panic her as she feels overwhelmed and under too much pressure to commit to you. This can often be fuelled by her close friends who, upon hearing that there's a new man becoming so quickly integrated in her life, start expressing deep suspicions or advise her to 'take things slower'.

If this happens and the woman suddenly appears uneasy or nervous about your relationship together, pull back and ease up on Communication and Proximity Overload. This entails fewer phone-calls and/or emails plus more nights off from one other. This is all that's needed here.

The usual result of 'pulling back' is that, by giving her some space: a) you have more time for Bastardly deeds elsewhere, and b) she will begin to miss your being around and keeping in touch with her. In the vast majority of cases, she'll come running back to you (much to the disbelief of her friends).

Burn out

She has seen you every day and you've been in constant contact with her. She may reach a point where she becomes bored of you. This problem may also affect you as well. After all, a Complete Bastard runs with several women at the same time and has the added pressure of having to operate while not getting caught by anyone in the process.

Again the solution here is to offer her some space away from you. Decrease both Communication and Proximity Overload and watch her come crawling back to you in time. Letting her miss you for a while also gives you a chance to catch up on your Complete Bastard backlog of misadventure elsewhere.

Fears to the fore

She now thinks that you could be 'The One' but perhaps she feels unready for a relationship or she's been hurt in the past. Suddenly she worries that you could hurt her like she's been hurt before.

Many men and women carry such deep-rooted relationship fears. If this woman has any form of gut instinct, alarm bells would be ringing, alerting her to the fact that you are a Complete Bastard. Luckily, you've given her enough 'evidence' to suggest that you are instead an intriguing blend of Magic (extravagant; extraordinary; exciting) and Mud (mature; caring; trustworthy). She should feel safe with you.

In case this still isn't enough to dispel all of her fears, be there to talk through her concerns. Sure, listening to someone's irrational fears is tedious to a Complete Bastard, but remember that this is part of your strategy to get her to fall for you. A quick-fix solution for quelling her relationship fears can be to remind her of the fun guy you are and the fun times you have together. Maybe at this point it's time to go on another fun date with each other and inject a little Magic back into proceedings.

She turns psycho

An avalanche of affection and empathy can have the nasty complication of turning a girl so much your way that she goes a little – or a lot – mad. What chance did she have? You expertly and cunningly invaded her life, cast her previous single life to the trash can, left her hanging on to your every word and craving you relentlessly in her bed.

To control the situation at her end, she can become obsessive about you. She gets paranoid when you take private phone calls or you refuse to meet with her one evening. Her mind strives for ways to better control you and this can overspill into deeply erratic behaviour. In short, you've created your own Frankenstein's monster, armed with bunny boiling tendencies and a stalker's toolkit.

To combat the 'psycho woman', you need to have your wits about you. Attempting direct conflict such as some of the more extreme methods of dumping (see chapter sixteen) might not be the best solution. Often dumping will simply bring her psycho side more to the fore. Instead, you may have to use the 'softly, softly, get me the hell away from this monkey' approach of slowly weaning her off you, by subtly decreasing both Communication and Proximity Overload at a pace that she won't become suspicious of. Sadly, having an infatuated psycho on your hands is never an easy situation to get out of. So if at all worried, go back over some of the earlier theory on 'Understanding Women' (chapter five) to get some of the early warning signs.

Putting it all together

You've now reached the end of this important chapter and should have learned that there is a whole strand of Complete Bastard work for you to do on your date to initiate that first connection (first kiss or the follow up date).

Then with a bond made, it's time to up the ante and use some particularly radical relationship tactics to turn up the heat on your relationship until it reaches boiling point.

There is much to gain and too much to lose from every relationship a Complete Bastard creates. To give you some idea of what these gains and losses are, we will now look at them in detail in the following chapter.

Crooked Fancy

When 'Hollysticks' fell for the Complete Bastard, he couldn't believe his luck – until he fell out of lust.

This is a tale from my early days of online dating when I was using the personal ads on one of the biggest free classified advertising sites. You take your chances on these sites, but occasionally you can find and get in contact with a real cutie.

'Hollysticks' was one such example. She was a 26-year old wine seller from the city. For both of us at that time, online dating was a new way of meeting people and we had an instant attraction to each other.

She had just come out of a long-term relationship with some guy who had treated her like shit for two years. She was fragile and disillusioned with the idea of dating, but I offered her a large dose of Magic with just enough Mud to keep reminding her that I was a truer, more genuine and better guy than she'd ever had in her life before.

Before I knew it and within a solitary week, she was infatuated.

'Hollysticks' would call me virtually every hour of every waking day. I'd also receive countless text messages from her, from saying just, 'Hi', to some steamy suggestions as to what we should get up to when we met up later. There were emails with cute, sickly, 'I love you' messages and invites to go out with her friends and to visit her family. I played along just as gamely, because Communication Overload is the key to winning the minds of your lovers.

We saw each other almost every day (Proximity Overload) and I spent most nights at her house and in her bed. Her housemates hated me – but that was probably just because, not only was I was devouring the entire contents of their fridge by day, but I was loudly banging away with 'Hollysticks' by night. Sex with 'Hollysticks' was the best part – passionate, wild and very naughty.

She was fun company too, if a little too compliant to my every whim and fancy. In time, I began to spend 'Hollysticks' money faster than she earned it. She was sinking into debt as I demanded more meals out, trips abroad, and even a new wristwatch. Well, it was a birthday gift!

Often my work would keep 'Hollysticks' and I apart (at least, that's what I told her). She would then offer to perform private webcam shows for my delight which were strictly for Adult Eyes Only. These were cynically aimed to keep me lusting after her.

Truth be told though, I quickly became bored of 'Hollysticks' and her smothering attentions.

I'd Flooded her and now she was Flooding me back. The perks were nice but, as she sank deeper into debt after a few weeks, the arguments between us began to flare up and the perks stopped coming.

There is an old adage of Papa Bastard's which goes: 'Give a Bastard a fish and he will eat for a day. Give him his own rod and he'll snap it in two and say: "Where's my f****** free fish?!"' I was missing going fishing.

The time had come to Shoo 'Hollysticks' out of my cyberlife and Dump her in my private life. Having someone infatuated with you is fun for a while, but the expert Complete Bastard must always know when the party is over.

'Hollysticks' sure was fun while she lasted, though.

Date Her, Dupe Her, Dump Her

– 14 –
Introducing Duping

What is Duping?

Most books that tell you how to succeed with women would have ended by now. Their final chapters assuming that all you ever wanted from life was to find the girl of your dreams and 'live happily ever after'. The Complete Bastard always likes to take things that one step further, however. And this chapter goes where other books fear to tread.

If falling in love or getting more sex were all that you are after, then we bid you happy hunting. You should now have enough know-how to achieve these goals. But for those who want to learn how to really indulge in some Complete Bastard behaviour, then the rest of the book will truly shock and astonish. It takes you into devilish new territory and shows you how to achieve results that would never have seemed possible from the innocent act of online dating.

What you can gain from beginning the pursuit in front of a computer screen is huge financial and social benefits. This is through the art of Duping. For the Complete Bastard, Duping is an essential part of his dating strategy.

Let me first define what Duping is: it is the act of lying, cheating and conniving to one or a network of potential or current sexual partners in order to gain the upper-hand at online or offline dating. It is a learnable set of skills, made up of the three main components as stated:

Lying: This is the act of being consciously and deliberately untruthful. Lying is used by the Complete Bastard to convince others that he is who he says he is, does what he says he does and, in the future, will be who he says he will be. Lying also covers the falsities that he says to others to make them like him more and convince them that he's a worthwhile lover.

Cheating: This is having multiple sexual partners. As soon as you have more than one sexual partner, you are an active cheat. That bit is obvious. The hard part is not getting caught if you are such a character and the next chapter gives you some handy hints to make sure you're a Cheating Champion, not a Cheating Chump.

Conniving: To collude secretly with another or a group in order to protect yourself from being exposed as a Complete Bastard. It's the riskiest of the three elements of Duping because it relies on the involvement of others. This runs the risk that they may betray you and inform others about some of your Bastardly activities. This naturally increases the likelihood of your getting caught as more mouths mean more chance of information straying into the wrong ears. It also means that you must carefully manage your relationship with your fellow conniver(s), which adds a further stress to any act of connivance.

With all the trickery and deceit I've shown you with regard to online and offline dating, you may be thinking that Duping is but an extension of this area of my instruction. However, it should be pointed out at this stage that there is one major difference between dating and Duping. With dating you show your best qualities to attract a woman and get her to agree to a first date. You then continue to play her until she falls for your charms.

Duping is the opposite though. At Dupe stage, you must hide your deviant nature and succeed in not being exposed as a Complete Bastard. It is a roguish sport of 'Duped or Be Done For' while you seek to win back your Man Mantle as a successful womaniser with the best quality of women to choose and to use. And when you've re-asserted your Manned Up status, you can begin to look at the perks to be gained.

Perks of Duping

So you've just learned what Duping is. In the next chapter, you'll learn exactly how to lie, cheat and connive until your Complete Bastard heart is content – and how to get away with it. Before that, I'm sure you're far more interested in finding out what are the perks of Duping.

By reading on, you'll get a brief insight into the multitude of specific perks within each of these 'life areas':

Sex

You've just spotted the most stunning picture of a girl on a dating website. She's the perfect age for you, she's beautiful, her photos show she has a great body and, after reading her profile, you can see that she is intelligent, funny and highly successful in her career. The one overriding feeling you have for this babe is complete and unbridled lust.

If there is one main underlying reason behind a guy wanting to date or to seek a partner, it is the chase to secure regular sex. Sex is a natural, physical urge (for both sexes) and the drive to secure sexual pleasure is **the** major motivation for many who are dating. It is, therefore, no surprise to learn that most resources that teach you how to better seduce women focus on the sole goal of enabling the reader to get more sex than he ever thought possible.

Duping is also geared towards getting sex. It encourages you to attract and Juggle multiple sexual partners, where each partner is special and attractive to you – yet they are unaware of being anything other than the sole recipient of your affections and sexual attentions.

As a Complete Bastard, over the years I've enjoyed a whole plethora of sexual conquests and sexual perks including:

Regular sex: When you want it, where you want it. The secret to attaining regular sex is taking mastering seduction techniques and being able to dictate to women what sort of relationship you want. By learning how to infatuate them, win their hearts and their minds will soon follow.

Casual sex: One-night stands with women who are interested in you only sexually and are willing participants in 'no strings attached' sex which both she and you know is never going to turn into any other kind of a relationship.

Adulterous sex: Many bored housewives or women in long-term relationships are becoming dissatisfied with the sex they get from their tired, overworked husbands. The Complete Bastard is only too willing to give them the discrete sexual release that many of them are looking for.

Experimental sex: By knowing how to seduce women comes the bonus of getting from them rich, new and varied sexual experiences. From multiple women in one conquest to participating in kinky forms of sexual interplay – providing that women feel relaxed and comfortable around you, anything goes.

Cybersex: The confidence to flirt with women can still be done when she isn't even in the same room. Erotic email chat, filthy IM conversations and webcam sex shows are all to be enjoyed as your online flirting reaches epic proportions.

The Date-athlon: The '10 women in one week' method is where I first dated ten potential sexual partners and selected the best while dumping the duds. (See Dating Diary of a Complete Bastard, chapter five) It's for all Complete Bastards who want a challenge.

The Complete Bastard, while as sex-mad as the next hot-blooded male, understands that sex is not the only perk to be had as a result of dating, however. There are others. The Complete Bastard does not to fortuitously fall into new and amazing lifestyles. Rather he is conscious of the women he wants to date when he selects them as potential partners online. He is primed to look for clues to the personality of a particular woman and the type of life that she is leading.

So, sex aside, what else makes up the Complete Bastard lifestyle?

Cash and gifts

As I hope that you are beginning to understand, the Complete Bastard lifestyle can be **whatever you want it to be**. So why not aim high?

After sex, probably the greatest goal of a Complete Bastard is money and other material rewards for all his efforts. These can be achieved by finding the right woman and using the techniques described in this book.

Women have been getting these perks since the dawn of time – who hasn't heard the term 'gold diggers'? The Complete Bastard can become the male equivalent of a gold digger if he wants. There are many women around these days with a sufficiently high level of wealth and disposable income to spend it on a man who they invite into their lives.

So what do you want from them? A roof over your head? A little extra spending money? New clothes or a new car? Find the right woman and these perks could all be yours, and more besides.

Or maybe you are looking to increase your status in life? Fancy getting access to glamorous social, cultural and sporting events? You just need to find the right woman who gets the VIP tickets to every event and needs a 'Plus One' to take along with her.

New friends

Online dating can give you the opportunity to meet lots of new faces. Some of these people may turn out to be weird or not your type; some may think the same about you and not want anything to do with you. In the main though, you can find people online who you are attracted to, share much in common with or are just impressed by. And it needn't stop there. Anyone whom you meet online can be the opportunity to open a whole new world of related friendships and social outings that can introduce some fresh faces and adventure into your life. You've just got to learn how to play it.

Over the years, this Complete Bastard met girls who were highly connected either because of their families, as a result of their jobs, or through their extensive and very impressive network of friends and contacts. Some notable 'new friends' included:

- Celebrities
- People who lived abroad
- Highly attractive female friends
- Great new male friends
- Business and work contacts

Duping to make new friends is particularly useful if you've just moved cities or countries and don't know anyone at all in your new location. Through just a handful of dates, all coming from online dating alone, I've had girls introduce me to their friends, who introduced me to their friends, who introduced me to their friends, and so on, until I ended up with a large social network within just a few weeks of arriving in a completely foreign country where I didn't even speak a word of the language.

The Complete Bastard is a highly social animal and, though maverick and devious in his calculations, he is never introvert. He understands clearly the merits of using society for his own personal gain and that means charming people. Again some of the lessons given previously in this book, such as knowing what to wear (chapter four) or behaving with confidence (chapter three) can be useful when interacting with people connected with your date.

Travel

The opportunity to use your cunning at Duping to get the reward of world travel is not one that should seem outlandish or out of your grasp at all. 'How does that work?' you may be thinking. 'I join a dating website and next thing, I'm in Hawaii?'

Nothing is ever quite that simple, but it's also more of a reality than you might think. Look at the profiles of many women that are online. Just about every one of them either harps on about their love of travelling or includes pictures of them posing in front of the Pyramids or helping build mud huts for orphans in Zanzibar. Travelling conjures up notions of adventure, escape, the exotic, and romance.

When two people first meet and hit it off, it's described as a 'honeymoon' period. This encapsulates a phase of courting when everything seems perfect. It is also symbolic of the act of honeymooning or escaping in love to an idyllic setting to begin a new life together.

The Complete Bastard takes full advantage of the 'honeymoon period' he conspires to create around a new victim. He dizzies her, creates Magic (with an equal amount of Mud), and knows just when to suggest to his new date that, 'Perhaps a trip out to your parents' chalet in the Alps for the ski season may be just the tonic we need to inject a little verve back into our relationship?!'

The Complete Bastard can also look at securing the perk of travel with a long term view. One of the most rewarding pastimes for the usually pragmatic Complete Bastard is dreaming up new places he would like to go and visit. More often than not, these are at the expense of his new date! Think of yourself with an atlas on your lap and your newfound and easily-Duped stunning girlfriend in the kitchen making your favourite pancakes with maple syrup, as you call out: 'Darling, what about Rio for the Carnival?' You've got the whole wide world in your hands – make the most of the opportunity.

Career

Work and pleasure don't go together – or so you may think. Online dating can provide a great opportunity to not just broaden your success in romance, but to increase similar success in your career as well.

A Complete Bastard's desirable date is often selected based purely on the fact that she works in a similar area to you. Obviously it helps if you are attracted to her too, but I have dated many women who were unaware that my only bond with them was business.

My career as a writer was, at many times, served well by the women I dated and Duped for help in my work life that included:

- Help with compiling reports, articles and features.
- Aid with researching information and fact-finding.
- Access to a network of specialist creatives including web designers, artists and computer programmers.
- Contacts within the media industry across many sectors.
- Inside company information and story leads.
- Legal, medical and other specialist advice.

Many other benefits have come to me by accident rather than design. After all, everyone with a career has some sort of useful skill or provides a service that she is usually willing to give away free to those who are close to her. So why not take advantage of all that your dates have to offer?

So these are all some of the perks that it's possible to obtain through taking dating and Duping to their ultimate extremes.

Becoming a Duper

With these delicious perks to motivate you, it's time to give you an insight into the mind of a successful Duper. To give you an overview of the type of man a Duper is, I have broken down the seven compulsory traits of an effective Duper:

7 Habits of a Devious Duper
1. The Devious Duper has many women and their perks to draw upon

As I've constantly been mentioning throughout this book, the Complete Bastard keeps his options open. This means seeking a quality and quantity of women. To Dupe is to nurture a network of gullible, infatuated, and willing women then to maximise the potential for extracting as much as you can from them.

More important: these women should be loaded with perks. One of the first things an effective Duper does is to select the perks he wants and then finds the women that his waggish charms will work on to get these perks. Plus, never forget that all of these women can also be enjoyed as affectionate, well-liked sexual partners too. After all, the only reason that they are opening up their purses or lifestyles to you is because they genuinely like you, trust you, and are highly attracted to you.

To focus on just one woman is not a recommended strategy to be a successful Duper. Though you may argue that a monogamous relationship can still be a profitable one (in the Complete Bastard sense), it doesn't always work quite like that. One relationship means only one prospect for sex and one access point to perks. This means that if you ever get caught behaving as a Complete Bastard, then you will be left with nothing at all. To refresh your memory at this point, re-read my story in chapter two and you'll see how a one-woman loser ends up – alone and down-and-out!

So you should ideally look to Woo more than one woman at a time. The Complete Bastard adds more women to his life all the time, checking online dating site profiles and flirting with women whom he thinks could provide him with fresh opportunities. He is using the most convenient means out there to meet and seduce women.

The Complete Bastard is also getting rid of – often with a ruthless intensity – the women that he has used already, those who are causing him any kind of trouble or are high-maintenance. The magnificent thing about the Complete Bastard way is that, instead of all this 'ducking and diving' with women turning you into a shifty-eyed, snaggletooth love rat, the opposite occurs. Instead you become more confident around women as you begin to seduce them in increasing numbers. No single woman's response to you will take on too much significance, especially negative responses. You will find yourself more at ease in women's company – livelier, and less worried about their unpredictable reactions. In fact, women will ultimately become very predictable as they begin to find themselves attracted to you and attached to you in no time. Do some of the women you attempt to seduce show you too much resistance or simply reject you? Who cares? There are plenty more where she came from and the Complete Bastard is adept at making the Numbers Game work for him.

But before you slip on your tuxedo, light up a Cuban cigar and log in to your favourite dating site, some words of warning: juggling many women is a strategy which needs to be carefully managed by a Complete Bastard. More women equal more opportunities to be found out and exposed as the user you are. In the next chapter entitled 'The Art of Duping', you will learn how to minimise the risks of this occurring.

2. The Devious Duper dictates every Dupe and is in full control
A major theme of this book has been to prove to you that it's time that men won back some, if not all, of the power in the Dating Game. For too long, we've skulked away from dates not knowing what went on in the woman's head, stared into empty inboxes wondering why no one ever writes, and suffered in dead-end relationships

where the only reasons for continuing in them was to avoid feeling lonely. It's not been easy investing heavily in women (both emotionally and financially) and getting very little back in return.

But one heavenly hope for men remains. That hope is held only by those who make it to the end of the Path to Bastardom and rise to become fully-fledged Complete Bastards. These admirable men are winning back power for men, Manning Up, and proving themselves as desirable and worthy lovers for women.

The Complete Bastard knows that online dating is his new best friend in finding and flirting with women. From the teachings contained in the earlier chapters of this book, you will have seen just how easy and effective online dating can be for a Complete Bastard, enabling you to win back control in the pursuit of women. Also, and contrary to the teachings of many charlatan dating experts, the male does not need to be initiating every step of a romantic encounter whether online or offline. The Complete Bastard knows how to make any system work for him and he applies that to online dating.

The outcome of a successful online dating campaign is that you will encourage women to get in touch with you (to Coo you) just as much as you pursue (Woo) them first. That is a revelation compared to how women have been seduced in the past.

3. The Devious Duper always Dupes for more

Right from the very first moment you start reading an online dating profile that you like, you should be thinking about Duping. Prospecting for what you think you can get out of the situation if you Woo and win over this person is a vital trait of the Complete Bastard. Why? Because without recognising that women can be enjoyed and used for other more Dupe-worthy gains than just sex or a standard emotional relationship, you are missing out on a whole world of other greater opportunities. I've showed you what these perks are. Surely they are far more than you ever thought possible from a situation that starts with a little gentle flirting on a dating site?

For the highly effective Duper, his quest does not end online however. While online dating is recommended as being the most convenient 'hunting ground' for fit, fallible chicks, bear in mind that these girls have female friends and family members too. You will be introduced to other women as you start to attend new social events and embrace a better, more lavish lifestyle. You will grow more successful within your job or meet new girls at the new and better job you may get as a result of Duping.

In short, women are everywhere and, with your newfound confidence and knowhow with them, you can gain more and more from being in their company and in their beds.

4. The Devious Duper knows what he wants – and gets it

Many people who join an online dating site enter the arena with a rather limited and fixed idea as to what they want to gain from it. Some seek a long-term relationship which they hope will culminate in marriage. Others are looking for quality people – better than the ones who they are currently meeting at bars or clubs – or worst case, not meeting at all. Some folk are just after a fling or sex and they may wrap that rather base pursuit up in romantic gloss just to get what they want. All these people have one thing in common: they have slotted themselves into rather limited pigeonholes in terms of their needs and wants. This starts the rot by seriously limiting the number of suitors they will attract and the amount of perks ripe for the picking.

The Complete Bastard is never so narrow-minded. He understands that there is a plethora of perks out there held by many women. He goes into dating with a set of outcomes in mind. These could include:

'This girl may be attractive to me, but she's also got a great job, says she adores travel, and boasts of having lots of great friends. I can get myself a share in that.'

'Wow! This woman is not only beautiful but her connections in the field of -_____ could really help my own career.'

'I'm not sure if this girl is right for me long term – but for a night of sexual pleasure, she looks like she'd be a lot of fun.'

If the Complete Bastard comes across as cynical, it's because he is. He is goal-oriented to a tee. But then again, who isn't? Everyone goes about their lives with some sort of a plan. And when it comes to relationships, the person we settle down with is rarely chosen on looks and personality alone. Their social life, career success, range of interests, and status in life are all factors that we appraise when selecting them as a partner.

So, when you take the next step to becoming the most devious Duper around, make sure you think with a particular outcome or outcomes in mind. By now, you've surely learned that there need be no limit to what you can get from women and life.

5. The Devious Duper empowers women for his own selfish gain

To illustrate the ways in which an effective Duper empowers women, some example scenarios may be effective:

Scenario A:

You're online and chatting with a potential date. You know that she likes you, but you want to avoid showing her that you're too keen. So you pull back with the direct flirting and begin to cool off in your pursuit of her. You tell her that you are unsure as to whether you should see one another – you've been hurt before and you don't want to be hurt again with the wrong woman.

Scenario B:

It's your first date with a girl. Everything is going well. You look great, she looks great and there's more flirting going on between you than the last dance at a nightclub. You crave her sexually, but you don't want to go and spoil it by coming on too strong. You announce that it's getting late and so you should catch your last train home.

Scenario C:

You've been dating this great chick for a few weeks now. She's beginning to get a bit suspicious and annoyed that she seems to be the one who is paying for everything while the 'great guy' you initially seemed to be now seems to be nothing more than a louse who just sits around her house saying that he's looking for new work and that he doesn't feel 100% committed to her. She confronts you and your response is to ask her if she wants to end the relationship.

In each of the three examples – A, B, and C – the Complete Bastard has handled a tricky situation by putting the onus for making the final decision on the women. He has empowered them with the control of both their destinies.

This may seem an almost certain forehead-slapping blunder. Surely, when a woman is given control, she will feel uncomfortable and return back to her mysterious, all-powerful ways that you have worked so long and hard to understand and control?

Wrong. By empowering her, you have given **her** the headache of having to make a quick decision to keep you or lose you. Unless she's as artful a game-player as you are, with multiple partners on the go, she'll not give up someone she likes and is attracted to on a whim. Instead, she will admire you more for giving her 'control' of the situation. She'll also like the way you have behaved in a potentially deal-breaking situation – that you are a thoughtful and emotional individual (Scenario A); that you appear willing to play a patient game with her and not pressurise her into sex (Scenario B); or that you have acknowledged that there is a problem in your relationship (Scenario C).

The great news is that the three situations above are likely to result in the following outcomes: she'll flirt more with you to re-awaken your sexual interest in her (Scenario A); she'll invite you to stay at her place (Scenario B); and she'll beg you to keep the relationship alive (Scenario C). With regard to the last scenario, perhaps at the point of resolution with her, you should suggest that a cosy meal for two in your favourite (i.e. expensive) restaurant may be a nice way to celebrate your fresh start in style. Her treat, of course!

6. The Devious Duper never boasts of his conquests

In chapter two, I told you of my rise from loser to user thanks to some expert tuition from Papa Bastard. He showed me many things, but his key teaching was giving me the confidence to take control of my own destiny. Though I quickly began to win the affections of women and the admiration of men as my Inner Bastard grew, one decision I made early on was to never boast of my conquests – never mind my duplicity – to any man or woman.

Over the years, I've had a lot to brag about. Many men and women have asked me how I do it: 'Why do women fall for you?'; 'How do you manage to lead a lifestyle that far outstrips what you earn?'; 'How do you get away with dumping women then replacing them with someone else so quickly?'

My answer is always: 'No comment.' They're two words that are used by politicians and celebrities to keep a prying media at bay and their privacy intact. They know that if they do comment, their words will be twisted, misinterpreted, changed, and then fed to a baying public who'll believe the media's every word. The same vigilance must be adhered to by the Complete Bastard. Boast and you're toast.

Men will applaud your jolly japes to your face but, behind your back, they'll taint you as sinister and untrustworthy. They're jealous. Lesser men will also worry that if you'd Dupe a women as beautiful as the one they saw you with at that party last week, then what's to stop you Duping their girlfriend or wife?

Women should be treated with even greater caution. What woman, upon hearing that one of her fellow 'sisters' has been Duped, would let that go? She may giggle at your bawdy tales of roguish romance and philandering in front of you but, give her a little time away from you, and your reputation will be in shreds.

A lot of people are spiteful gossips who seek and invent 'monsters' to hang their own failings upon. As a Complete Bastard, you are an easy target to become that 'monster'. So the best policy is to banish boasting for now and save your escapades for your memoirs when you're a shagged-out, grizzled old man. Plus, think about it: who really wants to hear talk from a cocksure braggart who's getting laid more than they are anyway?

7. The Devious Duper never gets caught

As the proverb goes: 'Play with fire and you will get burned.' And getting 'burned' is a major concern of any Duper. He is playing a game with the opposite sex so very delicious yet dangerous that, should he become exposed as a duplicitous parasite, he will incur the unwavering wrath of the people who are romantically close to him. And that's just for starters.

An effective Duper will be so integrated into all his women's lives that he has a lot to lose – the sex, the roof over his head, the cash, the flashy lifestyle, the social events, the free holidays, and maybe even his career. This is the double-edged sword that is Duping. But if you live by the sword, with some care and vigilance, you don't have to die by it. In the following chapter, you'll be given all the tips you will need to ensure that you avoid getting caught for your misdeeds.

To Dupe or not to Dupe?

At this stage on the Path to Bastardom, you may be feeling unsure, perhaps even afraid, that you will never be able to find the gall to become the Complete Bastard. After reading the '7 Deadly Habits of a Devious Duper', you should now clearly see that Duping is how many of us behave anyway, though we either deny these 'dark' urges or are blissfully unaware of them. The unenlightened or the gutless don't unleash these urges to their full potential. With the belief that you too can be a devious Duper, lying, cheating and conniving will simply feel right – a natural step in between dating and dumping women.

It is important that you embrace the concept of Duping if you are to truly embrace the whole philosophy and system that is the Path to Bastardom and beyond. You've seen the perks – so now go forward and do the Dupe. It's a lot more than simply 'robbing the rich to help the poor'. Duping and getting away with it will boost your confidence still further, will furnish you with a roguish charm, and put you firmly in control of all that you can achieve in life. This goes far beyond success at seduction. You'll also see radical improvements in your career, lifestyle and social life if you Dupe well. So, go on! Delight in Duping and watch your wildest dreams come true.

In conclusion, the Path to Bastardom doesn't advocate that men go out to intentionally plunder and lie to women. Rather it's a 'call to arms' for men to start behaving with the same cunning and social intelligence that women have been using for centuries. Women were the ones that demanded equality. Now they have it – and good on them. But they need to learn that they can't have their cake and eat it too – equal opportunities for earning should also mean equal opportunities for Duping.

Being a Complete Bastard is about proving to them that **the wrong man is the right man**. It is important to note that the wrong man is not an immoral man, a criminal or a misogynist – three charges that are levied at the Complete Bastard and are vehemently denied as follows:

The Complete Bastard is not immoral to women

There are many books on online and offline dating that forewarn users (usually women) of the 'dangers' from online dating. Their authors warn of the 'sinister characters' out there, ready and waiting to wreck lives and break hearts. As outlined earlier in this book, online dating has many pitfalls for unsuspecting users and these people can also fall victim to a number of dubious characters (male and female) who involve themselves with online dating.

The art of Duping actually also gives you the means to step around the game playing that has always been rife within dating. It is a proactive means of avoiding the hurt and pain that can go with opening yourself up emotionally and losing out in love to the opposite sex.

Duping does not set out to intentionally attack or victimise anybody – and certainly not those people who you may deeply care about. It is, therefore, not some sinful, black-hearted conceit found lurking within the DNA of horrible Complete Bastards. Rather, it is instead a learned set of social skills that should be used in self defence as a means of asserting control over dating, while ensuring that you are more able and more in control to achieve the goals that you want from life in general.

The Complete Bastard is not a criminal

Lying, cheating, conniving – hardly the most valiant of behaviours, admittedly. But neither are they criminal acts. The Complete Bastard never commits acts that are illegal, criminal or that cause direct harm to others. The Complete Bastard is way too smart to participate in a life of crime.

For a start, the Complete Bastard doesn't need to. He understands his situation and knows how to behave legally, effectively and to profit within it. Furthermore, what women would be attracted to a man who is committing criminal acts? There are a few gangsters' molls who might but, in the main, a life of crime never pays. It cannot be denied that the Complete Bastard is a maverick and a rule-bender. This does put him in murky waters with regard to what is 'ethical' behaviour, but his behaviour is certainly not criminal.

Duping should be viewed as a perfectly legal, non-criminal activity that focuses on how to best influence others for your own selfish gain. What's wrong with that? This is the how politicians, business people and even religious leaders operate every day of their lives. It is also how women have been Duping men for millennia, using exactly the same tactics – yet no one bats an eyelid. It has just come to be accepted as part of the natural order.

The Complete Bastard is not a misogynist

A misogynist is a man who hates women. Surely the Complete Bastard can be considered as one of them? Nothing can be further from the truth. Complete Bastards **adore** women. They certainly don't hate them.

When seeking potential online partners, Complete Bastards seek only the best. A prerequisite to guaranteeing 'the best', is selecting strong-minded, successful, highly attractive women. There is little benefit in focusing energies on the weak, the emotionally damaged or High Risk Wobblers. (These are women who are liable to fall hopelessly in love on a first date, become stalkers, bunny boilers, psychos, and so on, and who may require a restraining order or a zapping from a Taser gun).

The Complete Bastard enjoys the chase and the company of women. Nothing is more delicious a prospect to him than a romantic liaison with the fairer sex. Though, for Dupe extras, if the Complete Bastard can wing a free holiday in the sun, a few platefuls of gourmet cuisine, or a gutful of champagne – and all at her expense – then so much the better.

So you've now had your introduction to Duping. I hope you can see that it is a proactive means to get yourself the women of your dreams, as well as protect yourself from the pitfalls that dating throws up. But how do you go about the process of actually getting the perks out of her and protecting your duplicity against getting caught?

For that we move to the darkest of all the chapters – where you will learn the secret of **how** to Dupe her!

DATING DIARY OF A COMPLETE BASTARD

Travelling the World on a Dupe

The Complete Bastard journeys into the darkest recesses of his ingenuity to pull off one of his best dating coups ever.

'Miss_Penelope' was one of the wealthiest and most prominent women I ever dated. She was an International Funds Manager for a large global company and had written to me after she'd 'laughed herself sober' reading my cheeky online profile on one of the more exclusive, illustrious sites for people seeking 'high calibre' partners.

Though nearly a decade older than me, 'Miss_Penelope' and I hit it off right from our first date. In addition to being stinking rich, she was attractive, smart and funny. She didn't seem bothered that I wasn't some high-flying executive or wealthy socialite. Instead she liked my easy company, my brash self-assurance and she found me attractive. 'Miss_Penelope' was soon to become my greatest Dupe ever.

A Complete Bastard like me loves to go a-travelling. With a work-shy ethic and not a noodle of application, seeing the world should be an impossible dream. But what if, one evening, you're in bed with your older lady friend, grumbling of the frustration in life of trying to break through as a travel writer, when she gets all doe-eyed and makes you an offer so irresistible that you nearly fall out of her mahogany four-poster bed with glee?

> 'Sweetie, if it's the world you want to see, then hop along with me. You know I'm in a different country nearly every week. You'd get some great travel writing out of that, surely?'

> 'What? ... Oh, no. I couldn't possibly... Could I? How would that work? Where would I get the money? No!'

> 'Expenses, Sweetie. Expenses!'

I knew she flew Business Class all the time and her house was crammed with souvenirs from all the exotic places that she'd visited. Unbeknown to 'Miss_Penelope', I'd been dropping hints about this very idea for weeks. You may have heard of some dating 'gurus' dabbling in NLP to hypnotise chicks into dating them. Well, I had my own form of brainwashing chicks. I call it CBB – 'Complete Bastard Bullshitting' – and it works a treat.

And so began my 'all expenses paid' tour of some of the world's most exciting destinations. As 'Miss_Penelope' went about her business meetings, I either lounged around the pools and spas of five-star hotels or savoured every sight and sound of the fantastic places we stayed in. Every night, I ate and drank like a king on her expense account. For desserts, I had the added bonus of having my attractive bed partner as a lover.

I saw the world in style – from the chipped streets of Havana to the ultra-modern metropolises of Tokyo and Shanghai; the bustling souks of the Middle East to the glittering boutiques of Paris and New York. From Bangkok to Burma, Cape Town to Cairo, I visited them all and more. It was a heady adventure.

I didn't write a single word about the whole experience, but 'Miss_Penelope' cared not one bit. She was now besotted with me and having me with her gave her company, sex and fun. She never asked me for a single dime. My only commitment to 'Miss_Penelope' was appearing grateful for as long as it took for me to see the world.

Six months passed. I'd begun to get bored of all the travelling and, sadly, of 'Miss_Penelope'. Standing waiting for your suitcases on the carousel in some far-flung airport or unpacking your toilet bag in another luxury hotel's bathroom meant I wasn't able to surf for fresh talent on dating sites or Woo any other women. I began to miss the old life when **I** was the 'exotic destination' for a girl on a date.

I dumped 'Miss_Penelope' soon after. I'd seen more of the world in six months than most folk see in a lifetime. I'd also discovered that seduction can gain the most eye-opening rewards. But, as Papa Bastard once told me: 'A man gets to missing where he feels most at home.'

And it was the dating sites and the company of women which were what made me feel free and most alive. But Freedom was not a place 'Miss_Penelope' was willing to put on her expense account.

– 15 –
The Art of Duping

The Duper's 5-Point Plan

Now you know what Duping is, the perks to be gained from it, and the characteristics of an effective Duper, it's time to show you how to put Duping theory into Bastardly practice. What follows is a simple, step-by-step framework that will help ensure your Duping desires become a reality.

It is the **Duper's 5-Point Plan**:

1. Set your goals

A Greedy Bastard wants it all. The Complete Bastard knows that he can't have it all. He understands that: the higher the rewards, the higher the risks that come with securing them. So, wisely, he is careful to not outstretch his capabilities or else all of his hard work will quickly have ended up being in vain.

Defining what it is that is most important to improving your life is the first step to understanding who and how you must Dupe to get it. In the last chapter, you learned what these perks could be, including sex, cash, career advancement, travel, making new friends and obtaining an enriched lifestyle. Only you know what specifically it is that you want or need.

If you don't already know what it is you want, the time to think about it is **now**. You should work out **exactly** what you would like to get out of Duping women before you sign up for an online dating site – and then list them in order of priority.

Getting certain perks requires different strategies. If the reward you most want is more great sex, you will achieve the results best by remaining free and single for as long as possible rather than getting too close to any one particular woman.

Conversely, if your primary goals are more material in nature – money, travel, possessions, a roof over your head, and so on – then your strategy will be to focus all of your attention on one particular (preferably stinking rich) woman. At this stage, you may need to target more exclusive, more expensive dating sites that will afford you to access to richer, more successful women.

If you decide that a chick is worth Duping big time, then it's time to make your move. But there is a snag – for her to release these perks, she will demand a lover who is committed, honest and trustworthy. You are none of these things. You run around like a waggish rogue with a harem of women. This places you at an ultra-high risk of being exposed as a Complete Bastard. In this situation, you must make the Ultimate Duper's Sacrifice – and focus your attention on just one woman.

Be prepared for your Perk Priority List to shift over time because you will almost certainly find that your needs change. Satisfy one area of your life and it'll only expose another area as empty and perk-less. Therefore, the best advice here is to learn how to constantly be improving your Duping skills so that you can achieve more of them simultaneously.

2. Pinpoint the perks

Through your know-how of using online dating sites and creating a killer profile that will attract attention to you, you should also see that the information contained in women's profiles is your starting point for discovering what's on offer in terms of perks. But how do you know for sure who holds what perks?

You will soon learn that online dating profiles are highly detailed information sources that reveal lots of useful facts about the women who create them. For example, while most people rarely state exactly which company they work for, they will often give you clues about their income status: 'I'm a wealthy, self-made businesswomen who is now looking for love after many years working hard,' or; 'Life alone is no fun as a struggling student living in the city – I want to meet a young guy to wine and dine me!'

Of the two statements, it's easy to tell which one is worth Duping for cash and free meals out and which one will leave you footing the bill.

Checking out their pictures can also provide a lot of clues. Do they live in an upmarket part of the city? Are they well-dressed? Does the background of their pictures show them in a designer apartment or a slum? Do they have expensive hobbies such as skiing? These can all be accurate indicators that can help you pinpoint a person ripe for Duping.

As you read through profiles, start categorizing the women according to their potential perks until you end up with different 'hit lists' – one for sexual partners, one for financial perks, another for women who can advance your career prospects, and so on. As the proverb goes: 'Variety is the spice of life'.

By careful scrutiny of her dating site profile, you can discover whether a woman is worth Duping. You'll then find out more about their assets on the first and subsequent dates. It is a constant task for the Complete Bastard to be striving to discover as much as possible about women's assets and liabilities to know the upper limits of what he can hope to obtain from them. Always remember that the Complete Bastard is not an evil character – you're not looking to break her financially – just to convince her to give her excess to a deserving cause (i.e. you).

Maybe you got it wrong. Maybe she is a Faker who said that she was loaded just as a come on to attract some younger, hotter 'toy boys'? Maybe she has her own business, but she's having big problems because of the economic climate? If so, then don't be such a heartless Bastard as to take what little she really has left – the kindest course of action for you both is to Dump her and move on to a better target for some conscience-free Duping.

3. Plan your plunder

Now that you know the perks are there for the picking, it's time to work out how you are going to get your mucky paws on them – or her.

If, for example, casual sex is your primary goal, your aim is now to Woo this chick (see chapter eight), get her to your first date (chapter nine), bowl her over with your Inner Bastard confidence (chapter three), dress and move like a seductive man (chapter four) and start the seduction from first kiss (chapter twelve) to infatuation (chapter thirteen). The Duping of her in this instance will usually involve getting her to believe that you are in a monogamous relationship with her when, in fact, you are sleeping with many other women at the same time.

Duping chicks just for sexual gain tends to be a short term strategy that is commonly followed by the dump if things take a course for the worst. It is women with more perks worth Duping for who require a more carefully hatched long-term approach.

Say you've spotted a woman online who is obviously wealthy as well as being highly attractive. In this case, your goal is to not only date her and get her infatuated with you, but to go one step further. You want her to spend, spend, spend her money on you. Duping now requires you to get yourself into a position where she wants to 'share her good fortune' with you, instead of your amazing her by showing the woman what a magical, self-sufficient guy you are.

At first glance, this seems like a tricky balancing act that you need to perform. On one hand, you need to Woo her using your status as a Confident Bastard who excites her in your every move. Yet, on the other hand, you must convince her that you need something from her, which exposes you as being needy.

The secret here is to go back and re-read the Magic-Mud technique (in chapter thirteen). You will have learned that the 'Mud' part of the technique involves your opening up to her emotionally by sharing your fears with her. You make sure that your 'fears' include those of a financial nature. The key here is to be subtle about them and to try and brush them aside, in a heroic, stoic fashion. Here is an example of a conversation I've had many times with women:

> **Her:** 'You're looking rather down this evening, darling. Is there something the matter?'
>
> **You** (glumly): 'No ... no ... not at all, baby... I'm sure that everything will turn out all right in the end... It's nothing that you should be worried about.'
>
> **Her:** 'Come on now, darling. There's obviously something that's bothering you. Please tell me what it is.'
>
> **You:** 'I really don't want to burden you with this...'
>
> **Her:** 'Please, darling, you know I care about you deeply.'
>
> **You:** (sigh) 'Well ... it's just ... well, I'm two weeks behind on my rent now, and if I don't pay up by the end of the week, the landlord says that he is going to throw me out.'
>
> **Her:** (puts a reassuring hand on your shoulder) 'Oh, don't worry about that, darling. It's only a few hundred after all, isn't it?'
>
> **You:** 'But ... but ... no, I couldn't possibly ...'
>
> **Her:** 'Don't be silly. It's nothing at all, honestly.'
>
> **You:** (smiling sadly): 'I'll pay you back soon, I promise you. You're ... you're such a kind, generous warm-hearted person. I think I'm falling in love with you.'

'Infatuate first – and all else will follow' is the simple rule. When you have won her affections, you can be far more malleable with your own personality and with what you ask for. This is why the Complete Bastard's way is to accelerate the process to get her completely infatuated with you. Only then, can you begin to ask for perks.

4. Reap the rewards

The previous conversation shows a very simple Dupe in action. It's not always going to be as easy as that – particularly as you start asking for more and more out of her.

In order to get your more extreme requests granted, it is useful to think of the process in terms of a negotiation, just in the same way that you would try and get a pay-rise out of your boss, or haggle with a market trader. Negotiation involves two parties trying to come to an agreement to both get what they want out a situation.

You might think that she is the one holding all of the cards at this stage – after all, she has money, power, a roof over her head, useful contacts, and more, whereas you have nothing (or very little).

But you would be wrong. If you have mastered the earlier stages of the book and she is well and truly infatuated, you have your continued love, affection and happiness to use as a bargaining chip. Women are intensely emotional beings and, if you have found the key to her heart and brought intense happiness into her previously loveless life, then she will do anything – give you anything – in order to continue in her current state of happiness.

Never forget the very powerful position that you should now have gained within this woman's life – and milk it for all it's worth.

5. Don't get caught

It seems an obvious thing to say, but getting away with being a Complete Bastard is the defining moment when you realise that you are one. The Complete Bastard, in whatever his pursuit, spends much of his life bending rules and subverting systems. As this book has nearly finished showing you, he is able to bend the rules of online dating and use it to further his success as a seducer and Duper.

The Incomplete Bastard must find the confidence to play women with the persistent risk of being caught out. This is a real 'white knuckle ride' you are now on and Duping is the Complete Bastard's blackest art. Do not stray from my teachings in this book. Put into practice many, if not all, of my handy tricks that I've learned and used myself over the years to good effect. It will soon become clear that, the closer you are to feeling like you might get caught, the more exciting the dating game becomes. But watch out! Don't let arrogance or complacency set in or the consequences can be devastating. In the penultimate instalment of the 'Dating Diary of a Complete Bastard' you'll see just what the negative consequences can be.

The next section of this chapter reveals an array of devilish Duping tactics and handy hints that will help you to avoid being exposed as a Complete Bastard. Together, they provide a fool-proof method for getting away with any one or all of your devilish schemes.

Getting away with it

In case I have lulled you into a false sense of security, be warned – the Complete Bastard needs to be always on his guard for having his Bastardly sins exposed. Without a thorough understanding of how to hide your tracks and keep her from knowing your ulterior motives, all of your hard work will be for nothing. It is now time to open the Complete Bastard's Toolkit once again, and reveal to you some of the best and most effective ways to get away with Duping women for your gain.

Here are the four key areas that teach you the art of 'getting away with it':

Nailing the negotiations: Best practice for persuading women to give you what you want.

Looking after your lies: Making sure your fibs don't expose the truth, i.e. that you're a consummate liar.

Checking on cheating: Being caught as an unfaithful lover will get you dumped, so here are some helpful hints to avoid getting caught out.

Cunning at conniving: The people who can help you and hinder you as you Dupe. Plus, how to spot them and use them to your benefit.

Nailing the negotiations

Getting what you want in terms of perks from a woman is a constant pursuit of a fully fledged Complete Bastard. The devious Duper is always prospecting for more and greater rewards from his women and he must be adept at knowing how to effortlessly get these in the quickest timescale possible. Here are some tips to help you hone your negotiation skills when involved in a one-on-one Perks Plundering Attempt:

Begin small: This is the Dupe tactic where you begin by getting little perks from her (free meal, loan of some cash) and work up to getting bigger and better perks (moving in, bank loan in her name). This works on the premise that, with each perk she gives you, she loves you more and more – the more she loves you, the bigger the perk. It is also a good tip for 'testing the waters'. Rushing into a relationship and demanding a Rolex watch after one week rarely works – no matter if you're a Complete Bastard or not.

Open high: Once you know that you have got her truly infatuated, and she has already given you many smaller 'presents', you can adopt the opposite tactic. This is where you ask for the ultimate result that you would like her to give you: 'A new Mercedes sports car, please'. You state your demand confidently and give reasons as to why you need it. She can't afford a Mercedes, so you haggle with her for a while before settling on something that she can afford. So you end up with an Audi instead. You've still done a lot better out of the negotiations than if all you had asked her for was a second hand banger.

'Us' not 'me': The more perks that you can show her are for 'our relationship' and not just for your own selfish gain, the more likely she will be to invest. For example, moving in with her can always be viewed as you taking advantage of her kindness. However, show her that your contributing to the rent or her bills – as well as being together more – will benefit her just as much as you. Another example is travelling: 'Wouldn't a romantic weekend out of the city be a great way for us to relax?' you ask her. She'd never suspect you just wanted to try out your new set of clubs on a golf course close to the luxury hotel she paid for, while thinking you'd be spending your time 'driving up her fairway.'

Confidence is king: You're probably sick to death of reading the word 'confidence' in this book, but I make no apologies for using it yet again as it is so integral to the entire Bastardly Process – especially this part of the Bastardly Process.

Be prepared to hold your ground when asking for what it is that you want from her. Don't back down too quickly or else she will soon realize that it's easy for her to simply say 'no' to you. Be organized when it comes to making your request. Make sure that you spell out all of the benefits that will come from her giving you what it is that you are asking for.

Keep questioning: If she is still saying 'no' to your demands, then ask her the reasons for her rejection. Then just shut up and listen to what it is that she has to say. If she says, 'Because it's too expensive', ask, 'Why is it too expensive?' Keep on ploughing the same line of questioning long enough and you will force her into a situation where she would need to admit that she just doesn't want to spend that much money on you – which would be the same as her admitting that she loves her money more than she does you. Chances are that she's never going to want to risk losing you by telling you this, so she will eventually give in to your demands.

Say thank you: The gesture of thanking her after every one of her acts of 'charity' is a great way to prove to her that you are genuinely grateful and it is a form of repayment for her nice nature. Think about it: you get a new set of clothes; she gets, not only a better dressed lover, but the swell inside her little heart that she's like some guardian angel, watching over you. If only she knew you were nothing but a Duping Devil!

Use conditioning: You need to 'condition' her by gently 'rewarding' her for the times when she gives you what you want with smiles, gratitude and more of your love and happiness, or gently 'punishing' her by being moody, stressed out and/or not giving her the love that she has grown accustomed to. In some ways, it's no different to how you train a dog – chocolate drops for when she does her business outside; or rubbing her nose in it when she's a 'Bad Girl' and gives you shit. Be careful not to overdo the 'punishing' side of the equation though, or else you could piss her off on a permanent basis. So make sure the punishing sulkiness doesn't last for too long. Go back to your regular charming self and try again at some other point in the future.

Favours for favours: From time to time she will ask you for a favour – probably something minor involving your time, as she is probably working 12 hours per day whereas you're sitting around watching daytime TV in your underpants for much of the time. The perfect Complete Bastard phrase to come out with at this point is: 'If I do this for you, what will you do for me?' You need to keep it a bit light-hearted to avoid coming over as a completely evil, manipulating asshole, but it can sometimes gain you some minor rewards. Otherwise, remember the 'great sacrifice' that you made for her next time you are planning for asking her for something – or think of them as Frequent Bastard Points that you can cash in for a greater reward at some point in the future, i.e., 'You can't even do this one little thing for me after all the things I've done for you?! Have you forgotten how I helped you with X, Y, and Z?'

Milk the mayhem: Having a few problems in your relationship with her can be an ideal opportunity to get a Dupe in. Women like nothing better than the moment of tenderness and resolution that follows a major bust-up. It is during such heart-warming moments that the Complete Bastard will savour the opportunity to enjoy some great make-up sex, as well as suggest a slap up candlelit dinner for two to get things back on track. Watch her little eyes light up in joy – if you can take your eyes of her gold credit cards! And if the candlelit dinner for two goes well, then why not suggest a nice little weekend away to the country? And if the romantic weekend away goes well, why not start planning a long holiday abroad for the following month... ?

Escalate for effect: Use the power of 'escalation' to leverage her happiness that comes from her spending money on one activity to press for her to spend more on a bigger and better activity in the knowledge that it will lead to even greater happiness for the pair of you. Get her 'addicted to giving' in the same way that a junky starts off smoking a little pot and ends up by lying in the gutter jacking up on heroin as he constantly searches for bigger and better highs all the time.

Close the deal: She's definitely coming around to your way of thinking now – you just need to close the deal. One trick that a lot of salespeople use here is the 'alternate choice' close – which gives just her a choice of a couple of options to choose from, i.e. 'So where shall we go then? Hawaii or Jamaica?' or 'Shall we go to the Italian or the Chinese?' As soon as she chooses one of them, the deal is sealed and she can't back out of it.

Follow up quick: Once you have got what you want from her, summarize what you have agreed to with her so that there can be no ambiguity left at the end of the conversation. 'So we're going to Hawaii then, right?' Once she has agreed, you shut up or else you might make her have second thoughts about her decision or come up with other ideas. Instead, you need to put the plan into action as soon as possible, i.e., 'Shall we book it now? The longer we leave it, the more expensive it's going to be.'

Nibble for extras: She's agreed to all of your requests. So now what do you do? Why, you ask for even more from her, of course! Well obviously you can't go to a five-star resort in Hawaii dressed in the rags you're wearing. It just wouldn't be right at all. Obviously you'll need to go shopping so that you don't show her up in such a high-class environment! Salesmen call this tactic 'the nibble'. If you've bought some shoes and ended up with some shoe polish you didn't really need, or gone to buy a burger and said 'yes' to the question about whether you want some fries with it, and yes again to getting an extra-large portion, you'll know that it often works. So keep on 'nibbling' while the going's good until you start to feel some resistance.

Expect the unexpected: Always have a good idea in advance as to how you'll respond if things do not work out as you planned. If she won't buy you X, ask for Y. If she says 'no' now, then sulk for a while and maybe ask again in a week when the idea has settled in her mind. Above all, realise that Duping is a shifting game of negotiation. The better you get at it, the more you get!

Hopefully, after reading the above, you'll understand that, with some well-honed Bastardly negotiation skills, you have tremendous possibilities for getting everything that you want from a woman as long as she is completely infatuated with you and she can afford to spend this amount of money.

Look after your lies

Lying, as you now know, is a key part of the Complete Bastard's Duping strategy. But being exposed as a liar can see you shift from 'hero' to 'zero' in the eyes of a woman within a matter of seconds. For that reason, it is vital to lie and get away with it. Knowing how to lie and how to avoid showing yourself up as a liar are key skills to learn. Luckily, I am about to reveal to you some simple ways to make sure the lies that you tell don't reveal your duplicitous ways:

Control your body: Make lots of eye contact, be animated with your facial expressions – not limited and stiff – and use lots of wide-sweeping arm and hand gestures to show that you're really a passionate truth teller. Nervously touching your face, throat and/or neck with rapid hand movements is a sure-fire signal of lying. Also, face your accuser head on – turning your head or body away from her is a sign that you're uncomfortable and have something to hide. Nothing exposes a liar faster than his coming over as a shuffling, clenching, bag of anxiety whose eyes never leave his feet.

Sync your emotions: An effective liar knows that he must get the timing and duration of his physical gestures in tandem with his emotions. Imagine you're given a gift by a friend. You absolutely hate it, but a good liar will learn to smile, look happy and say, 'I love it!' all in one smooth, synchronized action. Poor liars will pause between the verbal element and the facial gesture, exposing themselves as ungrateful, lying fiends. Even worse – they may inadvertently frown while still saying, 'I love it!' – making it even more obvious that the gift is soon destined for the charity shop. It's vital to make sure that what you want to say is qualified with a genuine expression of positive emotions.

React with reason: A guilty person, when challenged, gets defensive, whereas an innocent person will often go on the offensive. So, next time you're confronted about cheating, boldly counter her as best you can, i.e.: 'How can I have been cheating on you?! I was with Steve that evening. You're just being paranoid!' As long as you have an alibi or a reasonable story to defend yourself, stick with it and weather your accuser's storm of questions.

Bluff the bluffer: Often someone who thinks they know you well will try and catch you out by saying something like: 'I know when you're lying – I can tell by your face.' This is guff and just a desperate attempt at trying to catch you when they have absolutely no evidence against you at all. A simple shrug and a, 'Well, if you did know me at all well, you'll know I'm telling the truth,' will put that interrogator on their back foot.

Pander to pauses: Liars usually hate uncomfortable pauses where they're made to squirm and so try to fill them with unnatural and unnecessary waffle. An effective liar will keep his cool, embrace the silence and face her with confidence. Ideally, you should be looking at her directly, palms outspread and open to her (another sign of honesty) with an expression on your face which tells her that you think she may be losing her sanity to accuse you of such 'ridiculous crimes'.

Watch your words: The words you say and the way that you say them should not differ from your regular style of speech. People who are lying often mumble their words and speak in a monotonous tone, muddling up the structure of his sentences. Liars also often repeat their accusers' exact words when phrasing a response and their speech will be more formal, avoiding contractions. For example, take Bill Clinton's famous, 'I did **not** have sexual relations with that woman'. If he was a better liar, he'd have simply shrugged his shoulders, shaken his head and said, 'I didn't do it.'

Check your cheating

There are a myriad of ways of getting caught cheating. This section will point them out to you and provide you with some common sense help to avoid this fate. You will go on to see how every aspect of your life – from the technology you use, to subtle changes in your lifestyle – can have a dramatic impact on alerting those who are infatuated with you to your hidden dark side. Only by taking control of your cheating and being vigilant to your potential pitfalls, will you keep your status as the Complete Bastard – and one who gets away with it all.

Beating the technology trap

One of the most common ways to get caught at cheating at online and/or offline dating is through the technologies that you use every day. There are two main ones to be careful of: your **computer** and your **phone.**

According to the Oxford University Internet Unit, a UK research team who study how people behave online, 20% of all people read their partner's email and text messages, while 13% check their partner's browsing history. And these statistics are for 'normal' people – a Complete Bastard is going to find himself under much closer scrutiny than most.

You know the potential fun to be had from online dating – and so do the women that you've met online. You flirt and Juggle. Maybe they do too. So, when you get into a relationship, any sign that you're spending more and more time online will look highly suspicious. Here are some ways of trying to hide your tracks online and making sure your computer doesn't get you caught:

- Make sure your surfing history is disabled so that she can't tell which sites you've been on.

- Ensure your email accounts are password protected and never used 'saved' passwords that allow your accounts to be accessed by any user on your computer.

- Don't re-activate your old dating site profile if the pair of you have agreed to take them down. Very few women will be so naive as to never check if your profile is active or not.

- Avoid placing new profiles on other popular sites that show your pictures as she could very well check these as well.

- If you have a particular 'type' and you see a girl on a site who seems to be 'too good to be true', then beware. It might be the woman in your life (or a friend of hers – see the section on 'Wing Women' below) laying some bait in order to try and entrap you.

- Avoid unusual, sneaky late-nights staying up alone at the computer, 'Just looking at holidays for us, darling'. She will guess you are up to something.

- Don't go sneaking online at home when she is around. If she spies you constantly closing your browser whenever she enters the room, she'll quickly figure out that something is up.

- Don't email her from somewhere you're not meant to be. It's easy to determine the location where an email was sent from by checking IP addresses.

- Set up your computer so that it does not accept 'cookies'. Even if your history is disabled, it's still possible for a sneaky snoop to check on what sites you've been to by checking what 'cookies' you've collected.

- Have a good anti-virus program running on your computer in case she is using any key-logging software.

One major problem with being overly secretive with your computer by clearing your history and passwords and by password protecting it is that your very secrecy could start to arouse her suspicions. After all, why go to all of this trouble if you have nothing to hide?

It's a tough problem to solve, but here are some sneaky solutions. One option is to go to the following site:

www.mojopac.com

By downloading the software, it allows you to turn any hard drive or Flash memory device – even an iPod – into a replica of a PC. Armed with this cunning little device, you will be able to do all of your Bastardly Business on the MojoPac drive, leaving your main computer completely free of any incriminating evidence.

Alternatively, Internet Explorer 8 comes with a feature that is a godsend for the Complete Bastard. It allows you to open what they call an 'InPrivate Browsing window'. While using the browser in this mode, no records of your online activities are kept.

If you need to save files, ideally keep them online rather than on your own PC. If you have to keep the files on your own PC, save them with a very bland file name and then save them somewhere deep within the recesses of your hard drive where no one ever looks, such as in your Windows folder.

An even more potentially incriminating piece of technology, unless you take great care, is your mobile phone. Receiving the wrong phone call or wrong text message from the wrong person at the wrong time is one of the fastest ways for a cheat to find himself busted.

Don't think that taking phone calls out of the room or not taking certain calls in her presence are going to solve the problem either – such actions will simply arouse suspicion still further. You need to ensure that your phone trail is carefully managed to show her that your social life – bar your male friends – is empty. Here are a few handy hints for keeping your phone free of accusation:

- Delete all incriminating sent and received text messages as soon as they are read.

- Regularly delete your call history.

- Store girls numbers under male or business-related pseudonyms.

- Put your ringtone on vibrate and deactivate the ringtone, so that any incoming calls or text messages are received unnoticed.

Despite taking all of the precautions above, your mobile is still always going to put you at great risk of discovery if you are living together with one woman and cheating on her with others.

One potential solution is to have a second, secret phone to use just for your naughty, cheating business and only ever give out this number to the other women in your life. You better make sure that you keep it well hidden though because, if your main partner ever discovers it, you're dumped.

Beating your habits

The other area of your life that needs Complete Bastard vigilance is your everyday general habits. This is the set of behaviours that include your appearance, your routine, and your personality. Any sudden or drastic change in any of these aspects of your life will arouse deep suspicion and threaten your capture as a cad. Once again, the secret to success here is planning well in advance. Before you start getting close to one particular woman, you should plan your lifestyle around your eventual Duping of her.

Is your future goal to move in with a rich chick so that she looks after your every whim and need, but you find monogamy to be such a bore that you know that you'll want to fool around from time to time? The solution here is to tell her that every Thursday is 'Boys Night Out' with your old friends from school – always has been and always will be. This allows you at least one night a week when you can fool around without arousing too many suspicions.

In addition to this general rule about introducing any new woman to your Dupe-Friendly lifestyle, there are a number of other areas you should be particularly careful of:

Hiding house habits
Given the choice, a Complete Bastard will always play his games away rather than at home. If it's a choice between going back to her place or yours, then always try to make it hers. One advantage of this is that you will be drinking her drink and eating her food rather than vice versa, and another is that she gets to clean up the mess after you've gone.

The main advantage of playing away though is that there is no chance of there being any evidence left in your apartment should you invite another girl over to your place. Women have keener senses than men generally and just the smallest pieces of evidence left in your apartment can give you away as the dastardly cheater that you are. Little things can be big mistakes – a lone blonde hair left on your pillow when your main girlfriend is a brunette, lipstick smudges on a hurriedly washed-up wine glass, the faint lingering smell of perfume in your bathroom, a used condom left in the garbage can – any one of these minor discoveries is enough to unravel all the best-laid plans of mice and Bastards.

If you have no choice but to bring a girl back to your apartment, you must always be fastidious when cleaning up after she's gone. This means tidying up and washing all your bed linen. Also remove all of your garbage to somewhere where it can't be connected with you in case an already suspicious woman decides to go through your dumpster.

Minding your mail
Perhaps the age of writing love-letters is all but behind us. However, this isn't the paper trail that will get you caught (unless you're **really** careless). In today's modern

age, data such as your spending patterns and your whereabouts can provide just the right information to entrap you.

Your bank and credit card statements can lay your Bastardly life open to anyone who sets their eyes on them. From details of gifts you have bought for people, restaurants you have taken them to, locations where you used ATMs where you weren't supposed to be, to showing that you have a healthy bank balance while claiming to be broke, the evidence that can be found here is usually highly incriminating.

Make sure also that you pay any parking tickets received for illegally parking in a place you shouldn't have been or else it's not just the law that you'll be in trouble with.

The bottom line is that you should never leave your mail lying around where she can read it. If you are living with a woman, for total security get yourself a mailbox and have all your mail delivered there. Shred or burn as much of your mail as possible once you have read it and carefully hide anything you need to keep well away from prying eyes.

Covering your car

The Complete Bastard who's living with a woman while spreading his wild oats around will begin to value his car as the means for getting him out of his neighbourhood and into the arms of other women. But your car can get you caught. So watch out for these tell-tale signs:

- You've just done the dirty with a six-foot stunner and your steady girlfriend gets suspicious as to why the passenger seat in the car has been moved back and is not in the usual position.

- Don't leave any evidence in your glove compartment.

- Is there 'mysterious' extra mileage on the car? If so, make sure that you have an excuse ready.

- As with your home, ensure that there is no trace of any 'female forensics' left inside.

Watching your wallet

It's the easiest thing in the world to do – after paying for a romantic dinner for two, you scoop up the change and the receipt together and put it in your wallet. Big mistake. If she suspects you of cheating, your wallet is going to be one of the first places she will look in order to try and gather some evidence of your wrong-doings. So make sure that you don't keep any unnecessary paperwork such as receipts, business cards, scribbled-down phone numbers and so on, in your wallet or pockets.

And as for keeping a spare condom about your person in case of emergencies – are you completely insane?!

Breaking your routine

A change in your daily routine can sound internal alarm bells for any woman who thinks she's the person you've scheduled your every waking hour around. And you've given her good reason to think this in the early stages of your Wooing, as you Flooded her with phone calls and dates.

A sudden loss of interest in her and you'll soon start wanting to find new faces to spend your time and money on. A change in your routine can be a signal that you are doing just that.

The excuse that you're 'working long hours' needs to be carefully backed up with evidence that proves you were at your workplace and not somewhere else. This is where a Wing Man (see later in this chapter) becomes a very valuable ally to you. He can provide you with an alibi whenever you desperately need one.

Ideally you will have prepared for the inevitability of your cooling interest by building in some free time for your other activities into the relationship right from the start. If not, then at least try to change your routine slowly and gradually over time so that it is less noticeable.

Masking your movements

You're locked in a passionate embrace with a gorgeous girl in the dark corner of a secluded bar. As you disentangle your body from hers, you look up. Glowering above you is the woman with whom you have supposedly been having a monogamous and loving relationship with for the past six months.

The classic scene in countless movies and TV shows, this is as bad as it gets when it comes to being discovered as a cheater. No matter how much of a Complete Bastard you are, there are no tricks available to you to use that will extricate yourself from this mess. You've just been caught red-handed and exposed as a cheater.

For this reason, you need to take great care when it comes to choosing the location for your philandering. The smaller the city you live in, the harder this exercise becomes. In a large city, it's quite easy to agree to meet your dates in areas that your regular partner would have no reason to ever visit, but in smaller towns and cities, this is probably not an option.

You need to learn the type of places that your regular partner would never want to visit and choose these as the location for your dates. Maybe your partner hates Chinese food, or would never set foot in a Sports Bar. These are then good venues for your dalliances. Never take a date to one of your partner's favourite places and avoid the parts of the city where she has reason to go to quite often.

Adapting your appearance

You now know the importance of looking good all the time as an integral part of your Bastardly seduction routine, but when you get into a relationship, it's natural to relax with how dress and behave, returning to become the lazy slob that is your natural character – there simply isn't the need to dress to impress her every day and night. So what happens when you meet someone else and you start dressing for attention again? You immediately arouse suspicion in the very person who wonders why you are dressing up for going out and not for her. So watch out that you don't give out these tell-tale signs:

- Suddenly taking an unusual interest in your physical appearance for 'unknown reasons'.

- Joining a gym, losing weight, visiting tanning salons, and so on.

- Buying and wearing stylish new clothes, getting a new haircut, wearing cologne more often.

The Complete Bastard prides himself on always looking good, but excessive buying of new and different clothes again shows you as dressing for someone else.

The way to avoid any suspicions in this area is to never stop looking your best in the first place. Not only will it keep the main woman in your life very happy, but it will also avoid her suspecting that you are up to anything. It also increases your chances of randomly hooking up with new women when you are out and about that you wouldn't otherwise have attracted if you had gone back to your slovenly pre-Bastard ways.

Managing mood swings

You may not even notice it at the time, but if there's a new woman on your mind, your thoughts will be on her and not the woman that you're currently dating. You'll not want to be distracted in your pursuit of her, but with another women vying for your affections, watch out that your daydreaming doesn't get you caught. Be wary of and try to curb:

- An unexplained indifference or aloofness in the relationship.

- Snappiness and irritability with your long-term partner.

- Giving your partner less affection and/or sex.

- Asking her detailed questions about her routine (so that you can find time to cheat on her while she's away).

- Bringing her flowers and 'guilt' gifts 'for no reason' when it's out of character for you to do so.

If the above list shows you just how much hard work it is to not get caught cheating, I make no apologies. This is why I said at the start of this chapter that, if you are planning on getting very close to one woman to go for the 'Big Dupe' on her, then you will probably have to forego the pleasures of having multiple partners unless you have the attention to detail of a brain surgeon. Only you can decide whether it's worth it and how good your chances are going to be for getting away with it.

Cunning at Conniving

As stated earlier, conniving is when you collude with another to further your potential as a Complete Bastard and to avoid getting caught while behaving as one. The Complete Bastard is a social animal and he is fully aware that there are those who can help and those who will hinder his Bastard deceits. In the following section, you'll meet an ally (the Wing Man) and an adversary (the Wing Woman). Know how to behave around them both.

Use your Wing Man wisely

Your best friend (or 'Wing Man' as he is known among parts of the seduction community) can be a powerful ally. Firstly, with regard to offline dating, hitting bars and clubs alone can be seen as suspicious or sleazy. Hanging out with a friend though is natural, should give you more confidence when you're part of a pair and can also make you appear more attractive to women as it makes you look more popular when you are seen to have a great friend around you. Also, how many women go to clubs alone? Very few. So having a Wing Man means that you can both chat up a couple of girls and both make your moves. You only need your Wing Man there until you've both scored. After that, you're back to being a Solo Bastard.

Probably the best use of a good Wing Man though is that he can provide you with an alibi. This is particularly useful to have once you are quite advanced in a relationship with one particular woman, are living with her and spending almost every night with her. Once you are sharing your life with one woman in this way, it can become quite difficult to 'escape' from her from time to time in order to continue with your Bastardly Agenda.

The Wing Man is a godsend in this situation as he gives you an excuse to get away from her, as in, 'I'll be back late tonight, darling, because I'm going round to Simon's place to watch the football.' You need to make sure that your Wing Man is always kept informed about what lies you have involved him in so that he can always corroborate any stories if she gets suspicious and tries to test him.

Conniving can also work with online dating. Unless you trust your Wing Man completely, it's never a good idea to tell him what girls you are flirting with online. This is, sadly, because he may pull a fast one and get in touch with the girl himself and disrupt your little game play. But you can let him into the game in part. There are thousands of girls online – someone for every man's tastes – so there's no reason for you and him to squabble over girls. Be upfront with each other and enjoy the rich pickings.

The advantage of involving your Wing Man in your online dating activities is that he can be a handy snoop for you. Remember the 'cyber crimes' I listed back in chapter eight? Well, let's take a situation where you have been flirting online with a girl, but you suspect her to be a Juggler. You like her so, exposing her at this stage as a Juggler means: a) you know where you stand; b) you can adjust your Duping strategy to Woo her, and; c) you can think about Dumping her if need be. It's time to get your Wing Man involved.

Wing Man begins flirting online with the girl. He sends her sweet emails and tries to win her attention. Sure, she just may not be interested in Wing Man anyway, but if she enjoys the attentions of most guys who come onto her, you'll soon out her as a Juggler. A delicious tactic that I love to use is when I confront a girl about such a situation. Apart from being hilarious to watch them squirm, you'll often find that, if they do like you, they'll stop their Juggling act and concentrate all of their attention upon you and you alone. So never think all is lost – you've only discovered a female version of yourself, after all!

Watch out for 'Wing Women'

Where men have their close friends and associates in the dating game, women have theirs too. In many ways, women have a far easier task recruiting a loyal friend who will help her do her Duping. This is because women tend to be on guard from sinister or threatening male behaviour. There is something of the 'we women must stick together' ethos at work here. Women tend to be more jealous creatures than men as well, and so you might find that your girl's best friend might try to ruin your relationship with her simply to bring your girl back down to her singleton level.

Vigilance against Wing Women is paramount. Note however: though called 'Wing Women', in some cases this could be a male friend who helps her to catch you. Here are a couple of scenarios to look out for:

- A girl you are flirting with online thinks you might be a player. So, she gets her best friend – also a member of the dating site – to write you a message and flirt with you, testing to see whether you are really exclusive or not. You fall for it and you're instantly 'Deleted' by both of them.

- You've been exaggerating again in your messages to a woman. She's suspicious and gets one of her friends to check that you do work for company X. When it's found out that you don't, that's two women you won't be dating!

- The Wing Woman agrees to ask another friend of hers – someone who you don't know at all – to follow you when you head off to your regular 'Boys Night Out' session to see if you really are partying with boys – or girls.

Although you might loathe the scheming witch of a friend, never reveal this fact to either your girl or her friend as it will force your girl to take sides. And there's a good chance that she will take the side of her friend over you.

Instead, you need to use your Wooing skills on the friend too – not to such an extent that your own girl will think that you're flirting with her friend, but just enough so that the friend also comes to think of you as a really great guy. If the friend comes to like you, and you become a good (platonic) friend of hers too, she will less likely want to conspire against you if asked.

Final words

Through reading this chapter, you should now have an excellent understanding of exactly what you can get from women by Duping them, how to put a Dupe into practice, and finally how to get away with it so that you can carry on Duping her (and other women) over and over again.

Duping is a lot more than simply manipulating others. Duping and getting away with it will boost your confidence still further, will furnish you with a roguish charm, and put you firmly in control of all that you can achieve in life. This goes far beyond success at seduction. You'll also see radical improvements in your career, lifestyle and social life too.

So, again I implore you: delight in Duping and watch your wildest dreams come true!

Purging Sin

When the Complete Bastard naughtily sneaks a chick back to his partner's place, he has more than his cheating ways to hide.

Advice is easier to give than follow. One tale I must tell you about occurred a little while back. I was in a steady relationship with a lovely, eminent lawyer's daughter called Hermione. Happiness is a movable feast though, and I still found myself bursting to be with other women. So, like a bee who seeks pollen, I couldn't stop myself making a return to my old Bastardly ways.

I found the adorable 'Lovely_Lisa' on a dating site. Obviously my girlfriend was under the assumption that I'd removed myself from all sites. However, unknown to her, I'd set up a number of fake profiles which allowed me to lurk on sites whilst evading capture. I'd made a pact with my Inner Bastard that, if I was going to allow myself the risky pleasure of ruining a perfectly good relationship, I would only use internet cafes and never be so foolish as to store my surfing trail on my laptop or our shared computer at home.

'Lovely_Lisa' and I decided on an afternoon date. If it went badly, I'd have the evening free and, more importantly, my girlfriend was off on a shopping spree with her friends and would be gone until early evening. This Complete Bastard, I figured, was entitled to a little flagrant consuming for himself.

So there I was, in 'The Riverside' wine bar, flirting like a Complete Bastard with my online date. 'Lovely_Lisa' sank a few glasses of fine wine and, because it was on her credit card, I felt obliged to quaff a few myself. Soon we found ourselves in an amorous embrace inside the bar. The filthy minx was angling to come back to my place to finish off our unfinished business. Her apartment, after all, was the other side of the city, she argued.

Against my better judgement and due to the fact my dick was winning the spat with my brain over the shameful fact that I hadn't had a fresh lay for weeks, I thought that it was worth the risk. And so I decided to sneak 'Lovely_Lisa' back to my – or to be more accurate, my girlfriend's – place. This was high risk stuff indeed. I lived with my perk-a-plenty long term girlfriend in her apartment. As Papa Bastard would say, 'Never piss on your own doorstep, for when things cock up, you may find yourself sleeping on it.' Bah! What did he know?

I had lied to 'Lovely_Lisa' that I was house-sitting for my sister for a few weeks. That would explain all the girlie stuff that was around our place when she arrived there. I also texted my best mate, Steve, who was instructed to call me after a few hours with a 'something's come up at work' excuse. Thereby, I could shift 'Lovely_ Lisa' out in good time before my girlfriend returned from her shopping trip.

'Lovely_Lisa' and I arrived home. Passions quickly inflamed as we kissed and held one another in lustful embrace, before cavorting around in the lewdest of fashions. The girl was one easy pull and, in no time, I had had my wicked fill of this tasty chick.

We sat tired and naked on the sofa. She was running her fingers through my hair and asking me when I'd like to see her again. Just as I was fumbling for an answer, Steve rang on my mobile. A good Wing Man is worth his weight in gold and, in no time, 'Lovely_Lisa' was dressed and on the bus home. It was now time to ensure that no evidence was left behind that could possibly catch me out as a cheat.

I had ample time – my girlfriend wasn't due back for hours yet. But a Complete Bastard is a Thorough Bastard. I began deleting all the text messages from 'Lovely_ Lisa', removing the unused condoms from my wallet, and even shredded an ATM slip from a bank I'd used around the corner from 'The Riverside'. It may seem paranoid, but Duping is all in the detail.

Suddenly, out of the window, I saw my girlfriend's car pulling up. What the hell was she doing back?! She was well early. And if I didn't hurry this clean up operation, the early bird would catch this Bastardly worm!

I swiftly plumped up the cushions on the sofa, ran with half-full wine glasses to the kitchen and gave them a quick rinse. (I even made sure to check for lipstick marks on the rims). I ran to the bedroom and threw on a fresh t-shirt. The old one smelt alarmingly of sweat and, though I did check, could still have had a few stray strands of blonde hair on it. With no point in taking chances and my girlfriend a brunette, I shoved the t-shirt to the bottom of the laundry basket.

I ran back into the room and looked around. Everything looked to be in order. You would never have known there had been a lustful gambol here but thirty minutes earlier. And then I spotted it...

In a moment of passion with 'Lovely_Lisa', I'd dropped a used condom on the floor. There it lay, glistening with pure menace. And worse still – I could hear the key in the lock now turning. I sprang upon the item, seizing the gloopy latex bag. My brain was now reduced to jelly with panic as I searched everywhere for a quick hiding place to put it. Seeing none, I scurried to the window. Thrusting it open, I lobbed the sperm parcel into the air and sent a thousand spent Baby Bastards heavenwards.

Just in time, for I could hear my girlfriend was now inside the apartment.

'Hi, darling. I'm back early, I know. How's your day been?'

I swung around to face her, instantly relaxing my tense body language into a carefree shrug and a smile.

'Oh, quiet,' I said brightly. 'Fancy a meal out tonight? I'm famished.'

My girl looked hot in her winter coat and she had a flushed face. I almost got a pang of Unbastardly remorse for the act I'd just committed behind her back. Almost.

'Your treat or mine?'

Ah, she was a joker this one.

'I think it's your turn, isn't it?' I said. (Then again, wasn't it always!)

* * *

The next morning, my girlfriend left for work. I figured I'd have another few hours in bed, then I'd get up, read the papers, do a little writing, and maybe shout Steve a beer at the bar later for his loyal work as my alibi in the 'Lovely_Lisa' fiasco. My thoughts of another lazy day to add to all the other lazy days a Complete Bastard enjoys were broken by Hermione's scream.

'Oh-mi-god! Baby! Come quick! It's horrible!'

I sprang out of bed, threw on some clothes, and ran out down to the street below. It was a chilly January morning and there stood my girlfriend, slipping on a pair of pink rubber gloves, with a dinner fork clutched in one hand. I looked at her puzzled and could see that she was very upset.

'Bastards!' she screamed, looking straight at me. 'Complete bastards!'

I was speechless. Did she know? Surely not! How on earth did she catch me?

She walked over to the car, dejected, and started hacking with at the hood of her with the fork. I was stunned by this. Here she was exposing me as a love-rat and vandalising her own BMW to avenge me?! It was only as I peered a little more that I saw what she was doing.

'How could they be so **disgusting**!' she wailed.

Whereupon she starting using the fork to chisel off an object stuck to her car. With a horror that almost chewed the very marrow of my bones, I recognised the object instantly. She was hacking away with wilful frenzy at my used condom from yesterday!

It had obviously landed on her car after I'd tossed it out the window and frozen solid overnight. My poor girlfriend was unwittingly destroying the only piece of evidence that I'd not properly taken care of. She, however, innocently assumed that some local gang of jokers had played some heartless prank on her.

As she scraped and cursed in anger, I turned and left her to it.

'I'm just going back to bed, darling. Any chance you could bring me a coffee when you're done?'

– 16 –
Dealing with Dumping

Dating means dumping

Introducing a shocking fact: the more successful you get at dating, the more frequently you'll be dumping. And here's another startling piece of information: ending relationships is about to become fun.

If both of these statements make you feel out of your comfort zone, then you better start rewiring your brain to cope – because what you have just read are two hugely significant truths which you must accept.

The Complete Bastard, who prides himself on having multiple sexual partners, all attractive and loaded with perks, also knows that most, if not all, of his sexual relationships are temporary. As a Duper, he is committing acts of deceit on an almost daily basis, manipulating women to get out of them what he wants for selfish gain. His deceitfulness is a necessity for him to get away with it all. One key reason why the Complete Bastard evades capture is that **he** is the one to make the decision as to when to dump a partner or lover, not **her**.

Dumping – the Complete Bastard way – is the act of terminating relationships by knowing when to end them, how to end them, and to minimise the loss of perks in the process. It's a vital Bastard skill.

This chapter will show you how to positively relish dumping your dates, plus how to put the *enfant terrible* back into the sober adult world of emotional breakups. If that sounds a little reckless, then realise this: without mastering the art of dumping, you will:

- Always be a loser in love and the heartbroken victim in every relationship you have.

- Always give the control for your relationships ending to the women in your life.

- Find yourself too scared to end relationships and often be trapped in them.

- Learn that dumping is part of a long-term strategy that will preserve your Complete Bastard sanity, while ensuring that you keep the perks rolling in.

- Not make it as a Complete Bastard and finish your journey on the Path to Bastardom.

Never before in the history of love and relationships has a book actually advised you to go out and dump for such pleasurable gain.

You dump her

Everyone knows that dumping is difficult. It is a highly charged and emotional experience for both parties. But it is important for the aspiring Complete Bastard to learn how to end a relationship in the most effective way while preserving any of the perks that he has managed to get his hands on.

The fact that the Complete Bastard is able to dump – and to dump with aplomb – may astound you. It is tempting to conclude that it must be something dark and twisted in a Complete Bastard's misanthropic character that leads to this lack of integrity and callous attitude. Yet the explanation is more logical science than black art. It is **because** the Complete Bastard has developed the confidence and the commitment to dump that he is so brutal in his craft.

Let's look at confidence and commitment in turn and understand that it is imperative to get you into the mindset of a devoted dumper in order to carry out what is otherwise not an easy exercise to do.

Gaining the confidence to dump

Much of what you learned in chapter three is also applicable to becoming a successful dumper – the same techniques apply. First, it's essential to Man Up – there are no two ways around it. Dumping means finding your Inner Bastard and having the mettle to take control of your relationships. As you come to have multiple sexual and perk partners, that means dumping as you go along.

Another confidence booster will come from just behaving as a Complete Bastard leading up to the dumping stage. If you are reading this book from cover to cover and have yet to embark on your Path to Bastardom, the idea of casually dumping someone with no regrets might seem to be way outside your comfort zone. However, remember that you have a long way to go before you reach the dumping stage. You will find your confidence growing of its own accord as you successfully complete each stage of the journey and your success starts exceeding your wildest dreams.

The dumping stage is also a time to dispel a few inner demons. One of the main reasons why so many Wimp Chimps are petrified of the thought of dumping is the fear that, 'I'll never find anyone else as good as her again.' Hopefully, by now, you will already have realized that the Complete Bastard has little to fear in this regard. Most of the times when you will be dumping a girl, it will be because you have already found someone better.

So if you have any fears that you don't have the pluck for the cold-hearted dump just yet, then leave the rest of this chapter until you're ready for the final test. Go find your Inner Bastard first and make sure you have the confidence to dump.

Finding the commitment to dump

The Complete Bastard has a dilemma: he has already decided to play the field and assemble a harem of women that he can use for sex. He is also using women for other reasons (money, a home, enriched lifestyle, advanced career, and so on). The commitment to dump has added complications, therefore.

The key difference between someone who dumps and someone who is dumped, is that the dumper is the one who has made the decision to break the relationship. For each woman you become involved with, you need to ask yourself these questions: 'Does this woman have the qualities and characteristics that I seek?' Plus, 'What are the perks that I gain by staying with her?' Understanding what these qualities, characteristics and perks are, is a critical step. You require a measured overview of them to let you judge the pros and cons of staying in a relationship with a woman or getting out of it.

Dumping, for the Complete Bastard, is more of a tactical decision than a heartfelt one – there is a colder, more rational, decision-making process and action at play. Committing to dump, means keeping your cool emotionally. One of the most important aspects of being able to dump without the emotion that goes with breaking up is to circumvent the drama of dumping.

Dumping is rarely a 'quick chat and it's over' scenario. There are many cases of unhappy relationships that ended for a while before the couple got back together again. In some relationships, such situations can happen over and over again, like a rollercoaster, where the 'theatre' of breaking up is almost part of the thrill of the ride. I call this phenomenon 'Dumping Turbulence'. It is a condition that affects men and woman who are too blinkered and emotionally stunted to realise that their relationship is unhealthy, resistant to changing for the better, and long past its Dump Date.

Let it be stated: the Complete Bastard never stays in relationships that are past their Dump Date or prone to Dumping Turbulence because:

- All negative relationships drain the Complete Bastard of confidence, and confidence is necessary to feed his Inner Bastard.

- Knowing when to get out of a relationship is a sign that you understand that the relationship is holding you back from attaining your goals as an individual. Chances are it is also doing the same for your partner.

- The Complete Bastard will not return to an old relationship because he knows his ability to find and seduce new women is legendary.

- The Complete Bastard will remain committed to his decision to dump in a relationship and has the confidence to carry out the act of dumping with cutthroat relish.

You should now be starting to see that dumping doesn't have to be such a highly emotional and dramatic affair. The Complete Bastard is able to take full control of his emotions and rationalise why dumping happens and why it is inevitable.

Why dump her?

This book has stated time and time again that the Complete Bastard seeks far more than just sex from women. The Complete Bastard is all about perks and he is a fervent believer in the fact that seducing many women is his best route to getting these perks.

When the issue of dumping arises, Naïve Bastards may argue that a key theme of the Path to Bastardom is that the Complete Bastard nurtures his network of dates and is careful not to get caught by his many women. He keeps all of them because they are precious resources. However, the reality is that, like running a business with staff, sometimes a few heads must roll to keep the greater wheels of efficiency turning.

You might want to keep as many hot women in your harem as possible, yet there's no Bastardly way around the fact that you only have 24 hours in one day. There are physical and mental limits as to how many women you can cheat on at the same time. As you start to take advantage of your newfound Complete Bastard seduction skills, you may very well want to use them to score as much sex with as many women as you possibly can. Go ahead – there's nothing wrong with that.

However, as you get more proficient going about your Bastardly business and see the advantages of Duping, chances are that you will be Juggling more women than you can handle. You'll start to realize that the **quality** of women can bring you greater perks than the **quantity**. This in turn means that some of the less useful and interesting members of your little gang are probably going to have to go as you concentrate on the Bigger Better Deals.

A cunning Complete Bastard also advocates that a relationship which may be less than perfect – may be one that is not even enjoyable – should still be maintained as long as there are perks for the picking. However, this theory does fall down in certain circumstances with certain women types. Here are a few such characters to look out for on the 'Must Dump' hitlist. They are so destructive to the motivation and schemes of the Complete Bastard that they must be gotten rid of – and quick:

She's for sex only

Both of you are interested in a short, intense period of fornicating fun and not much else. The reason why you want to dump in this situation is relatively straightforward: you see no mileage in a relationship, physically you are bored of her now, the seduction (or chase) has been won, and there are no perks (other than sex) that you can get from her. More importantly, she is beginning to show a deeper interest in you and you are keen to avoid being lumbered with a girl who is beginning to exhibit some avoidable personality traits (see chapter five, 'The Four Women Types')

She's not your type

Sometimes, despite all your best efforts and seduction techniques, you just don't click with someone. Maybe she has an annoying habit or two. Maybe her opinions rile you so much that you now want to smash her collection of antique teapots with a polo mallet. Maybe the way she styles her hair makes you want to plunge a breadknife into your eyeball, then set fire to your manhood. Whatever the reason, when two people have a personality clash, it can be painful to endure and impossible to salvage anything good from staying together. This is particularly true in relationships which are in their very early stages (usually under one month). The girl is driving you mad and it's time to make a fast exit. Get out fast before she gets even more annoying and dangerous to your health (see 'She's psychotic!' below).

She's psychotic!

In chapter five, 'Understanding Women', we looked at the Four Types of Women framework. Each type had her good points, but there was also a section within each of their profiles forewarning of potential psychoses that lurked inside these creatures. From being over-needy, through having violent mood-swings, to being a complete bunny boiler, the Complete Bastard always has his radar switched on to detect such personality disorders. For any guy who has encountered a deranged loony lover, the results can be highly unpleasant – having your clothes cut up, your car vandalised, physical harm inflicted, malicious rumours spread to friends, family and work colleagues, and worse – it's all nasty stuff. Keep your own sanity and avoid psycho women at all costs.

She's blowing your cover

You've spent weeks, maybe months, nurturing this woman, but despite all of your best efforts at hiding your sneaky activities (see chapter fifteen, 'Checking your cheating), she's become suspicious that you are a cheat. The signs are there after all – you're spending a lot more time on the computer and she's sure she saw your profile on a dating site. You covet your phone like it's a kidney, and have started taking calls out of her earshot. She's been seeing a lot less of you since you started regularly taking those 'out-of-town business trips', and you seem to be buying lots of new clothes and generally becoming less of a lazy slob. She's on to you and could be close to blowing your cover as a Complete Bastard. It's now time to take control and dump or be dumped.

She has no perks

There are two types to avoid here. The first is the woman whom you've realised has little to offer you in terms of real perks. She's certainly beautiful, but she lives in a hovel, has a lowly salary and believes that all men should pay their own way. There are no exotic holidays to look forward to and her social network is her cat. This well is truly dry and it's time to seek pastures new.

The second type is the woman who you've bled dry already. She is beginning to tire and has become suspicious of the fact that you're more interested in the contents of her bank account than the contents of her bra. She is beginning to realise that you're not quite the charmer she first met and is starting to think she's being taken for a ride. It's time for you to ride out of town before things get nasty and she invoices you.

She's worse than you!

There are some women out there who may quickly start to exhibit many of the behaviours more associated with the Complete Bastard. These include gold diggers or women who have made a career out of sapping men's minds and money for their own selfish gain. Two gold diggers in one relationship means bankruptcy for at least one of them. Don't let it be you – dump with ruthless vigour.

Look out also for the female dating game players. A good game player will know how to thwart and torture a Complete Bastard, never mind the average male. She will be cheating on you, constantly flirting with other men and is as perk-hungry as you are. She is an energy sapper and, quite frankly, the Smart Bastard will find easier and more malleable prey elsewhere.

She's wasting your time.

What is more frustrating than trying to arrange a date with a woman who is constantly cancelling on you or telling you that she has no free time? It's hardly the stuff of romance and a complete inconvenience to a Complete Bastard who finds himself unable to go about his own shady affairs due to this woman's busy schedule. Get your revenge by filling your own diary with anything else other than spending time with she who is best referred to as a 'diary demon'.

She's got kids

Another dating type who will make you compete for her time is the single mother.

Always a much pitied figure of society, don't be duped by this woman's artfulness at sucking you for everything she can get from you as well as trying to morph you into husband/father material. It's also a case of you versus the kids here. There can be only one winner – and it's not you. Single mothers can be the easiest of all women to dupe, but there are always her little ones to think about. What the kids say goes and no self-respecting mother will put you before her offspring, no matter how finely-honed your Complete Bastard skills are. You're way too much of a brat yourself to put up with the competition for long anyway and so either avoid the single mother or get set to dump her after the sex goes stale.

She's a Dump Dragon

Finally there is the mother of all dating evils and the ultimate 'Must Dump'. These are the Dump Dragons. For an illustration of this type, read the 'Dating Diary of a Complete Bastard' at the end of this chapter. It is a classic illustration of the type of women for whom no amount of wealth and other resources can compensate for their ability to drive even the most accomplished Complete Bastard to despair. These are heartless, dangerous women and should not be welcomed into any man's life under any circumstances.

How to Dump Her

Now that you know the types of women who you should dump and why you must rid yourself of them, it is time to learn **how** to dump them.

There are seven ways that you can dump, including the final technique (dumping by inducing hate), which, as you will read, is the absolute preserve of only the most composed Complete Bastard. Before we look at that approach though, let us go through some other ways to dump:

Dumping online: This is where you or the girl simply ceases communication while interacting online. It can happen at the first hurdle – i.e., she ignores your email message. Or, it could take place much deeper into your online bonding – perhaps after just a few or even many exchanges of messages. Either way, dumping at this stage can take the form of a polite 'no' via email to your advances and interest, or an immediate and bemusing severing of all virtual ties. This means she simply ignores you and isn't looking for you to do anything other than take the hint.

Dumping by ignoring: You want to remove an ill-fitting date from your social life; so what could be more Bastardly than completely body-swerving the issue and denying the situation completely? You owe this woman nothing and nothing is exactly what she will get in terms of an explanation as to why you have blocked her telephone number, won't answer her emails or text messages and have spread rumours that you have re-located to Brazil. A cold-hearted dumper's preserve is this one.

Dumping by SMS: This is viewed as one of the most callous ways to dump another. With only 160 characters with which to perform the evil deed, it is a clipped and cutting way to confront an issue that may be highly emotional and hurtful to the dumped individual. Often the sender does not expect or want a response and so the message tends to be frank and often brutal.

Dumping by telephone: This is better than receiving an SMS, but it still lacks the face-to-face confrontation that most dumpees demand and believe they deserve. Often it is easier to be bolder and more forthright over the telephone than during a face-to-face meeting. And, for many, they avoid having to endure and receive the bawling and begging for mercy that goes with being dumped. Finally, if the dumping isn't going as planned, there is always the option to hang up, move to a different technique or just ignore.

Dumping face-to-face: If you're a Right Honourable Bastard, then this is the method for you. You meet with her, tell her calmly that it is time for the pair of you to finish the relationship, giving her the reasons why it must be so, and then calmly leave it at that. Your conscience is (relatively) clear knowing that you've done the right thing in the right way, however the downside is that you will have to brave the ups and downs of the emotional rollercoaster that she'll make you ride with her during the process, possibly leaving you with a major guilt trip on your hands at the end of it.

Dumping by escalating arguments: It's a rare relationship that doesn't suffer from lover's tiffs, squabbles, tantrums, arguments and even screaming matches. The Clever Bastard who wants out of a relationship can use these natural potholes on the road to true love to his advantage through purposefully escalating the disagreements until one or both of you are so enraged that she either tells you to, 'Get out!' or you tell her, 'That's it – we're finished!'.

The plus side to this method is that she will usually think that she was the one responsible for the break up and so you will avoid her undying hatred and the possibilities of any retribution on her part. The downside though is that she will constantly be trying to get you back, which can come to be a tiresome irritation to you for weeks or months to come. Only you can decide whether this price is too high for coming out of the relationship still smelling of roses.

Dumping by inducing hate: This is the Complete Bastard's platinum dumping technique. Completely opposite in its effects to the strategy mentioned above, it's where you save yourself the hassle and time of having your victim go through the messy, 'But I still love you!' stage and move straight to having her hate your guts.

It starts off in the same way as the previous method, with your beginning to do things around her that are intentionally rude, annoying or designed to rouse her. As the Day of Dumping draws near, you continually up the frequency of such behaviour and, if you're feeling especially Bastardly, deliver her a revelation so despicable that she has but one option and that's to dump you first. Some examples could include telling her that you've been cheating on her or that you've spent all her savings at the casino (the truth that you actually spent it all on dating her best friend may actually kill her!)

The Complete Bastard methodology goes one step further here. If you really want to dump her (perhaps some vengeance is desired here as well as an exit strategy), then reveal to her that you are a Complete Bastard. Don't stop there – give her examples and instances of your despicable ways. Shock her into realising she has been sharing her life and body with the most loathed, contemptible, hideous, deceitful scum known to women.

Surely this is one step too far? Actually it's not. In the 'theatre' of dating and romance, the Complete Bastard is a controversial character, both dastardly and delicious. Where would love be without the cad to shake it up a little? With the swagger and confidence to be the Complete Bastard, your ego should swell and you should be ready to unleash the *coup d'état* of Bastardom – the revelation that you're a Complete Bastard and proud of it. Watch her shrivel like a worm in your shadow.

Warning: Use all the knowledge that is contained within the above technique wisely. It's an extreme method of dumping and should only be used by fully actualised Complete Bastards who are well prepared for the inevitable aftermath.

What to do if she dumps you

Learning to dump is one thing, but learning to survive being dumped is just as important for a Complete Bastard.

On your journey down the Path to Bastardom, chances are that you are going to stumble from time to time – it's all part and parcel of the learning process. Maybe you will overdo it when it comes to asking for perks, or maybe you will become careless at hiding the tracks of your cheating. If so, chances are that you are going to get dumped.

Sometimes even a Complete Bastard – one who has followed the instructions contained within this book to the letter – will be the victim of a dump. Women have their own goals and agendas from relationships – many of these are very different from the sneaky, perk-plucking, emotionally carefree goals of the Complete Bastard. And so, on occasion, the Complete Bastard receives a dumping. The difference is that he knows how to handle the pain of a break up and may even have orchestrated it so that the onus for a dead relationship was passed to his partner to clean up. This section will explain to you why you might get dumped and how to ensure you survive.

Why she might dump you

This book has provided you a blueprint for becoming the type of man that most women want from a partner. Fail to follow the instructions and you will be less than perfect for her, providing her with a good reason to dump you. In particular, beware the following:

Low value lover

Relationships are complex. There are fluctuations in the balance of liking each other, sexual attraction to one another and the decision-making power within the relationship. However, the measure of who is liked the most, is most sexually attractive and who tends to control the majority of decisions within the relationship is the one who is valued more highly by the other. And the one who is valued highest, holds the power to dump.

'Value' is a shifting resource. It moves within the terrain that is an emotional, sexual and loving relationship. Dumping is the moment when one person decides that their partner's value has reached 'below market value' and so terminating the relationship is the only option.

For the Complete Bastard who is both showman and strategist, losing value is not so much a threat as it is for other lesser men. The Complete Bastard is a high value lover. There is, however, one far greater threat to the Complete Bastard than being undervalued in the eyes of a woman. It is the threat of himself.

The 7 Deadly Sins of the Complete Bastard

Living life as a Complete Bastard can bring you the greatest of joys and change your fortunes like you could never before have imagined possible. A competent Complete Bastard will use his newfound knowledge and powers wisely and carefully. A Complacent Bastard will err from the Path of Bastardom. This latter path can easily end in nasty consequences. Here are the Seven Deadly Sins that can manifest themselves in a Complacent Bastard. Not only can these behaviours get you dumped, but they can also expose you as the Duper you are. Bastard, beware!

1. **Lust:** Your constant desire for more and more sexual partners.

2. **Gluttony:** You're acting spoilt by the riches she has bestowed on you.

3. **Greed:** Seeking too many more perks on top of those you've already received.

4. **Sloth:** Forgetting that perks have to be worked for and don't come to you by being lazy, or being sloppy at hiding the evidence of your duplicitous behaviour.

5. **Wrath:** Losing your temper when perks don't always come your way.

6. **Envy:** Coveting perks that another Complete Bastard has.

7. **Pride:** Over-confidence in believing that you now have her so infatuated you can do no wrong.

You've now learned what type of actions can get you dumped, but what can you do when you realize that it's now too late – when you've crossed the line and realize that the shit has hit the fan and you're about to receive a dumping?

Dodging the dump

This section offers a number of effective coping strategies for dodging the dump:

Dump her first

This is Complete Bastard coping strategy number one. You've been exposed; she knows your game. Now it's damage limitation time and it's time to walk. This is not a cowardly backdoor escape tactic at all. This is a mature, unemotional and adult course of action. You've dated and it didn't work out. It happens. The next phase is moving on, learning from your experience and realizing that the relationship was flawed all along.

Nothing destroys a Complete Bastard's mojo more than being in a negative or highly uncertain relationship. Such relationships suck your energies into avenues which are not conducive to happiness or gain. One of life's most important teachings is that we can't always live happily ever after and that things get messy from time to time, no matter how much we may try and prevent them.

Sometimes, however, you don't get that opportunity. Perhaps she takes you by surprise, there is a reason you never second-guessed, or she has uncovered something about you that you didn't realise. Whatever the reason, she may have dealt the dump before you.

Beg forgiveness

So, you've been caught and she knows you're nothing but a lousy lying, cheating, conniving son-of-a-bitch. Clearly, you didn't follow my advice on 'Getting away with it all' in chapter fifteen. And now look at what a fine mess you've gotten yourself into!

You are on the brink of losing a perk-packed relationship. Her feelings of infatuation have curdled to hurt and hatred towards you. She knows now that you've duped her all along and every perk she gave you out of love, now just feels like a dirty trick she fell for.

In this situation, things are usually looking pretty grim. However, there is a chance you might salvage the situation by begging her for forgiveness. This will involve admitting your duplicity and seeking her mercy. But what Complete Bastard wouldn't give it a shot?

The key technique here is to get down on your Bastard knees and beg for her to take you back using every pathetic, fawning cliché under the Bastard Sun: 'I can change!'; 'What do you want me to do?!'; 'I'm sorry for everything!'; 'I love you!'; 'You have to take me back – I've just been diagnosed with a terminal illness!' In short, whatever it takes to grind her into submission.

Note: Begging for forgiveness is a high-risk, low-gain strategy. Firstly, if you have been exposed as a Complete Bastard, it is unlikely that she will forgive you. Secondly, unless you change your Complete Bastard ways completely, you will now find yourself in a relationship which is curbed of all perks and under her constant and intense scrutiny. Duping her again will be almost impossible – even for a Complete Bastard as adept as you. Would you really want a relationship like that?

Fight to win her back

If you find yourself dumped against your will, you may want to save your relationship. Perhaps you really liked her and the sex was great. Maybe you've hit the jackpot by hooking up with an ATM with breasts and aren't quite ready to cash in your meal ticket just yet, even though she's starting to tire of your constantly using her. With the right will and the right tactics, it is possible to avert a dumping and win back her affections.

Here is a simple-to-use checklist that should cast aside all those sleepless night of self-analysis and drowning your sorrows at the bar. Apply it to your Complete Bastard personality and your broken heart should quickly mend:

The 7 step plan to winning her back

1. Isolate what, not who, went wrong.
2. Fix the problem.
3. Let her stew for a while.
4. Show her that the problem is fixed by flooding her with messages, whether by email, phone or texts.
5. Be bold and be Bastardly in all that you say and do now – make sure you tell her what she will get in no uncertain terms – don't be vague.
6. Don't rush the outcome.
7. If all fails – walk away fast.

Run, Bastard, run!

For the ultimate relationship exit strategy, read on. If all else is lost, the chips are truly down, she hates you, and there's a lynch mob forming baying for your blood, then get the hell out of there! Run, Bastard, run!

If there is one final piece of advice for any would-be Complete Bastards who are on the Path to Bastardom, then it's this: travel light. Whatever you carry into your Faustian pact by behaving like a Complete Bastard, you must be prepared to lose along the way. This can ultimately mean the things you value in life the most. At best, life as a successful Complete Bastard has the potential of becoming some of your happiest times ever. However, be warned – as the next and final instalment of the Complete Bastard's Dating Diary shows – err from the Path of Bastardom and they can also turn out to be your unhappiest times too.

Final words

You should by now have learned that getting dumped or doing the dumping is a natural part of dating. You should also have started to lose the fear of ever being dumped and embraced the fact that you can now begin to take control over your relationships. That means being proactive in your commitment to, and confidence in, dumping the wrong sort of women for the lifestyle you seek. You are even better at salvaging relationships that were on the brink of break up.

The fear of being dumped is a major reason as to why many people are afraid of even entering into a new relationship to start with. No one wants the pain, heartbreak and resentment that dumping is so associated with. As this chapter draws to a close, you should have learned that dating and dumping the Complete Bastard way are two sides of the same coin. As will be the case when you begin to start enjoying dating and getting real success with women, dumping will actually become an enjoyable part of your role as seducer too.

The final part of your Complete Bastard education is now almost complete. There is one final instalment of my Dating Diary extract to go and it's a dramatic tale of what can happen to the Foolish Bastard who strays from my teachings. It is worth reading if only to remind yourself that you now have knowledge and power that can help you achieve incredible sexual success with woman and profit handsomely in all other aspects of your life at the same time.

For every Complete Bastard who has now gone down the Path of Bastardom, it is also important to see your journey does not stop now. It has only just begun. Never forget the perils of lapsing into a Complacent Bastard and committing any of the seven deadly sins: Lust, Gluttony, Greed, Sloth, Wrath, Envy and Pride. Committing just one of these sins with the wrong woman at the wrong time can lead you to Complete Bastard ruin. So be the best Bastard you can be when it come to handling the tricky subject of dumping and, at every stage remember, Bastard beware!

Mimi, the Dump Dragon
The Complete Bastard meets his nemesis – the Ultimate Dumper.

Mimi was a remorseless relationship-ruiner who breathed fire on every man she dated. I dubbed her 'the Dump Dragon' after I crossed paths with this vile creature in a tale that was to take my life to the very brink of despair.

She was a well-known character on the dating scene – a rich socialite, three times divorced, and heiress to her late father's fortune. She now ran several very successful businesses of her own. Mimi was also beautiful and highly charming – at least on first impression.

One of her sidelines was organising Date Parties for single men and women whom she got in touch with through online dating sites. She'd invite them to bars or clubs for private soirées. Apart from profiting off their need to meet new people, it also afforded her a rich network of eligible single men for her own pickings.

I got invited to several of her parties in my online dating heyday. Around this time, I was Top Dog on a number of dating sites. My reputation as a roguish player and insatiable womaniser was at its height.

Mimi was one of the most flirtatious and exciting women I'd ever met. She had the most mischievous sparkling eyes, dressed impeccably, and had a womanly hourglass figure. I was utterly flattered when, during one of her parties, I was summoned to her table. We hit it off together instantly, with the result that she invited to go on a date with her. At that point, I couldn't believe my luck.

Over the next few weeks, Mimi and I hooked up several times. This woman certainly knew how to Dupe, for she had me footing the bills for a string of weekends away in posh hotels, meals in expensive restaurants, and I even found myself – against my better Bastard judgement – lavishing her with an array of expensive gifts.

With her millions in the bank, her homes across the world, an amazing social circle of jet-set friends, plus her drop-dead stunning looks, here was a woman I was sure would make me – if I was just able to tame her. Mimi was the Ultimate Catch.

Except, Mimi wasn't for the catching – no matter how hard I tried. She was far too self-centred, resourceful, and had no intention of settling down with one man. With hindsight, it was perhaps inevitable but, at the time, I was completely taken by surprise when an email from her arrived in my inbox:

'Dear Marcus, I'd always heard what a Complete Bastard you are. Women talk. Unfortunately for you, lots of women whom you have used and whose hearts you have broken have told me of your terrible treatment of them. It wasn't until I saw your despicable game first hand that I realised you were the lowest form of male life. Being a player is a hell of a blast – I should know! But sadly for your sake, you got complacent and now – out of a sense of kinship for Womanhood – it has fallen to me to set the axe to fall upon your neck.

Love and kisses, Mimi'

I quickly wrote an email in reply, assuring Mimi that she had made some terrible mistake and that she should not listen to the spiteful gossip of others who were obviously trying to split us apart. I vowed to avenge these mischief-makers and I ended by re-stating my adoration of her.

Unknown to me, however, some darker trickery was at play. Mimi was a close associate of 'Miss_Penelope', the wealthy business woman who I had callously dumped some months before (See Dating Diary extract, chapter fourteen). 'Miss_Penelope' had got talking with Mimi and told her everything, from my adept game play on the dating site, to how I was able to deceive her into funding my round-the-world adventure. 'Miss_Penelope' had seemingly never forgiven me for my Bastardly treatment of her and, together, she and Mimi had hatched my downfall.

Those heartless hounds did truly unleash a dose of Female Vengeance upon my life like I had never seen the like of before. It began when my email account began receiving hundreds of spam messages every hour of every day from Viagra and penis growth advertisers. The venom continued as they created and uploaded mock profiles on several dating sites that I was a member of. These profiles were all black-humoured parodies of my own profiles and contained insult after insult. Finally, the dating sites themselves, upon being informed of my roguish misdemeanours, deleted my real profiles and blacklisted me.

The women somehow also managed to hack into my private email and social networking accounts. They messaged my contacts, including both female and male friends. They wrote to them detailing what a lying, cheating piece of garbage I was, and giving them solid proof that I was nothing more than a Complete Bastard.

The knock-on effect was catastrophic. I began to get message after message from angry women who were furious that I'd used them. They all swore their own form of retaliation, which took a variety of forms.

I was clearly in deep trouble. Mimi and 'Miss_Penelope' had wreaked havoc upon my Bastard lifestyle and torn my carefully spun web of deceit to shreds.

I ran to Papa Bastard for advice. Surely he, if anyone, could help me?!

'Oh, Son, what wicked seeds we sow when first we commit to going down the Path to Bastardom. Complacency and misjudgement have steered you on the Road to Ruin and you must take the consequences. Your final lesson to learn is that a Duper must never get caught. And now you must face the penalty of your dark deeds.'

Thanks, Pop! Even the Sly Dog had washed his filth-stained hands of me. I was lost and alone.

The final straw came a couple of days later when I received a lawyer's letter saying that I must repay many thousands of pounds back to 'Miss_Penelope'. She and Mimi had also orchestrated my sacking from an editing post which 'Miss_Penelope' had got for me through one of her friends. I was broke, without a job and potentially facing a lawsuit or maybe even jail.

Perhaps in the minds of the many women I had hurt in the course of my great online dating adventure, I deserved my comeuppance. The game of dating is a fickle one. You must always be aware that even the most successful seducers are still fallible to the unpredictable scorn of a woman (or women) hurt in love. I **had** grown complacent. Playing with the like of Mimi and 'Miss_Penelope' so flagrantly had been an error of judgement that finally bought about my demise.

And so down I fell. Cast from the Heavens and down into the murky depths of a womanless, penniless, jobless Hell. I knew what now lay before me. It was time for me to put into play the final and most desperate act as contained within this book: escape.

It was time to Run, Bastard, run!

– 17 –
Final Words

What's stopping you becoming a Complete Bastard?
You've probably spent a lifetime believing that you don't deserve great-looking women – believing that great-looking women belong on the arms and in the lives of other men better than you – men who are more handsome, have better physiques, men who are more successful in their careers, men who have more money and better personalities than you.

You are, after all, just an 'ordinary guy'. And what woman is attracted to mediocrity?

Hopefully this book will have shown you a few uncomfortable, but nevertheless revealing, truths. One is that **confidence** is the key to believing that you can be attractive to women. That same confidence is the key factor that you'll require to start successfully seducing women too. By adopting the attitude of the Complete Bastard, you can begin to internalise more confident feelings about yourself that will increase your self-esteem and make you happier about how you feel inside.

Another important factor in developing self-confidence and impressing women is **improving your external self**. How you look, dress, carry yourself and act around women is critical to your success with them and all of these elements can be improved with the knowledge set out in this book. Some of these improvements can be made in a matter of minutes or hours – others could take a high degree of effort on your part – but all are achievable. After all, isn't the woman of your dreams a prize worth a bit of hard work?

With the right attitude and the right style, you can now start developing your **technique with women**. Finding a source of a high quantity and quality of women is the obvious starting point and this book advocates that the best place to meet women is online through dating sites. It is on the Web that the Complete Bastard is able to conveniently select, meet and seduce women whom he will go on to meet in the real world.

By teaching you how best to **promote yourself online** with your profile, how to most **effectively interact online** with interested women, and even how to **seduce women online**, you can begin to reap the rewards of being a Complete Bastard

227

internet dater.

But there is a lot more to gain from using online dating than to seek love or a relationship with one woman. The motto of this book is: 'The more the merrier'. And that implies, by **creating a carefully crafted and tightly managed network of admirers,** you can begin to enjoy the perks of knowing many more women, most of whom will be highly attracted to you. This can lead to an improved sex life with multiple partners, often more attractive than you would ever have dreamed possible.

It doesn't stop there.

The Complete Bastard is able to manoeuvre himself into situations where he is the recipient of an expanded and improved social life, a better and more lavish lifestyle and substantially improved career prospects. Women are the catalyst to all these benefits and more. You are the charming seducer – wringing every last drop of pleasure from your wonderful new world.

Central to this book is the need to learn the skills necessary to develop a meeting from someone online to getting along with them in the real world. **Dating** is that crucial bond builder. With an array of tips and techniques to deal with any date scenario, you should now feel well-equipped to not just cope with the uncomfortable social outing that is a date, but to positively revel in the experience. The Complete Bastard has no fear of dating because there is no fear of failure – only the opportunity for heightened success. Hopefully you will now understand why he thinks like this.

Surviving dates may be what got you reading this book, but now you have hopefully realised that it is the possibilities **beyond dating** that make the life of a Complete Bastard so very tantalising. You have been shown a secret insight into how the mind of such a cunning character works in the chapters about **Duping**. Here you read what amazing perks can be gained by the careful application of some easy-to-master techniques and how you can get away with it all in the eyes of others or have to do a little **dumping** along the way.

You have also met and read the **story of a Complete Bastard** – my story. The 'Dating Diary of a Complete Bastard' is a true-life account of just what is possible – scrapes and all – from playing the dating game at full throttle and taking it further than you ever thought imaginable. I am but one of a growing legion of Complete Bastards who have realised that destiny is of their own making and the time has come to play women at their own game – a game they have been mistresses of for centuries.

So what's stopping **you**? Reading this book is one thing – putting the lessons that you've learned into practice is quite another. So now it's time to for you to give the Complete Bastard method a go and show the world that you're made of stronger stuff.

It's now time, my new friend, to become... **the Complete Bastard**. But just before you set off on your own Bastardly adventures, why not find out what happened to your hero in the final adventure of my Dating Diary?

The Fall

After some time on the run, the Compete Bastard finds himself captured with little chance of escape.

The baking sun beat down; sweat oozed from my every pore. In the corner of the tiny room I was kept in, a busted mattress served as my bed and my only furnishing. I was fed on food so terrible that surely stray animals must have eaten better. My every waking hour was spent in confinement; each day followed the next, and always under the watchful stare of my captor.

My captor was Papa Bastard. With no one else to turn to and women baying for my castration back home, my former mentor had lured me to his hideout in North Africa and imprisoned me like his dog.

Day and night that Old Bastard made me work, typing out page after page of my debauched story. It began with my past life as a luckless flop with women, to how I emerged to become one of the most successful seducers in the city.

'Buy back your innocence, Son. Show every man and woman how your finesse as a womaniser made you rise to unfathomable heights of success, but warn them how your folly was to finally ruin you after your Icarian fall. Write it all down and purge yourself of your shameful sins.'

Strange – from what I remember, all my 'shameful sins' had come straight from the advice that he had given me. But, like always, I obeyed Papa Bastard. And so I began to write.

Days turned to weeks, and weeks into months. The merciless heat followed me everywhere, from the lowly bed upon which I lay, to my calloused fingertips as I typed page after page of my tale.

Then suddenly, after one long, hard, dull day that was like every other – my story was borne. I had finished putting down my tale. Papa Bastard came to me and led me outside into the sunlight.

We stood side-by-side, like father and son, on his huge balcony looking over the moored fishing boats, ramshackle mule carts, and bustling souks below.

My adventures with women I knew had made me The Complete Bastard. I had wooed women on online dating sites, wowed them on dates, and won their hearts and minds. My extraordinary mastery had taken me to bedrooms and beyond as

I plied my devilish techniques on some of the world's most eligible and beautiful women. Over the years, I'd travelled the world, lived off girlfriends, and won the adoration of scores of gullible females.

And now it was finished. The most exciting adventure of my life had reached its climax. Fortunately – by fair means or foul (he never did tell me) – Papa Bastard had managed to sort out my problems with 'Miss_Penelope' and Mimi back home while I had been writing the book.

As the sun began to set and the sound of the call to prayer broke out around the city, Papa Bastard turned to me: 'Son, I have a little reward for you after all your hard work. How would you like to meet a pretty woman tonight and enjoy the pleasure of her company – just you and her?'

I stared in utter disbelief at the Old Man. After all I'd been through? His eyes twinkled with pure deviousness. I laughed a throaty, mischievous laugh and replied: 'I couldn't think of anything better.'

And so ends my sordid tale of how I became The Complete Bastard. My life has never quite been the same since I took those first, fateful steps on the Path to Bastardom. By reading my words and practicing my teachings, you too can begin taking your own personal journey. Wherever it may lead, I wish you every Bastard success.

Also Available

How to Get Into My Pants

One Woman Reveals the Hidden Secrets to Understanding Women's Minds on Dating, Love, Romance & Sex

By Claudia Fox

For too long, women have made it difficult for men to understand exactly what they want – saying one thing, but thinking and doing something completely different. Not any longer.

One woman has broken ranks with her own gender, to bring to men's attention the definitive guide to understanding women.

In **How to Get Into My Pants**, Claudia Fox tells men exactly what they've always been trying to figure out for themselves. The book offers men a step-by-step system for attracting, romancing and seducing all women – and takes the guesswork out of deciphering the female mind.

If you've been of the opinion that women are strange alien creatures, then **How to Get Into My Pants** is the book for you.

Never again need you use manipulative 'circus tricks' to try and win a woman's affections. **How to Get Into My Pants** shows you genuine know-how with women that really works.

For any guy who has been banging his head against a brick wall trying to figure out women for himself with little success, this book is a must-read.

Release Date: Mid 2009

ISBN: 978-0-9561448-2-9

For more information on all Complete Bastard titles visit:
www.completebastards.com

Also Available

Shameless Writing Whore

The Complete Bastard's Guide to Making Big Money Writing Non-Fiction

By Nick Pendrell

Nick Pendrell got bored on holiday back in 2007 and started looking around properties in Egypt. As a result of his obsessive-compulsive nature, what was supposed to be a few thousand words turned into a full book which was immediately picked up by a small publisher and released as a book a few weeks later. Through the book alone, Nick came to be perceived as a property 'guru' and went on to sell over 220 apartments in the following 12 months.

With **Shameless Writing Whore**, Nick explains in simple terms how anyone who can string a few sentences together can replicate his success. All it takes is to do a little research in order to find a topic that people are prepared to pay money to find out more about, to read a few books on the subject and do a little Googling to become an 'instant expert'.

The book provides a step-by-step guide to producing your first book – coming up with an idea, researching it, writing it, publishing it as inexpensively as possible, marketing it and then using it as leverage to make the big money from the back end.

Release Date: Autumn 2009

ISBN: 978-0-9561448-6-7

For more information on all Complete Bastard titles visit:
www.completebastards.com

Also Available

Business Blagging & Bullshitting

The Complete Bastards' Guide

By Nick Pendrell and Oscar Maxwell

Have you an idea for a business yet have practically no cash to start it with? Or have you got a small/medium sized company that has been hit by the recession so now you need to slash costs to keep it alive? Or maybe you don't really want a business at all, but want to create the illusion of having one in order to reap the benefits that the appearance of one would give to you?

If you answered 'yes' to any of these questions, **Business Blagging & Bullshitting** is just for you. The book is written in two parts: the first explains how any company can harness the power of the Web plus new technology to give the appearance that you are the CEO of a mega-corporation, even if you're just sat in your underpants, working from your bedroom. The second part deals with the psychology of blagging and bullshitting – showing you how to use these tools to their maximum effect to get things for free or at greatly reduced prices.

So whether you want your business contacts to think that you are the head of a corporation with offices all over the world, or want something as simple as pretending to be a journalist to get yourself easy access to many places and situations out of bounds, you'll find that **Business Blagging & Bullshitting** reveals the formula for your future success.

Release Date: End 2009

ISBN: 978-0-9561448-4-3

For more information on this and other titles, visit:
www.completebastards.com

Lightning Source UK Ltd.
Milton Keynes UK
UKOW031907250112

186057UK00009B/82/P